I0820266

OKODAKICIYE WAKAN ODOWAN QA OKNA
AHIYAYAPI KTA HO KIN

HYMNAL
WITH TUNES AND CHANTS

ACCORDING TO THE USE OF THE

EPISCOPAL CHURCH

IN THE

NIOBRARA DEANERY

OF THE

DIOCESE OF
SOUTH DAKOTA

Edition of 1951

Reprinted 1966
Reprinted 1981
Reprinted 1996
Reprinted 2025

ACKNOWLEDGEMENT

Those who have prepared this work for publication desire to acknowledge very gratefully their obligations to the authors and owners of the tunes herein contained. With but one exception, cheerful consent has been given by all whose ownership could be traced to the free use of their music in this mission hymn book for the Dakotas.

Church Publishing
19 East 34th Street
New York, NY 10016
www.churchpublishing.org

A record of this book is available at the Library of Congress.

Print ISBN: 978-1-64065-865-3
eBook ISBN: 978-1-64065-866-0

The Rt. Rev. WM. H. HARE, D.D., S.T.D., Bishop of South Dakota, All Saints' School, Sioux Falls, S.D.

Dear Bishop:

The committee appointed by you to examine, revise, and prepare for publication the Dakota Church Hymnal, with Tunes, Chants, etc., arranged by Mrs. Jessie W. Cook in fulfillment of a long-cherished purpose of her late husband, the Rev. Chas. S. Cook, has, we trust under the guidance of the Holy Spirit, completed their work.

On this first anniversary of our lamented brother's death, we herewith offer to you the manuscript copy for your examination, should you so desire; and, if approved, hope to receive your authorization of its publication.

Your obedient servants in Christ,
WM. J. CLEVELAND,
JOS. W. COOK.
EDW. ASHLEY,
Committee.
Good Friday, 1893.
Madison, So. Dakota.

Missionary District of South Dakota, Sioux Falls, South Dakota, Easter Even, 1893.

To WM. J. CLEVELAND, JOS. W. COOK, EDW. ASHLEY,

My Dear Brethren:

The comfort and help which the Dakotas find in the hymns and music of the Church are so great and their enjoyment of them is so rich that I welcome the announcement of the completion of your work, and rejoice that it coincides with the anniversary of the death of the beloved brother who sympathized so keenly with his people in their need and in their love of sacred music. The publication of the Tune Book is hereby authorized, with grateful acknowledgement of your labors.

Your faithful brother,
WM. H. HARE, Missionary Bishop of S.D.

TABLE OF SUBJECTS.

TABLE OF SUBJECTS.

INDEX OF FIRST LINES

INDEX OF FIRST LINES

AUTHORS AND TRANSLATORS, ODOWAN KAUAPI KIN

A. J.	Andrew Jones
Com.	Committee
C. S. C.	Charles S. Cook
C. W. H.	Charles W. Hoffman
D. W. H.	Daniel W. Hemans
G. D.	George Dowanna
G. St. C.	George St. Claire
H. S.	Henry Swift
J. B. C.	John B. Chapman
J. C. T.	Joseph C. Taylor
J. H.	James Hemans
J. W. C.	Joseph W. Cook
T. K. T.	T. Kicosmani Taylor
L. C. W.	Luke C. Walker
P. J.	Philip Johnson
P. L. P.	Pierre La Pointe
P. M.	Paul Mazakute
P. W.	Philip Weston
S. D. H.	Samuel D. Hinman
T. W.	Thomas Wakanna
W. H.	William Holmes
W. J. C.	William J. Cleveland
W. M. R.	William M. Robertson
W. S. H.	Walter S. Hall
W. T. S.	William T. Selwyn

BI-LINGUAL HYMN LISTS

Hymns for bi-lingual use, in accordance with the bi-lingual Hymnal of 1946, with numbers of the regular Hymnals of 1916 and 1940. "s" indicates a difference in the number of stanzas between the Dakota books and the English language books.

TABLE 1. DAKOTA-ENGLISH

Dak.	First line	1916	1940
1	Lo, He comes	57s	5s
2	O come, Emmanuel	66s	2s
3	Love of Jesus	231	
4	Watchman, tell us	106s	440s
5	Saviour, again to	50s	487s
6	The sun is sinking	17s	183s
7	To the Name of our	89s	326s
8	On Jordan's bank	282	10
9	Joy to the world	101s	319s
10	Hail to the morn		
11	Carol, carol, Christians		
12	O come, all ye faithful	72	12s
13	Come, thou long expected,	55s	1s
14	Hark, the herald	73s	27s
15	Silent night	546	33
16	Shout the glad tidings	75	15
17	Hark! what mean	81	
18	A few more years	443	
19	Jesus! Name of wondrous,	90	323
20	How wondrous fair		
21	Hail, thou once despised	191	357
22	Lead us, O Father	248s	433s
23	Triumphant Sion, lift	472s	381s
24	Hail to the Lord's	99	545
25	Just as I am	139	409
26	Rock of ages	217s	471s
27	O worship the King	255s	288s
28	Songs of thankfulness	96s	53
29	In the cross of Christ	152s	336s
30	Sweet the moments	157s	72
31	Nearer, my God	222	465
32	Saviour, when in dust	130s	332
33	Weary of self (earth)	129s	58s
34	Forty days	123	55
35	Glory be to Jesus	162	335s
36	Take my life, and let		408
37	Ride on, ride on	145	64
38	For the brave of		582
39	'Tis finished		
40	Bound upon the		
41	When our heads are	409s	79s
42	O who shall roll away		84s
43	Jesus Christ is risen	172	85
44	On wings of living	559	
45	The strife is o'er	173	91
46	Look, ye saints	185s	105s
47	Jesus lives! thy terrors	176	88
48	He is risen, he is risen	179s	90s
49	Crown him with many	190s	352s
50	Thou art gone up	189	
51	Fight the good fight	113s	560s
52	Hear us, thou that	524	
52-B	O Sion, haste	474	261s
53	Spirit of mercy, &	197	111
	O come, Creator		& 108
54	Our blest Redeemer	199s	368
55	The God of Abraham	253	285s
55-B	Onward, Christian Sol.,	530	557
56	Father of all, whose	206	
57	Holy, Holy, Holy	205	266
58	Pleasant are thy	467	392
59	Ye holy angels bright	264	600
60	We love the place	465	398
61	God of the prophets	451s	220
62	Lord, pour thy Spirit	450	219
63	O God, on high, in		
64	O Paradise	167s	588s
65	For all the saints	295s	126s
66	Let saints on earth	299s	397s
67	I love thy kingdom	315	388s
68	The Lord His help		
69	Glorious things	468s	385s
70	The Church's one	464	396
71	Jesus, thou Joy of	328s	485s
72	Shepherd of souls	324	213s
73	My God, thy table	329	203s
74	Bread of the world	336s	196s
75	According to thy	320s	
75-A	Here, O my Lord	334	208
75-B	And now, O Father	333	189
76	A little child	341	
77	O Lord, and Master	496	501s
78	Soldiers of Christ	346s	552
79	The gentle Saviour		
80	Do no sinful action		
81	Jesus, gentlest Saviour	322s	348s
82	Saviour, like a shepherd	355s	247s
83	Thine for ever, God	370	427s
84	Now the day is over	364s	172s
85	Brightest and best	95s	46s
86	O North, with all thy	107s	541s
87	For the beauty	425	296

DAKOTA-ENGLISH HYMNS (cont.)

Dak.	First line	1916	1940
88	When all thy mercies	237	297s
89	Go forward, Christian	535	553
90	O happy day		
91	Witness, ye men and		
92	O bless the Lord, my	318s	293s
93	More love to thee		461s
94	Asleep in Jesus	413s	
95	O God, our help in	445	289
96	Immortal Love	404s	360s
97	There's a land		
98	O what the joy	544s	589s
99	As the sweet flower		
100	Jesus, where'er thy	459	
101	O Master, let me walk	493s	572s
102	From Greenland's	476s	254s
103	Lift up your heads	186	484s
104	Arm of the Lord	487s	
105	Lord, while for all	431	
106	Come, pure hearts	288s	134s
107	Let us, with a		308s
108	My country 'tis of	427	141
109	Jesus, I live to thee	218s	
110	Father in heaven, who	367	506
111	We sing the praise	160	340
112	Christ, whose glory	4	153
113	Abide with me	18s	467s
114	Softly now the light	19s	177s
115	Our day of praise	49s	175s
116	The day is past	21s	
117	Lord, in thy presence	377s	
118	All praise to thee	25s	165s
119	Sun of my soul	20	166
120	How sweet the Name	232s	455s
121	City of God, how broad	470	386
122	All hail the power	192	355
123	Approach, my soul	303	
124	Jesus, Lover of my	223	415
125	How firm a foundation	212	564
126	Jesus shall reign	480	542
127	Jesus calls us	268	566
128	O Saviour, precious	526	349
129	Stand up for Jesus	538	562
130	Hasten the time	477	257
131	Round the Lord	207s	269s
132	This is the day	45	
133	Before the Lord (Before Jehovah's)	309	300
134	All people that on	249s	278s
135	O very God of	102	442
136	Praise to the holiest	259	343
137	O thou whose feet	365	507
138	For ever with the Lord	516	
139	There's a wideness	240	304
140	My God, I love thee	234	456
141	As pants the wearied	313s	
142	God, my king, thy	311s	280s
143	Praise to God, immortal	420	140
144	Soldiers of the Cross	115s	
145	Blest be the tie	489s	495s
146-A	O Light, whose beams,	40	
146-B	O Saviour, bless us	48	182
147	Awake, my soul	111s	577s
148	A charge to keep		
149	Light's abode	507s	587s
150	With broken heart	133s	60s
151	Oh, where shall rest		
152	One sole baptismal	463	
153	Hark! the sound of	297	125
154	Come, my soul, thy suit	304s	
155	Shall we gather		
156	Rejoice, the Lord is	521s	350s
157	Thy kingdom come	105s	544s
158	Jerusalem, my happy	514	585
159	Jerusalem, the golden	511s	597s
160	At the Name of Jesus	528	356s
161	O Land of the blest		
162	Sweet hour of prayer		
163	Hark! hark, my soul	290s	472s
164	Inspirer and hearer	34	
165	We walk by faith	270s	
166	Take the Name of Jesus		
167	Guide me (with refrain)		
168	Where cross the crowded	494s	498s
169	My soul with patience	314	439s
170	Through the night	539s	394
172	Call Jehovah thy	310	448
173	Jesus, the very	316	462
174	The Son of God goes	85	549
175	The head that once	188	106
176	My faith looks up	211	449

TABLE II. ENGLISH-DAKOTA

First line	Dak.	1916	1940
A charge to keep	148		
A few more years	18	443	
A little child	76	341	
Abide with me	113	18s	467s
According to thy	75	320s	
All hail the power	122	192	355
All people that on	134	249s	278s
All praise to thee	118	25s	165s
And now, O Father	75B	333	189
Approach, my soul	123	303	
Arm of the Lord	104	487s	
As pants the wearied	141	313s	
As the sweet flower	99		
Asleep in Jesus!	94	413s	
At the name of Jesus	160	528	356s
Awake, my soul	147	111s	577s
Before the Lord Jehovah's	133	309	300
Blest be the tie	145	489s	495s
Bound upon the	40		
Bread of the world	74	336s	196s
Brightest and best	85	95s	46s
Call Jehovah thy	172	310	448
Carol, carol Christians	11		
Christ, whose glory	112	4	153
City of God	121	470	386
Come, my soul, thy suit	154	304s	
Come, pure hearts	106	288s	134s
Come thou long expected	13	55s	1s
Crown Him with many crowns	49	190s	352s
Do no sinful action	80		
Father in Heaven	110	367	506
Father of all, whose	56	206	
Fight the good fight	51	113s	560s
For all the saints	65	295s	126s
For ever with the Lord	138	516	
For the beauty of the	87	425	296
For the brave of every race	38		582
Forty days and forty nights,	34	123	55
From Greenland's icy	102	476s	254s
Glorious things of thee	69	468s	385s
Glory be to Jesus	35	162	335s
Go forward, Christian	89	535	553
God, my King	142	311s	280s
God of the prophets	61	451s	220
Guide me, O thou great	167		
Hail, thou once	21	191	357
Hail to the Lord's	24	99	545
Hail to the morn when	10		
Hark! hark, my soul!	163	290s	472s
Hark the herald	14	73s	27s
Hark! the sound of	153	297	125
Hark! what mean those	17	81	
Hasten the time	130	477	257
He is risen	48	179s	90s
Hear us, thou that	52	524	
Here, O my Lord	75A	334	208
Holy, Holy, Holy!	57	205	266
How firm a foundation	125	212	564
How sweet the name of	120	232s	455s
How wondrous fair is	20		
I love thy kingdom	67	315	388s
Immortal Love, for ever	96	404s	360s
In the cross of Christ	29	152s	336s
Inspirer and hearer of	164	34	
Jerusalem, my happy home	158	514	585
Jerusalem the golden	159	511s	597s
Jesus calls us	127	268	566
Jesus Christ is risen	43	172	85
Jesus, gentlest Saviour	81	322s	348s
Jesus, I live to thee	109	218s	
Jesus lives! thy terrors	47	176	88
Jesus Lover of my soul	124	223	415
Jesus! Name of wondrous	19	90	323
Jesus shall reign	126	480	542
Jesus the very thought	173	316	462
Jesus, thou joy of loving	71	328s	485s
Jesus, where'er thy people	100	459	
Joy to the world!	9	101s	319s
Just as I am	25	139	409
Lead us, O Father	22	248s	433s
Let saints on earth	66	299s	397s
Let us, with a gladsome	107		308s
Lift your heads, ye mighty	103	186	484s
Light's abode	149	507s	587s
Lo, he comes	1	57s	5s
Look ye saints	46	185s	105s
Lord in thy presence	117	377s	
Lord, pour thy Spirit	62	450	219
Lord, while for all mankind,	105	431	
Love of Jesus, all divine	3	231	
More love to Thee	93		461s
My country, 'tis of thee	108	427	141
My faith looks up to thee	176	211	449
My God, I love thee	140	234	456
My God, thy table now is	73	329	203s
My soul with patience waits	169	314	439s
Nearer, my God, to thee	31	222	465
Now the day is over	84	364s	172s
O bless the Lord	92	318s	293s
O come, all ye faithful	12	72	12s

ENGLISH-DAKOTA HYMNS (cont.)

METRICAL INDEX

METRICAL INDEX

THE DAKOTA ALPHABET.

A little attention to the following explanation of the sounds of the characters used in printing the Dakota language will enable almost anyone to pronounce it with fair accuracy.

Persons who have no knowledge of the meaning of the words can thus, with a little care and practice, soon learn to sing the hymns and chants contained in this book, so that they would be intelligible to the native Sioux or Dakota Indians.

VOWELS.

The vowels, five in number, have what are commonly called the long Continental sounds. There are, properly, no "Short" vowel sounds, but each has one unvarying "Long" sound.

a (ah) the same sound as *a* in *Father*.

e (aye) the same as *a* in *place*.

i (ee) the same as *ee* in *see*, or *ea* in *sea*.

o (oh) the same as *o* in *no*.

u (oo) the same as *o* in *lose*, or *oo* in *smooth*.

CONSONANTS.

b (bee) the same as in English.

c (chee) the same as *ch* in *chain*.

ç (ch'ee) ch explosive. Formed by pronouncing ch with a strong pressure of the tongue against the roof of the mouth, followed by a sudden expulsion of the breath.

d (dee) the same as in English.

g (ghee) the same as *g* hard in English, as in *get*.

CONSONANTS.

ġ (ġhee) a rough guttural, formed by pronouncing *g* hard with a strong pressure of the organs in the back part of the mouth.

h (hee) the same as *h* in English.

ĥ (ĥee) a rough guttural, formed by pronouncing *h* with a strong pressure of the organs in the back part of the mouth.

j (zhee) the same as *z* in *azure*, or *s* in *pleasure*.

k (kee) the same as in English.

m (mee) the same as in English.

n (nee) the same as in English. The abrupt, or closed, nasal.

ŋ (iŋ) the same as *n* in *think*, or the French *n* in *bon*. The open, or unclosed, nasal.

p (pee) the same as in English.

p̧ (p'ee) p explosive. Formed by pronouncing *p* with a strong pressure of the lips, followed by a sudden expulsion of the breath.

q (k'ee) k explosive. Formed by pronouncing *k* with a strong pressure of the organs, followed by a sudden expulsion of the breath.

s (see) the same as in English, or *c* soft in *peace*.

ṡ (shee) the same as *sh* in *show*.

t (tee) the same as in English.

ţ (t'ee) t explosive. Formed by pronouncing *t* with a strong pressure of the tongue against the roof of the mouth, followed by a sudden expulsion of the breath.

w (wee) the same as *w* in *will*.

y (yee) the same as *y* in *you*.

z (zee) the same as *z* in *zebra*.

The apostrophe indicates an hiatus, as in *s'a*.

ODOWAN.

I. THE CHRISTIAN YEAR.

CHRISTIAN OMAKA KIN.

Advent.—U kte ciŋ.

1 "Lo! He Comes, with Clouds Descending." 8s. 7s. 4s.

"Waŋyaka po, mahpiya śapa kiŋ akaŋd u; uŋkaŋ wiciśta owasiŋ waŋyakapi kta."— Wayuo i: 7.

From "Tunes Old and New" by permission of Rev. Dr. Tucker.

2 Wowitaŋ waŋ wokokipe
Ed waŋyakapi kta ce;
Tona He anaġoptaŋ śni
Tka ihahapis'a qoŋ,
Ceyaya hciŋ
Christ iyekiyapi kta.

3 Miniwaŋca qa maka kiŋ,
U kiŋ oŋ napapi kta;
Śicedakapi hena e,
"Woyasu kta ed u po;"
He nahoŋpi
Oŋ yuśiŋyayapi kta.

4 Wopekitoŋpi kta taŋka
Waŋ apepi qoŋ u ce;
Tona Tawa kiŋ owasiŋ
Itkokipa yapi kta:
Aliluya!
Woyasu aŋpetu u.

5 Haŋ, ohouŋdapi kta ce,
Toyaŋke wakaŋ kiŋ ed;
Wowitaŋ qa wowaśake,
Christ, dena Nitawa kta.
U ye, u ye,
Christ Wanikiya, u ye. AMEN.

1 Lo! He Comes with Clouds Descending. 8s. 7s. 4.

"Waŋyaka po, maĥpiya ṡapa kiŋ akaŋd u; uŋkaŋ wiciṡta owasiŋ waŋyakapi kta."—Wayuo i: 7.

SECOND TUNE. ST. THOMAS. (V. NOVELLO.)

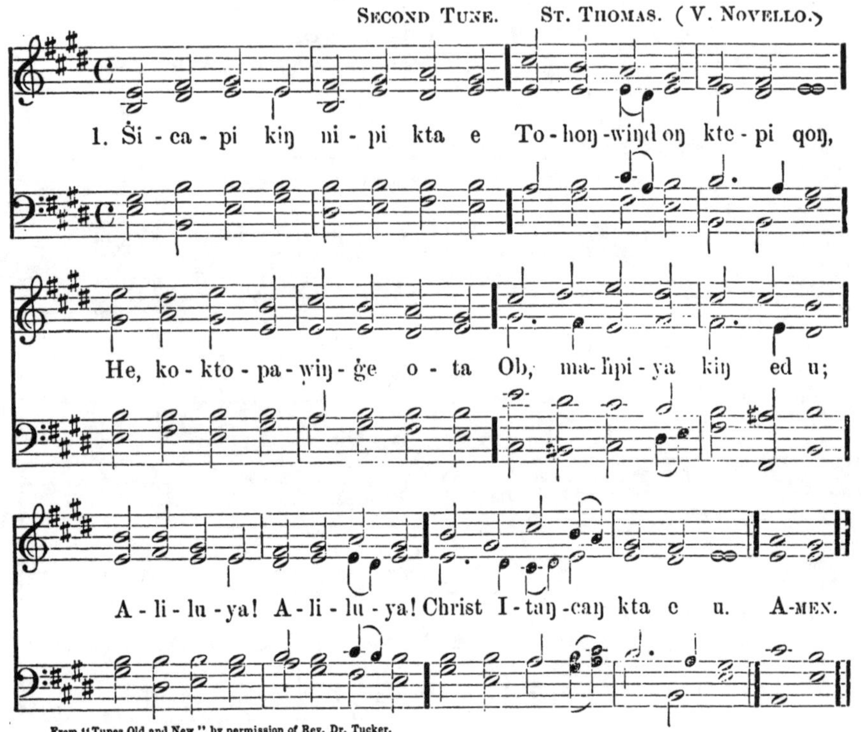

From "Tunes Old and New" by permission of Rev. Dr. Tucker.

2 Wowitaŋ waŋ wokokipe
Ed waŋyakapi kta ce;
Tona He anaġoptaŋ ṡni
Tka iĥaĥapis'a qoŋ,
Ceyaya ĥciŋ
Christ iyekiyapi kta.

3 Miniwaŋca qa maka kiŋ,
U kiŋ oŋ napapi kta;
Ṡicedakapi hena e,
"Woyasu kta ed u po;"
He naĥoŋpi
Oŋ yuṡiŋyayapi kta.

4 Wopekitoŋpi kta taŋka
Waŋ apepi qoŋ u ce;
Tona Tawa kiŋ owasiŋ
Itkokipa yapi kta:
Aliluya!
Woyasu aŋpetu u.

5 Haŋ, ohouŋdapi kta ce,
Toyaŋke wakaŋ kiŋ ed;
Wowitaŋ qa wowaṡake,
Christ, dena Nitawa kta.
U ye, u ye,
Christ Waŋikiya, u ye. AMEN.

2 "O Come, O Come, Emmanuel." Six 8s.

"Wopekitoŋ kiŋ Zion ed u kta." — Isa. lix: 20.

From "Tunes Old and New" by permission of Rev. Dr. Tucker.

2 O u ye, O Emmanuel,
Qa Israel kiyuŝka ye,
Wakaŋŝica nape etaŋ,
Qa wookiye kiŋ qu ye.

3 O u ye, Aŋpao Wakaŋ,
Caŋte waŝteuŋyaŋpi ye,
Wicoŋte ohaŋzi owas
Hena kahiŋdiyeya ye.

4 O u ye, O Itaŋcaŋ kiŋ;
Maȟpiyata tiyopa kiŋ
Ahiuŋkiyuzamnipi
Qa woteȟi anapta ye. AMEN.

The Christian Year.

2 "O Come, O Come, Emmanuel." Six 8s.

"Wopekitoŋ kiŋ Zion ed u kta."—Isa. lix : 20.

SECOND TUNE. MELITA.

From "Tunes Old and New" by permission of Rev. Dr. Tucker.

2 O u ye, O Emmanuel,
Qa Israel kiyuśka ye,
Wakaŋśica nape etaŋ,
Qa wookiye kiŋ qu ye.

3 O u ye, Aŋpao Wakaŋ,
Caŋte waśteuŋyaŋpi ye,
Wicoŋṭe ohaŋzi owas
Hena kahiŋdiyeya ye.

4 O u ye, O Itaŋcaŋ kiŋ;
Maħpiyata tiyopa kiŋ
Ahiuŋkiyuzamnipi
Qa woteħi anapta ye. AMEN.

Advent.

3 Martyn. 7s. D.

"Iyoyaŋpa mitawa qa Wanikiya mitawa kiŋ he Itaŋcaŋ Ee: tuwa kowakipiŋ kta he?" — Ps. xxvii: 1.

From "Tunes Old and New" by permission of Rev. Dr. Tucker.

2 Wowaśake niŋd wauŋ,
Qa wicaȟoŋwiŋ koyag;
Aŋpao wiyakpakpa
Christ iwaciŋwaya ce;
Conkaśke suta ȟce ciŋ
He Wakaŋtaŋka ee;
He nape uȟakiya
Mni wiconi kiŋ ekta.

3 Hed maȟpiya teca kiŋ,
Qa maka ko teca kiŋ,
Ed otoŋwe kiŋ wakaŋ
Heciya wauŋ waciŋ.
Heced oŋ tuwa waŝte,
He kiyuġatapi ye;
Taku śnije kte śni waŋ
Hed teśdagniyaŋpi kta. AMEN

The Christian Year.

4 St. George. 7s. D.

"Aŋpetuwi qa haŋhepiwi kiŋ okpaza icu kta, qa wicaḣpi kiŋ iś towiyakpa ekdakupi kta."—Joel iii: 15.

[*Spanish Chant, Hymn 32, may also be used.*]

From "Tunes Old and New" by permission of Rev. Dr. Tucker.

2 Tośikda Wakaŋtaŋka
Peta se idekiya,
Qa maka wicoḣaŋ kiŋ
Hena e ihaŋgyiŋ kta;
Woaḣtanitoŋ owas
Ceyaya heyapi kta;
"Hehehe! okokipe,
Woyasu hihuŋni ce."

3 Wowitaŋ Nitawa kiŋ
He ecena ḣciŋ suta,
Qa Nitokicoŋze kiŋ,
O Ate, wana hi ce;
Taku He kipajiŋ qoŋ,
Taku He oknayaŋ śni,
Hena e ḣuḣnaġiŋ kta,
Qa waŋjina hiŋ kte śni.

4 Jesus Christ Wanikiya,
Oŋ miye wani kta ce;
Qa Nitaaŋpetu de
Ed mioḣaŋ śice ciŋ
Miciḣuḣnaġa eśa,
Niś Niye waciŋciya,
Heced oŋ wani kta ce;
Wowitaŋ duha nuŋwe. Amen.

5 Eventide. 10s.

"Aŋpao wicaḣpi nina iyeġe ciŋ, he Miye." — Wayuo xxii: 16.

From "Tunes Old and New" by permission of Rev. Dr. Tucker.

2 Maka wicanaġi inajiŋ po,
  Niśtiŋmapi etaŋ kiktapi ye,
Wicakuje owas iḣpeya po,
  Iyoyaŋpa kiŋ ed omani po.

3 Qa aŋpa wipe kiŋ koyaka po,
  Wahacaŋka suta icupi ye;
Wakta awaŋiçikdag mani po,
  Waihaŋgye ciŋ he onidepi.

4 Ikduḣica po, aŋpa de wakaŋ,
  Aŋpetu de apiiçiya po,
Iyoyaŋpa wana hiyohi ce;
  Optaye opeya kdicupi ye.

5 Wakaŋtaŋka waśte, waoŋśida,
  Wanikiya waśte, wacaŋtkiya,
Qa Woniya waśte, wayuwakaŋ,
  Owihaŋke śni wowaśte yuha.
Amen.

The Christian Year.

6 Twilight. P. M.

"Wicaṭe ciŋ wicayasupi kte ciŋ wana hi." — Wayɹo xi: 18.

From "Tunes Old and New" by permission of Rev. Dr. Tucker.

2 Inajiŋpi kte ça
Owotaŋna
Hena wiconi kiŋ
Wicaqupi kta ce.

3 Tka tona śice ciŋ
Ecoŋpi kin,
Hed woyasu kiŋ ed
Iyayapi kta ce.

4 He oŋ wiconi kiŋ
Akita po;
Dehaŋd eccena
Oyakihipi kta.

5 Wakaŋtaŋka Ate,
Ciŋhiŋtku kiŋ,
Qa Woniya Wakaŋ
Wakaŋtaŋka Hee. AMEN.

Advent.

7 St. Thomas. 8s. 7s. 4.

"Wicoie kiŋ de wicakapi, Christ Jesus waĥtanipis'a niwicayiŋ kta e oŋ makata hi." — 1 Tim. i: 15.

First Tune.

From "Hymns Old and New" by permission of Rev. Dr. Tucker.

2 Jesus Christ makata hi qa
Hed wiconi kiŋ kduśtaŋ;
Tona He waciŋyaŋpi kiŋ,
He niwicayiŋ kta e.
He wiconi,
Christ Itaŋcaŋ kiŋ, ahi.

3 Jesus Christ makata hi qa
Wowakaŋ makoce kiŋ,
He etaŋhaŋ woyaka hi;
Wowicake ĥce ciŋ he.
He wiconi,
Christ Itaŋcaŋ kin, ahi.

4 Jesus Christ makata hi qa
Wowaśte yaotaŋiŋ;
He tuwe ihakab mani
Towaśte etaŋhaŋ qu,
He wiconi,
Christ Itaŋcaŋ kiŋ, ahi.

5 Jesus Christ makata hi qa
He Wahośiye waśte;
Towiconi taŋka ĥce ciŋ,
He hiyohiuŋyaŋpi.
He wiconi,
Christ Itaŋcaŋ kiŋ, ahi.

6 Jesus Christ makata hi qa
Wowaoŋśida yuha;
Awicakehaŋ wicani
Kta oŋ He Itaŋcaŋ hi—
He wiconi,
Christ Itaŋcaŋ kiŋ, ahi. Amen.

The Christian Year.

7 Sicilian Mariner's. 8s. 7s. 4s.

"Wicoie kiŋ de wicakapi, Christ Jesus waĥtanipis'a niwicayiŋ kta e oŋ makata hi." — 1 Tim. I: 15.

SECOND TUNE.

mp

1. Je-sus Christ ma-ka-ta hi qa Ed wi-ca-ce-ĥpi i-cu, Haŋ, wi-ca-śa ĥca i-ca-ġa, Qa Wa-wi-ci-ya wa-śte, He wi-co-ni, He wi-co-ni, Christ I-taŋ-caŋ kiŋ, a-hi. A-MEN.

Used by permission of Rev. Dr. Hutchins.

2 Jesus Christ makata hi qa
Hed wiconi kiŋ kduśtaŋ;
Tona He waciŋyaŋpi kiŋ,
He niwicayiŋ kta e.
He wiconi,
Christ Itaŋcaŋ kiŋ, ahi.

3 Jesus Christ makata hi qa
Wowakaŋ makoce kiŋ,
He etaŋhaŋ woyaka hi;
Wowicake ĥce ciŋ he.
He wiconi,
Christ Itaŋcaŋ kiŋ, ahi.

4 Jesus Christ makata hi qa
Wowaśte yaotaŋiŋ;
He tuwe ihakab mani
Towaśte etaŋhaŋ qu,
He wiconi,
Christ Itaŋcaŋ kiŋ, ahi.

5 Jesus Christ makata hi qa
He Wahośiye waśte;
Towiconi taŋka ĥce ciŋ,
He hiyohiuŋyaŋpi.
He wiconi,
Christ Itaŋcaŋ kiŋ, ahi.

6 Jesus Christ makata hi qa
Wowaoŋśida yuha;
Awicakehaŋ wicani
Kta oŋ He Itaŋcaŋ hi —
He wiconi,
Christ Itaŋcaŋ kiŋ, ahi. AMEN.

Advent.

8 Bartholdy. L. M.

"Wakaŋtaŋka niuŋ wicaśa owasiŋ Wanikiya tawapi, qa iyotaŋ tona wicadapi kiŋ hena."—1 Tim. iv: 10.

From "Tunes Old and New" by permission of Rev. Dr. Tucker.

2 Wiconi ohiŋniyaŋ kiŋ
He tawayapi kta keya;
Anaġoptaŋye ȟciŋ uŋ po;
Wiconi kiŋ duhapi kta.

3 Itaŋcaŋ Towaśte kiŋ he,
Maȟpiya kiŋ etaŋhaŋ e
Dena uŋhiyohipi ce,
Qa he owihaŋkiŋ kte śni.

4 Itaŋcaŋ Towaoŋśida
Maka akaŋd uŋqupi ce;
Owihaŋke waniciŋ kta,
Wiconi kiŋ iyakdeya.

5 Itaŋcaŋ, Jesus Christ, Iye
Waciŋyaŋpi hena owas
Owihaŋkeśniyaŋ waŋkaŋd
Kici ouŋyaŋpi nuŋwe. AMEN.

The Christian Year.

Christmas. — Toŋpi kiŋ.

9 Antioch. C. M.

2 Waŋji waŝte uŋyuhapi
Uŋyataŋpi kta ce:
Owihaŋke wanice ciŋ
Jesus Woekdaku.

3 Waĥtanipi kiŋ ota oŋ
Waciŋyaŋpi waniŋd,
Teĥiya ĥciŋ uŋṭapi, tka
Jesus Wanikiya.

4 Haŋ, Jesus, wowaŝake kiŋ
Owas Nitawa ce;
Haŋ, ceuŋniciyapi ce,
Jesus Wakaŋtaŋka.

5 Ateyapi wakaŋ, nakuŋ
Taniya he, tuka
Waĥtanipi kajuju kiŋ,
Jesus Initaŋcaŋ. AMEN.

10 "Hail to the Morn." 8s, 10s.

From Hollister's S. S. Hymnal, by permission of E. P. Dutton & Co.

Wo - e - ye ḣca taŋ- ka, wa-kaŋ; Ho-san-na, Hosan-na, He waŋkaŋd ti!

He ed o- kni - kde hi - pi ce, Beth - le- hem ed Christ toŋ - pi qed.

U - pi ye, dowaŋ, do-waŋ; U - pi ye, do-waŋ, do-waŋ; Ho-san - na, Ho-

san - na! Christmas ed Christ toŋpi ce; Ho-sanna, He waŋkaŋd ti! A- MEN.

2 Wookiye maka akaŋd;
Hosanna, Hosanna, He waŋkaŋd ti!
Wowaśte qa wookiye;
Hosanna, Hosanna, He waŋkaŋd ti!
Haŋ, He Wicaśayatapi;
Wiyuśkiŋyaŋ idowaŋ po.

3 Haŋ, haŋ, Wanikiya kiŋ hi;
Hosanna, Hosanna, He waŋkaŋd ti!
He qe waoŋśida ḣca ce;
Hosanna, Hosanna, He waŋkaŋd ti!
Christ de aŋpetu toŋpi ce,
Ho po, yataŋ idowaŋ po.

4 Jesus Itaŋcaŋ taŋka ce;
Hosanna, Hosanna, He waŋkaŋd ti!
Towaśake taŋka kiŋ oŋ;
Hosanna, Hosanna, He waŋkaŋd ti!
Ho po, Iye yataŋpi ye;
Christ He waoŋśida ḣca ce. AMEN.

The Christian Year.

11 "Carol, Carol, Christians." 6s, 5s.

"Itaŋcaŋ kiŋ iyuśkiŋyaŋ uŋkidowaŋpi kta." — Ps. xcv: 1.

From Goodrich's S. S. Hymnal, by permission of E. P. Dutton & Co.

The Christian Year.

2 Christ caŋtewaśteya
He idowaŋ po;
De aŋpetu kiŋ ed
Mary Jesus toŋ;
Haŋ, Wanikiya kiŋ
He wacinuŋyaŋpi,
Oŋ Taaŋpetu kiŋ
He ahopa po;
Dowaŋ, dowaŋ.

3 Qa wawicaqupi
Ota kiŋ etaŋ,
Towaoŋśida kiŋ
He sdoduŋyaŋpi;
Heoŋ Ti wakaŋ ed
Cekiyapi ye;
Itehaŋd yaŋke śni,
Qa naĥoŋ kta ce.
Dowaŋ, dowaŋ.

4 Qa tokatakiya
Ded maka akaŋd,
Wapaha waŋ Tawa
Owaŋyag wakaŋ,
He oĥdateya hed,
Wokicize ed,
Wowaśtedake oŋ,
Ho, bdiheca po.
Dowaŋ, dowaŋ. AMEN.

Christmas.

12 "Come Hither, Ye Faithful." P. M.

"Wana Bethlehem ekta uŋyaŋpi kta."—St. Luke ii: 15.

Adeste Fideles.

From "Tunes Old and New" by permission of Rev. Dr. Tucker.

2 Maĥpiya etaŋhaŋ
Ate kiŋ Ciŋca;
Witaŋśna ikpi kiŋ
Hitikda śni ce;
Christ kaġapi śni, tka
Icaġe ĥca ce.

3 Waŋkaŋta dowaŋpi
Nawicaĥon po!
Oknikde heyapi:
"Wakaŋtaŋka ce,
He, wowitaŋ ĥca oŋ
Yataŋpi nuŋwe!"

4 Haŋ, Jesus, nitoŋpi
Aŋpetu de ed,
Maka qa maĥpiya
Niyataŋpi nuŋ;
Wakaŋtaŋka ĥca, tka
Wicaśa ĥca ce.

CHO. O kuwa, kohaŋna,
O kuwa, kohaŋna,
Ohouŋdapi kta,
Inaĥni, u po. AMEN.

13 "Hail! Thou Long-expected Jesus." 8s. 7s.

"Oyate owasiŋ Caŋtiheyapi kiŋ He u kta."—Hag. II: 7.

[*Merton, Hymn* 30, *may be used.*] STUTTGART.

From "Tunes Old and New" by permission of Rev. Dr. Tucker.

2 Israel towaśake kiŋ qa
Tokicaŋpte kiŋ Niye;
Qa maka oyatepi kiŋ
Tehaŋ ĥciŋ apepi qoŋ.

3 Haŋ, oyate nipi kta e
Wowakaŋ yakpazo ce;
Qa Initaŋcaŋ kta e oŋ
Wokoŋze yakdohi niŋ.

4 Woniya owihaŋke śni
Oŋ uŋcaŋtepi yuha:
Qa Nitowaśake kiŋ oŋ,
Hed uŋkicupi ye, Christ.

5 O Wakaŋtaŋka, Ate kiŋ,
Qa Ciŋhiŋtku kiŋ nakuŋ,
Woniya Wakaŋ Hena ko,
Ohiŋni yataŋpi ye. AMEN.

Christmas.

14 "Hark! the Herald Angels Sing." 7s.

"Iyotaŋ waŋkaŋtu ekta Wakaŋtaŋka wowitaŋ yuha nuŋwe."
— St. Luke ii: 14.

[*St. George, Hymn* 4, *may be used.*] MENDELSSOHN.

From "Tunes Old and New" by permission of Rev. Dr. Tucker.

2 Christ, waŋkaŋd ohodapi;
Christ, Itaŋcaŋ ohiŋni,
Ohaŋketa hciŋ hi ce;
Mary he Ciŋhiŋtku kiŋ.

3 Qa Wakaŋtaŋka hca e,
He wicacehpi icu,
Qa wicaśa ob uŋ ce,
Jesus Christ Emmanuel

4 Wookizi kiŋ yuha,
Aŋpa qa wiconi ko,
He dehaŋd uŋkahipi,
Itkokipa po, owas. AMEN.

The Christian Year

15 Silent Night.

Christmas.

16 "Shout the Glad Tidings." P. M.

"Iho, wopida taŋka wootaŋiŋ waṡte oyate kiŋ owaŋcaya eced yiŋ kte ciŋ." — St. Luke ii: 10.

From "Tunes Old and New" by permission of Rev. Dr. Tucker.

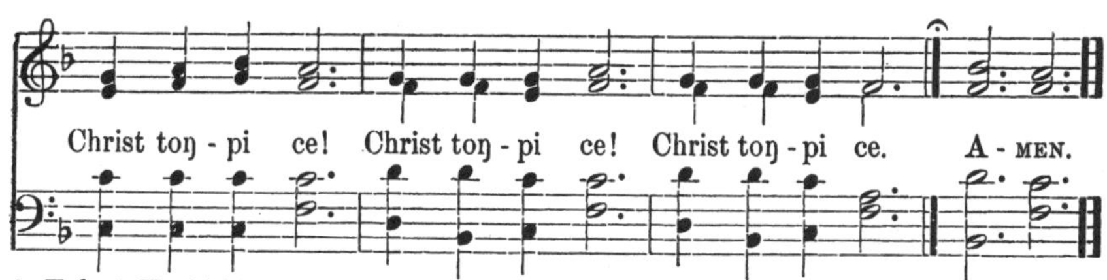

2 Toked He hi kiŋ, oyate owas ed,
Maka kiŋ sitomni oyakapi niŋ;
Waciŋyaŋpi kiŋ toked wiyuśkiŋpi, qa
Kdajujupi śni keś niwicayiŋ kta.

3 Woyataŋ taŋka uŋqupi waśteka,
Oknikde wakaŋ kiŋ ob iyakiś'a;
Maka qa mahpiya kiŋ okiwaŋjina
Christ Jesus Itaŋcaŋ idowaŋpi ye.
AMEN.

17 "Hark! What Mean those Holy Voices." 8s. 7s.

"Uŋkaŋ iknuhaŋna mahpiya ekta uŋpi kiŋ wicota oknikde wakaŋ kiŋ kici hiyeya, Wakaŋtaŋka yataŋpi."—St. Luke ii: 13.

FIRST TUNE. HOLY VOICES.

From "Tunes Old and New" by permission of Rev. Dr. Tucker.

2 Woyakapi kiŋ nahoŋ po!
Wiyuśkiŋyeh śkaŋpi ce;
Wowitaŋ Iye yuha nuŋ!
Haŋ! Tuwa waŋkaŋd uŋ He.

3 Wookiye taŋka hi ce,
Uŋkaŋ he oyate oŋ
Nipi kta ce, wiyuśkiŋpi
Qa dowaŋ po, nina hciŋ.

4 Jesus toŋpi, Christ Iyotaŋ
He; mahpiya qa maka,
Iyakiś'a po! Iye oŋ
Wowaśte iknipi ye.

5 Woohoda qupi ye, qa
Wopida waśte nakuŋ,
Heced ohaŋketa Ti ed
Ohiŋni yauŋpi kta. AMEN.

Christmas.

17 "Hark! What Mean those Holy Voices." 8s. 7s.

"Uŋkaŋ iknuhaŋna mahpiya ekta uŋpi kiŋ wicota oknikde wakaŋ kiŋ kici hiyeya, Wakaŋtaŋka yataŋpi." — St. Luke ii: 13.

From "Tunes Old and New" by permission of Rev. Dr. Tucker.

2 Woyakapi kiŋ naȟoŋ po!
Wiyuśkiŋyeȟ śkaŋpi ce;
Wowitaŋ Iye yuha nuŋ!
Haŋ! Tuwa waŋkaŋd uŋ He.

3 Wookiye taŋka hi ce,
Uŋkaŋ he oyate oŋ
Nipi kta ce, wiyuśkiŋpi
Qa dowaŋ po, nina ȟciŋ.

4 Jesus toŋpi, Christ Iyotaŋ
He; maȟpiya qa maka,
Iyakiś'a po! Iye oŋ
Wowaśte iknipi ye.

5 Woohoda qupi ye, qa
Wopida waśte nakuŋ,
Heced ohaŋketa Ti ed
Ohiŋni yauŋpi kta. AMEN.

New Year. — Omaka oihaŋke qa Teca kiŋ.

18 "A Few More Years shall Roll." S. M. D.

"Wana tokata kiŋ ptedyena." — 1 Cor. vii: 28.

From "Tunes Old and New" by permission of Rev. Dr. Tucker.

The Christian Year.

2 Ehake conana
Wi kiŋ mahed yiŋ kta,
Qa wi mahed iyaye šni
Kiŋ hed uŋqoŋpi kta:
Jesus, Niwe kiŋ oŋ,
Naġi mayuska ye;
Aŋpetu teca kiŋ he oŋ
Mayuwiyeya ye.

3 Ošiceca kte ciŋ
E conana ihaŋ,
Hehaŋd ošiceca cona
Kiŋ hed uŋqoŋpi kta
Jesus, Niwe kiŋ oŋ,
Naġi mayuska ye;
Abdakena kte ciŋ he oŋ
Mayuwiyeya ye.

4 Ehake conana
Teħi sdoduŋyaŋpi,
Qa woteħi yukiŋ kte šni
Kiŋ hed uŋqoŋpi kta:
Jesus, Niwe kiŋ oŋ
Naġi mayuska ye;
Aŋpetu waŋ wašte kiŋ oŋ
Mayuwiyeya ye.

5 Iye hi kte ciŋ he
Wana ikiyena,
Uŋnipi kta oŋ ṭe ciqoŋ,
Christ Jesus Hee ce:
Jesus, Niwe kiŋ oŋ,
Naġi mayuska ye;
Oiyokipi kte ciŋ oŋ
Mayuwiyeya ye. Amen.

Circumcision. — Bakiȟdayapi.

19 "Jesus! Name of Wondrous Love." 7s.

"Caje waŋ wicacaje owasiŋ isaŋpa waŝte kiŋ he qu." — Phil. ii: 9.

First Tune. Maidstone. (W. B. Gilbert.)

2 Jesus! He caje waŝte;
Ŝicapi hena owas
He wicayuska kta ce,
Oŋ piya ȟca nipi kta.
Jesus! He caje suta
Oŋ wicani kta Hee,
Tokeca waŋjina ȟciŋ
Oŋ wicaŋi kte ŝni ce.

3 Jesus! He caje wakaŋ!
Tawa kiŋ wicaŝa ȟca,
Tka Iye Wakaŋtaŋka;
Oŋ waciŋuŋyaŋpi kta.
Qa Ateyapi wakaŋ
Qa Ciŋhiŋtku kiŋ wakaŋ,
Woniya Wakaŋ kiŋ ko,
Wowitaŋ yuha uŋwe. Amen.

19 "Jesus! Name of Wondrous Love." 7s.

"Caje waŋ wicacaje owasiŋ isaŋpa waśte kiŋ he qu." — Phil. ii: 9.

SECOND TUNE. INNOCENCE.

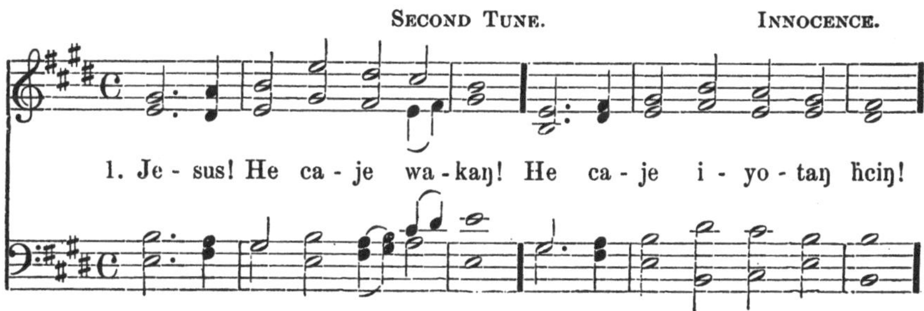

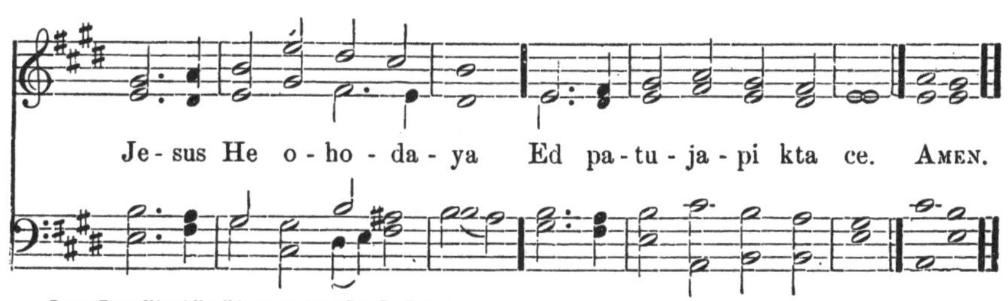

From "Tunes Old and New" by permission of Rev. Dr. Tucker.

2 Jesus! He caje suta;
Qa witaŋśna uŋ qoŋ he,
Jesus toŋ śni itokab
Gabriel he okiyaka.

3 Jesus! He caje waśte;
Sicapi hena owas
He wicayuska kta ce,
Oŋ piya hca nipi kta.

4 Jesus! He caje suta
Oŋ wicani kta Hee,
Tokeca waŋjina hciŋ
Oŋ wicani kte śni ce.

5 Jesus! He caje wakaŋ!
Tawa kiŋ wicaśa hca,
Tka Iye Wakaŋtaŋka;
Oŋ waciŋuŋyaŋpi kta.

6 Qa Ateyapi wakaŋ
Qa Ciŋhiŋtku kiŋ wakaŋ,
Woniya Wakaŋ kiŋ ko,
Wowitaŋ yuha nuŋwe. AMEN.

Epiphany. — Yuotaŋiŋpi kiŋ.

20 Dowanna. P. M.

"Wicaḣpi tawa kiŋ he wiyohiyaŋpata waŋuŋyakapi."—St. Luke ii: 2.

Air and words by GEO. DOWANNA (Native). Harmony revised by WM. W. ROSSEAU.

2 Haŋ, wicaḣpi waŋ wiyakpa,
Jesus He etaŋ,
Qa iyoyaŋpa ska
Hed otaŋiŋ ce;
Aya po, aya po.

3 Jesus Christ Wanikiya kiŋ
Wowitaŋ waśte
Oŋ ikdutaŋiŋ qa
Woniya uśi.
Aya po, aya po. AMEN.

21 Seraphim. 8s. 7s.

"O kuwapi ye, Itaŋcaŋ uŋkaǧapi kiŋ itokab caŋkpeŝka makakde inauŋjiŋpi kta."—Ps. xcv: 6.

2 Ho, owasiŋ Christ ed u po,
Jesus Christ He ded uŋ ce;
Cekiya, ohodapi ye,
Ded waoŋŝida uŋ ce;
Woaĥtani kiŋ owasiŋ
Nicicajujupi kta,
Qa niyuskapi kta, u po,
Jesus He Wanikiya.

3 Jesus Christ wana ed u po
He wacaŋtkiye ĥca ce;
He ekta ohoda u po;
Hee e Wakaŋtaŋka;
Tona He waciŋyaŋpi kiŋ,
Ska wicakaǧa ece;
Wopida kiŋ taŋka ĥca ce,
Heoŋ u po, Jesus ed.

4 Jesus ed u po, oyate,
He ti kiŋ ed nicopi,
Ed owas ohoda u po;
He niniyaŋpi kta ce:
He ekta yaipi heci
Wowaŝte wiconi kiŋ,
Ed Caje dataŋpi kta ce,
Jesus Christ ed upi ye. AMEN.

Epiphany.

22 Langran. 10s.

"Wakaŋtaŋka oŋśiuŋdapi qa Iye ite kiŋ aiyoyaŋbuŋyaŋpi nuŋwe."

From "Tunes Old and New" by permission of Rev. Dr. Tucker.

2 Maka akaŋd wicaśa uŋpi kiŋ,
Nicaje taŋka kiŋ yataŋpi kta;
Opewicayakitoŋ kiŋ he oŋ,
Oyate kiŋ iniyuśkiŋpi kta.

3 Qa woowotaŋna Nitawa kiŋ,
Qa woyasu Nitawa kiŋ okna,
Oyate kiŋ wicadasu kiŋhaŋ,
Nietapa kiŋ ed uŋqoŋpi niŋ.

4 Itaŋcaŋ kiŋ, Nitaokiyepi,
Owasiŋ wowaśte wicaqu ye;
Qa oŋ caŋku wiconi kiŋ okna,
Maĥpiyata sutaya ipi kta.

5 Wakaŋtaŋka waśte, waoŋśida,
Wanikiya waśte, wacaŋtkiya,
Qa Woniya waśte, wayuwakaŋ,
Owihaŋke śni wowaśte yuha. AMEN.

The Christian Year.

23 Wareham. L. M.

"Ojaŋjaŋ waŋ oyate kiŋ aojaŋjaŋwicayiŋ kte ciŋ."— St. Luke ii: 32.

First Tune.

From "Tunes Old and New" by permission of Rev. Dr. Tucker.

2 Itaŋcaŋ Toptaye owas,
Caje wakaŋdapi nuŋwe;
Wicoowotaŋna wi oŋ
Iyoyaŋbwicayiŋ kta ce.

3 Wanikiya waciŋyaŋ po,
Wateśdagyctoŋpi kta ce;
Qa Jesus Tokicaŋpte oŋ
Maka oyate nipi kta.

4 Wiconi kiŋ oyadepi
Owas Iyoyaŋpa kiŋ de
Ihakab u po, heced oŋ
Wiconi ed yaipi kta.

5 Ateyapi, Ciŋhiŋtku kiŋ,
Qa Woniya Wakaŋ kiŋ He,
Wakaŋtaŋka waŋjina kiŋ
He wowitaŋ yuha nuŋwe. Amen.

Epiphany.

23 Grace Church. L. M.

"Ojaŋjaŋ waŋ oyate kiŋ aojaŋjaŋwicayiŋ kte ciŋ." — St. Luke ii: 32.

From "Tunes Old and New" by permission of Rev. Dr. Tucker.

2 Itaŋcaŋ Toptaye owas,
Caje wakaŋdapi nuŋwe,
Wicoowotaŋna wi oŋ
Iyoyaŋbwicayiŋ kta ce.

3 Wanikiya waciŋyaŋ po,
Wateśdagyetoŋpi kta ce;
Qa Jesus Tokicaŋpte oŋ
Maka oyate nipi kta.

4 Wiconi kiŋ oyadepi
Owas Iyoyaŋpa kiŋ de
Ihakab u po, heced oŋ
Wiconi ed yaipi kta.

5 Ateyapi, Ciŋhiŋtku kiŋ,
Qa Woniya Wakaŋ kiŋ He,
Wakaŋtaŋka waŋjina kiŋ
He wowitaŋ yuha nuŋwe. AMEN.

24 "Hail to the Lord's Anointed." 7s. 6s. D.

"Iye Towitaŋ kiŋ oŋ maka kiŋ ataya ojuna nuŋwe." — Ps. lxxii: 19.

[*Montgomery, Hymn* 129, *may be used.*] HODGES.

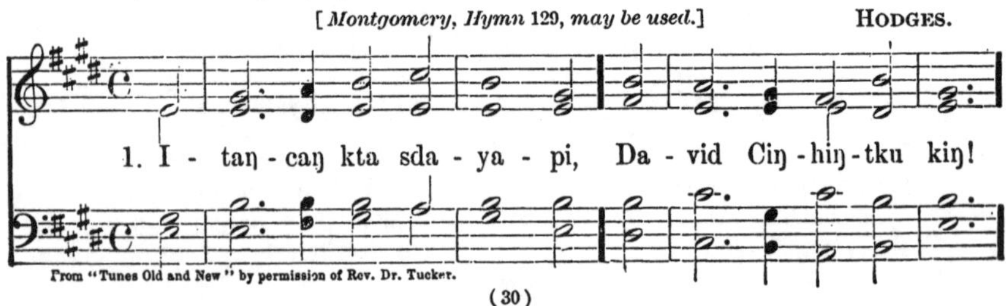

From "Tunes Old and New" by permission of Rev. Dr. Tucker.

The Christian Year.

2 Kakijapi hena qa
  Waȟpanicapi ko,
He owicakiyiŋ kta;
  Qa oŋśikapi kiŋ
Waśagwicayiŋ kta ce,
  Qa ceyapi tka qoŋ
Dowaŋpi heekiya
  Wicaqu kta e hi.

3 Iwaśtena maġaju
  Iyeced hi kta ce;
Qa wowiyuśkiŋ ȟce ça
  Wacaŋtkiyapi kiŋ,
Waȟca waśte iyeced,
  He Toye kiŋ okna
Icaȟ hinapiŋ kta ce,
  Maka sitomniyaŋ.

4 Qa wookiye kiŋ He
  Itokab yiŋ kta ce,
He ȟe owas iyahaŋ
  Qa eyaŋpaha kta.
Paha owas etaŋhaŋ
  Wicoowotaŋa
Mniyowe waŋ iyeced
  Kadus waŋkiŋ kta ce.

5 Nakuŋ ayaśtaŋśniyaŋ
  He cekiyapi kta,
Qa Tokiconze kiŋ he
  Ihaŋgyapi kte śni;
Caje kiŋ he suta kta,
  Owihaŋke waniŋd;
Wacaŋtkiyapi ȟce ciŋ,
  Caje kiŋ hec ce. AMEN.

Lent. — Akiĥaŋiçiyapi Omaka kiŋ.

25 "Just as I Am,—Without One Plea." 8s. 6.

"Itaŋcaŋ, tuwa ekta uŋyaŋpi kta he? Owihaŋke waniŋd wiconi wicoie kiŋ duhe ciŋ."—St. John vi: 68.

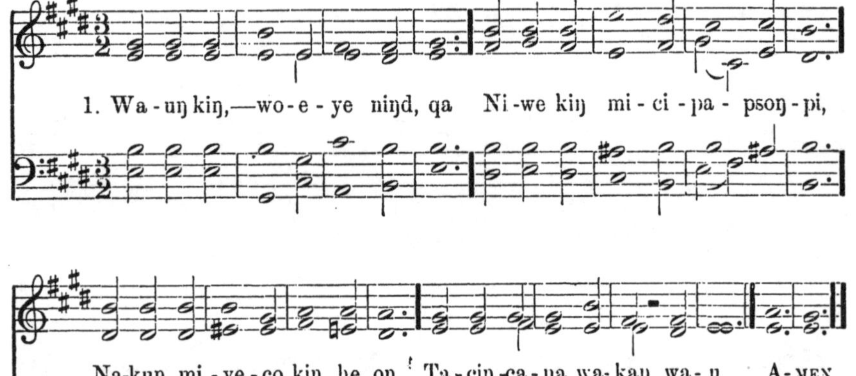

From "Tunes Old and New" by permission of Rev. Dr. Tucker.

2 Wauŋ kiŋ, — qa minaġi kiŋ
He ṡape ciŋ wakduska kta
E takuna ape ṡni ĥciŋ,
Taciŋcana wakáŋ, wau.

3 Wauŋ kiŋ, — haŋ, Niye ekta,
Niwe kiŋ woṡape owas
Yuska okihi kiŋ he oŋ,
Taciŋcana wakaŋ, wau.

4 Wauŋ kiŋ, — woceṭuŋkda oŋ
Kaĥodiyemayaŋpi s'a
Qa toketu taŋiŋ ṡni s'a,
Taciŋcana wakaŋ, wau.

5 Wauŋ kiŋ, — haŋ, mahetaŋhaŋ,
Akaŋtaŋ, wokipajiŋ ko
Qa wokokipe ota ṡa,
Taciŋcana wakaŋ, wau.

6 Wauŋ kiŋ, — haŋ, waĥpanica,
Iṡtaġoŋġa, qa oŋṡika —
Qa takuna bduhe ṡni ṡa,
Taciŋcana wakaŋ, wau.

7 Wauŋ kiŋ, — wowijice qa
Iṡta wicabdeza, hena
Niye ĥca ed iyewaya,
Taciŋcana wakaŋ, wau.

8 Wauŋ kiŋ, — haŋ, ĥmayacu.
Nakuŋ mayaduska kta ce
Miyeco kiŋ wicawada,
Taciŋcana wakaŋ, wau.

9 Wauŋ kiŋ, — haŋ, nitowaṡte
He wokaġi ihaŋgya ce,
Qa tawamayakiyiŋ kta,
Taciŋcana wakaŋ, wau. AMEN

25 "Just as I Am, — Without One Plea." P. M.

For remaining stanzas, see preceding page.

26 "Rock of Ages, Cleft for Me." 7s.

"Imnija oḣdoka waŋ mahed ecikde kta." — Kdi. xxxiii: 22.

From Goodrich & Gilbert "Hymnal," by permission of E. P. Dutton & Co.

2 Ohiŋni waceye ṡa,
Ohiŋni ḣtawani ṡa,
Oŋ wawaḣtani hena
Miciyuskapi kte ṡni,
Tka nimakiyiŋ kte ciŋ
He Niye niṡnana ce.

3 Wowiyuŋ manice ṡa,
Ed onicataŋpi kiŋ
He ecena yus wauŋ,
Wowaṡake ko waniŋd,
Woṡape kduha wau,
Jesus Christ mayuska ye.

4 Ni wauŋ hebaŋyaŋ ḣciŋ
Qa tohaŋd maṭe ciŋhaŋ,
Qa tohaŋd piya wani,
Qa waŋciyake ciŋhaŋ,
Iŋyaŋ Ohiŋniyaŋ kiŋ,
Hed Niye namaḣma ye. AMEN.

The Christian Year.

27 Hanover. 5s. 6s. 5.

" Nitowaoŋśida waśte taŋka kiŋ oŋ wawaȟtani kiŋ pajuju ye."—Ps. li: 1

From "Tunes Old and New" by permission of Rev. Dr. Tucker.

2 Aomakpaza,
Iyoyaŋpa niŋd
Onuniyaŋ ȟciŋ
Kakiśya wauŋ;
Christ Jesus Itaŋcaŋ,
Minaġi ni kta
E mayuteca ye,
Kici ciuŋ kta.

3 Wiconi duha,
Miś nuni wauŋ,
Wani kte ciŋ he
Iyecece śni.
Matiŋ kte śni e oŋ,
Ate wakaŋ kiŋ,
Nitowaoŋśida
Umakiya ye.

4 Wanikiyapi,
Waoŋśidapi,
Wakicaŋptapi,
Henakeȟ owas
Oyate wicekna
Kduotaŋiŋ ye;
Wicoŋṭe etaŋhaŋ
Niuŋyaŋpi ye. AMEN.

Lent.

28 Benevento. 7s. D.

"Tohiŋni aciyuśtaŋ kte śni qa iḣpeciyiŋ kte śni."—Heb. xiii: 5.

From "Tunes Old and New" by permission of Rev. Dr. Tucker.

2 Wowaśte Nitawa kiŋ
He uŋcaŋtepi ed uŋ:
Wowaśake kiŋ duha,
Qa minaġ'i qa taŋcaŋ
Koya oŋ waciŋciya.
Ohiŋni ohocida,
Ohni ceciciyiŋ kta,
Heced oŋ namaḣoŋ ye.

3 Wopida eciciya,
Oŋśimayakida kta;
Woaḣtani ota kiŋ
He oŋ micicajuju
Qa naġi mayuwaśte,
Qa caŋte mayuska ye;
Heced ceciciya ce;
Omayakiya nuŋwe.

4 Wowaciŋye taŋka kiŋ,
Qa Nitokaŋ wowaśte
He iyeyepica śni.
Niś Iniyotaŋ yauŋ;
Qa waoŋśiyadas'a
He kanipepica śni;
Wowaśte Wakaŋtaŋka
Yecidaotaniŋ ce. AMEN.

The Christian Year.

29 Ephrata. 8s. 7s.

"Iĥpemaye śni, nakuŋ amayuśtaŋ śni ye, O wiconi mitawa ta-Wakaŋtaŋka." — Ps. xxvii: 11.

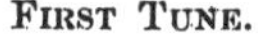

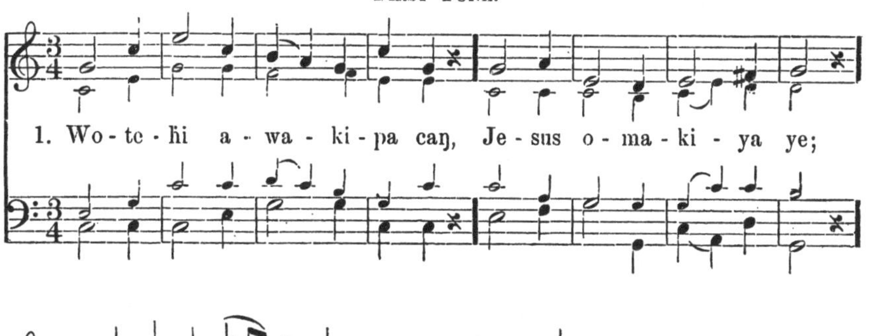

2 Niś caŋku waśte yakaġa
He okna bda waciŋ,
Qa maka abduśtaŋ qeyaś,
Jesus Niś waciŋciya.

3 Wowinape kiŋ mitawa,
Niś waoŋśiyada ce;
Wokokipe kiŋ owasiŋ
Ed nimayakiyiŋ kta.

4 Wawaĥtani kiŋ kajuju;
Qa iśtamnihaŋpe kiŋ
Koya micipakiŋta ye;
Jesus oŋśimada ye

5 Taku Jesus Christ uŋqupi
He wiconi taŋka ce;
Oyapapi kta iyeced
Oŋ taŋyaŋ oĥaŋyaŋ po.

6 Jesus Christ Nioĥaŋ kiŋ he
Wopida ĥca taŋka ce;
Qa waniyakiyiŋ kte ciŋ,
He dehaŋd otaŋiŋ ĥca. Amen.

Lent.

29 Turneau. 8s. 7s.

"Iĥpemaye śni, nakuŋ amayuśtaŋ śni ye, O wiconi mitawa ta-Wakaŋtaŋka." — Ps. xxvii: 11.

SECOND TUNE.

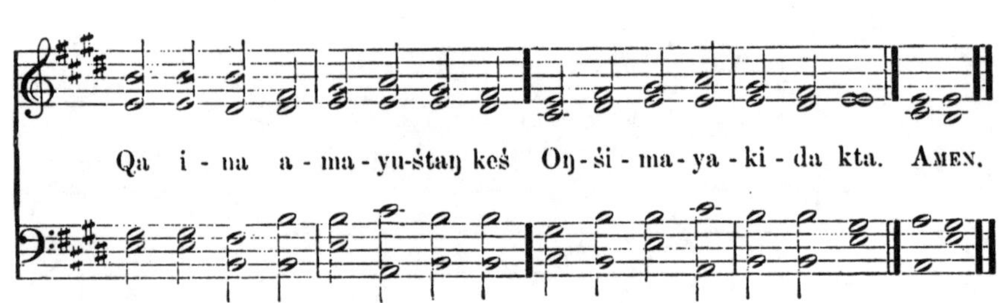

From "Tunes Old and New" by permission of Rev. Dr. Tucker.

2 Niś caŋku waśte yakaġa
He okna bda waciŋ,
Qa maka abduśtaŋ qeyaś,
Jesus Niś waciŋciya.

3 Wowinape kiŋ mitawa;
Niś waoŋśiyada ce;
Wokokipe kiŋ owasiŋ
Ed nimayakiyiŋ kta.

4 Wawaĥtani kiŋ kajuju;
Qa iśtamnihaŋpe kiŋ
Koya micipakiŋta ye;
Jesus oŋśimada ye.

5 Taku Jesus Christ uŋqupi
He wiconi taŋka ce;
Oyapapi kta iyeced
Oŋ taŋyaŋ oĥaŋyaŋ po.

6 Jesus Christ Nioĥaŋ kiŋ he
Wopida ĥca taŋka ce;
Qa waniyakiyiŋ kte ciŋ,
He dehaŋd otaŋiŋ ĥca. AMEN.

30 Merton. 8s. 7s.

"Wicaśa Ciŋhiŋtku kiŋ woaȟtani maka akaŋd kajuju kta okihi e he sdodyayapi kta." —St. Matt. ix: 6.

From "Tunes Old and New" by permission of Rev. Dr. Tucker.

2 Woaȟtani ota kiŋ oŋ
Ohiŋni wawaqiŋ, qa
Wowaśake niŋd wauŋ kiŋ,
Oŋ mayuwaśaka ye.

3 Woaȟtani oŋ maśica,
Qa nikiyena mni kta
E iyemacece śni, tka
Miś miyeco oŋ wau.

4 Awicakehaŋ wanuni,
Niś aciyuśtaŋ kiŋ oŋ,
Tka dehaŋtu ciksuye ça
Oŋ iyopemiçiya.

5 We Nitawa kiŋ hecena
He wayuska kiŋ ee,
Oŋ micaŋte qa mioȟaŋ
Miciyuecetu ye. AMEN.

Lent.

31 "Nearer, my God, to Thee." P. M.

"Iho Miś nici wauŋ, qa toki da eśa awaŋciyakiŋ kta."—Wicoicage xxviii: 15.

[*Bethany, Hymn 93, may be used.*] KEDRON.

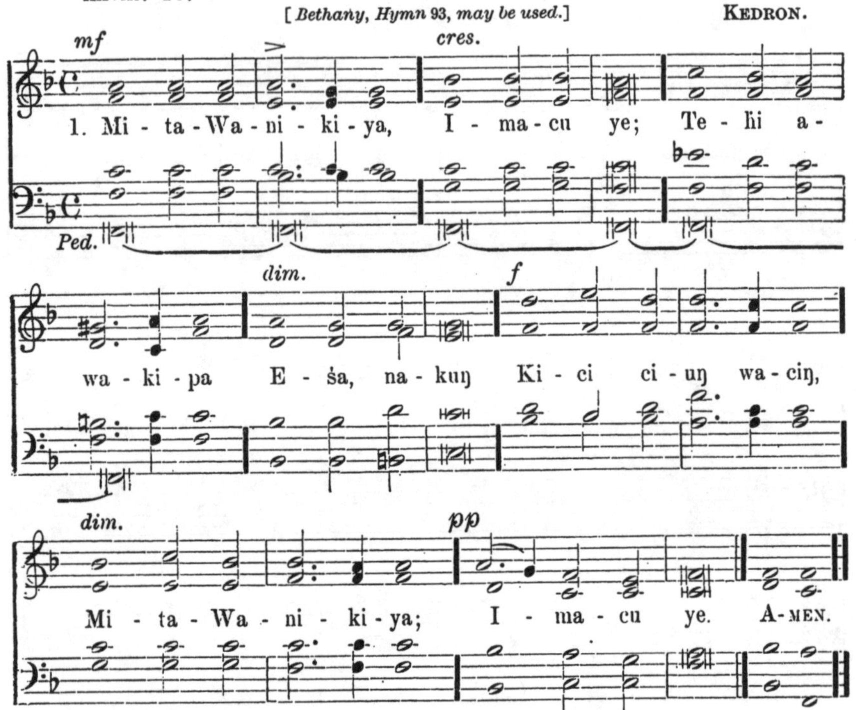

From "Tunes Old and New" by permission of Rev. Dr. Tucker.

2 Ḣewoskaŋd, okpaza
  Ed iŋyaŋ waŋ
Iwapahiŋ, nakuŋ
  Owaŋka niŋd,
Wiwahaŋbde ciŋ ed,
Mita-Wanikiya,
  Kici ciuŋ.

3 Maḣpiyata caŋku
  Makipazo;
Wakaŋpi kiŋ waŋkaŋd
  Yemaśipi,
Qa wowaśte kiŋ ed,
Mita-Wanikiya,
  Mayuha kta.

4 Waktaya ḣciŋ wauŋ,
  Teḣika śa,
Christ omakiya oŋ
  Bdataŋ kta ce;
Owayuśna kiŋ ed,
Mita-Wanikiya,
  Kici ciuŋ.

5 Qa wibduśkiŋ kiŋ oŋ,
  Wicaḣpi kiŋ
Wi ko awektoŋja,
  Waŋkaŋd ye se,
Icidowaŋ kta ce;
Mita-Wanikiya,
  Nikiyena. AMEN.

32 "Saviour, when in Dust to Thee." 7s. D.

"Iye iyutaŋyaŋpi kiŋ heoŋ etaŋhaŋ tona iyutaŋwicayapi kiŋ hena ewicakdaku kta okihi."—Heb. ii: 18.

SPANISH CHANT.

2 Qa Nitoŋpi kiŋ he oŋ,
Qa wicaśa tokope,
Tokakijcpi kiŋ ko,
Oyapa kiŋ hena oŋ,
Qa akiȟaŋniçiya
Ed wakaŋśica yakte,
Oŋ waceuŋkiyapi
Ed uŋkatoŋwaŋpi ye.

3 Qa iyonicisica,
Ceyakiye ȟca he oŋ,
Wowiśted śina yetoŋ,
Qa watcśdake pepe
Nuŋ, Niopi qa hehaŋd
Caŋ akaŋd niktepi qoŋ,
Oŋ waceuŋkiyapi
Ed uŋkatoŋwaŋpi ye.

4 Qa wicaȟapi kiŋ he,
Qa wicoŋṭe kiŋ nakuŋ
Ko ohiyaye ciqoŋ,
Oŋ niuŋyayapi kta;
Wowaśake waŋ wakaŋ
Wowitaŋ nakuŋ duha,
Oŋ waceuŋkiyapi
Ed uŋkatoŋwaŋpi ye. AMEN.

Lent.

33 "Weary of Earth, and Laden with my Sin." 10s.

"He oŋ wopekitoŋpi kiŋ uŋyuhapi, Iye we kiŋ oŋ, woaḣtani kajujupi kiŋ hee, Iye towaoŋṡida taŋka kiŋ eciyataŋhan." — Ephes. i: 7.

LANGRAN.

From "Tunes Old and New" by permission of Rev. Dr. Tucker.

2 Tka taku ṡica hed ouŋye ṡni,
Qa miṡ hemaceca sdodwakiya,
Eṡa wicaho waŋ hetaŋhaŋ ḣciŋ,
"U wo," emakiya nawakiḣoŋ.

3 Haŋ, nina ḣciŋ maṡice ciŋ he oŋ
Makoce waŋ wakaŋ kiŋ hed, nakuŋ
Oiyotaŋke ska kiŋ toked ed
Inawajiŋ owakihi kta he?

4 Maḣpiyatakiya yewacaŋmi
Tka ṡice ciŋ icakdaya mauŋ
Ṡa wokicaŋpte de nawakiḣoŋ,
"Owas okdaka yo, yani kta ce."

5 Hemakiye ciŋ Jesus Hee ce,
Imacu kta e oŋ nape uya;
Owas yuska kte ciŋ we kiŋ he e,
Waŋkaŋd amai kta okihi ce. AMEN.

Palm Sunday and Passion Week. — Jerusalem ed ya Aŋpetu Wakaŋ qa Ioko kiŋ.

34 "Forty Days and Forty Nights." 7s.

"Qa Woniya kiŋ Jesus makotahena ekta iyayeya; aŋpetu wikcemna topa hehaŋyaŋ Wakaŋṡica wawiyutaŋyaŋ. Uŋkaŋ aŋpetu kiŋ ḣena ed takuna yute ṡni." — St. Luke iv: 1, 2.

FIRST TUNE. HERNLEIN.

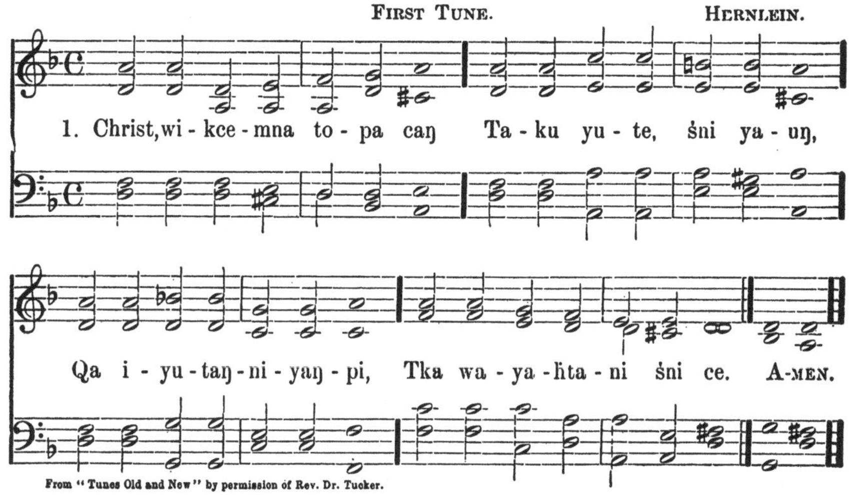

From "Tunes Old and New" by permission of Rev. Dr. Tucker.

2 Qa iyokiṡid yauŋ
He ed ouŋpapi qa
Ceuŋkiyapi kte ciŋ
He iyececa ṡni he?

3 Qa waŋkaŋṡica kiŋ he
Nina ḣciŋ uŋkuwapi
Ṡa, he ḣuŋkpaŋniyaŋ ye,
He eciŋ yaktena ce.

4 Heced wookiye ḣca
Oŋ uŋkakipapi kta
Qa Nitaoknikde kiŋ
Ouŋkiyapi kta ce.

5 O Wanikiya wakaŋ,
Nicakda uŋqoŋpi nuŋ;
Oŋ wicakini kte ciŋ
Ed inauŋjiŋpi kta. AMEN.

Palm Sunday and Passion Week.

34 "Forty Days and Forty Nights." 7s.

"Qa Woniya kiŋ Jesus makotahena ekta iyayeya; aŋpetu wikcemna topa hehaŋyaŋ Wakaŋśica wawiyutaŋyaŋ. Uŋkaŋ aŋpetu kiŋ hena ed takuna yute śni."—St. Luke iv: 1, 2.

SECOND TUNE. REDHEAD NO. 47.

From "Tunes Old and New" by permission of Rev. Dr. Tucker.

2 Qa iyokiśid yauŋ
He ed ouŋpapi qa
Ceuŋkiyapi kte ciŋ
He iyececa śni he?

3 Qa waŋkaŋśica kiŋ he
Nina hciŋ uŋkuwapi
Śa, he huŋkpaŋniyaŋ ye,
He eciŋ yaktena ce.

4 Heced wookiye hca
Oŋ uŋkakipapi kta
Qa Nitaoknikde kiŋ
Ouŋkiyapi kta ce.

5 O Wanikiya wakaŋ,
Nicakda uŋqoŋpi nuŋ;
Oŋ wicakini kte ciŋ
Ed inauŋjiŋpi kta. AMEN.

35 "Glory be to Jesus." 6s. 5s.

"Christ we teħike ciŋ." — 1 Peter i: 19.

FIRST TUNE. CASWELL.

From "Tunes Old and New" by permission of Rev. Dr. Tucker.

2 We waśte ħiyu kiŋ,
  Oŋ maka kiŋ he
Ohiŋni teħi kiŋ
  Ed waŋkiŋ kte śni
E opekitoŋ kiŋ,
  Ohiŋniyaŋ he
Woyawaśte taŋka
  Oŋ yataŋpi nuŋ!

3 Heoŋ ho taŋkaya
  Iyakiś'a po —
Haŋ, mnitaŋ e ħmuŋ se
  Iyakiś'a po;
Awicakeħaŋ ħciŋ
  We teħike ciŋ
Jesus we waśte kiŋ
  He yataŋpi ye! AMEN

Palm Sunday and Passion Week.

35 "Glory be to Jesus." 6s. 5s D.

"Christ we tehike ciŋ." — 1 Peter i: 19.

SECOND TUNE. ST. JOHN.

From "Tunes Old and New" by permission of Rev. Dr. Tucker.

2 We waŝte hiyu kiŋ,
  Oŋ maka kiŋ he
Ohiŋni tehi kiŋ
  Ed waŋkiŋ kte ŝni
E opekitoŋ kiŋ,
  Ohiŋniyaŋ he
Woyawaŝte taŋka
  Oŋ yataŋpi nuŋ!

3 Heoŋ ho taŋkaya
  Iyakiŝ'a po —
Haŋ, mnitaŋ e ħmuŋ se
  Iyakiŝ'a po;
Awicakehaŋ ħciŋ
  We tehike ciŋ
Jesus we waŝte kiŋ
  He yataŋpi ye! AMEN.

Palm Sunday and Passion Week.

36 Hollingside. 7s. D.

"Takuna oŋ imawiŋkta ṡni nuŋwe, Jesus Christ Itaŋcaŋuŋkiyapi caŋicipawega Tawa kiŋ hecena oŋ." — Gal. vi: 14.

[*Martyn, Hymn 3, may be used.*]

From "Tunes Old and New" by permission of Rev. Dr. Tucker.

2 Wosdodye waŋ tokeca
Takuna owade ṡni,
Christ miye oŋ caŋ akaŋd
Nina ȟciŋ kakiṡyapi;

Wosdodye decena ȟciŋ
Oŋ wiconi ȟca kta ce,
Oŋ wani kta hee e,
Christ okaȟniȟmayaŋ ye. AMEN.

The Christian Year.

37 "Ride On! Ride On in Majesty!" L. M.

"Wicota tokata yapi, qa tona ihakab·upi kiŋ iyakiś'api qa heyapi; David ciŋhiŋtku woohiye yuha nuŋwe." — St. Matt. xxi: 9.

ROUSSEAU.

1. Ya yo! ya yo! I - ni - taŋ -caŋ! Paŋ - yaŋ Ho - san - na e - ya - pi;

Caŋ-ḣa - ka qa śi - na kiŋ ko A - di ya yo, Wa - ni - ki - ya. AMEN.

From "Tunes Old and New" by permission of Rev. Dr. Tucker.

2 Ya yo! ya yo! Initaŋcaŋ!
Eśa, niţiŋ kta e ya yo;
O Christ, wicoŋţe kiŋ nakuŋ
De oŋ ohiyayiŋ kta ce.

3 Ya yo! ya yo! Initaŋcaŋ!
Maḣpiya ed wicobe kiŋ
Wanikduśna kte ciŋ de oŋ
Iyokiśid hiyeya ce.

4 Ya yo! ya yo! Initaŋcaŋ!
Ehake wokicize qed;
Niyate Toyaŋke akaŋd
Iye ape niyaŋka ce.

5 Ya yo! ya yo! Initaŋcaŋ!
Eśa niţiŋ kta e ya yo;
Nicakije ciŋ ohakab,
Nitowitaŋ ikikcu wo! AMEN.

Good Friday. — Aŋpetu Izaptaŋ waŝte kiŋ.

38 Spanish Chant. 7s.

"Awicakehaŋ wauŋyazaŋpi kiŋ hena Iye yuha, qa wicocaŋte ŝica uŋkitawapi kiŋ hena Iye qiŋ."—Isa. liii: 4

From "Goodrich & Gilbert Hymnal" by permission of E. P. Dutton & Co.

2 Jesus Christ Wanikiya,
De aŋpetu kiŋ ehaŋ,
Caŋicipaweġa kiŋ
Ed onicataŋpi ce;
Miŝ wawaȟtani hena
Oŋ niktepi he ehaŋ,
Tka miyecicajuju,
Oŋ waciŋciyiŋ kta ce.

3 Jesus Christ Wanikiya,
De aŋpetu ed, miye
E oŋ, wokakije waŋ
Oŋ teŝdagnicatoŋpi;
Tka tokata hee oŋ
Miŝ, Wakaŋtaŋka ti ed,
Wowitaŋ wateŝdake
Hee ȟca mayaqu kta.

4 Jesus Christ Wanikiya,
De aŋpetu kiŋ ehaŋ,
Mni waŋ p̣a niçupi ce;
Woteȟike tanka ȟca
Tka tokata, hee oŋ,
Miŝ, Wakaŋtaŋka ti ed,
Woyatke wiconi ȟca
Niŝ yatkemayayiŋ kta.

5 Jesus Christ Wanikiya,
De aŋpetu kiŋ ehaŋ,
Niŝ cuwi canipapi;
We, mini nakuŋ, hiyu,
Qa hetaŋhaŋ oŋ, dehaŋd
Woaȟtani kiŋ owas,
Oŋ maŝape ciŋ ee,
Micipajujupi ce. AMEN.

The Christian Year.

39 "'T is Finished; So the Saviour Cried." L. M.

"Wana yuŝtaŋpi ce, eya ; hehaŋd pa makata iyeye ça taniya kiŋ hiyuya."—St. John xix : 30.

FIRST TUNE. REDHEAD, 12.

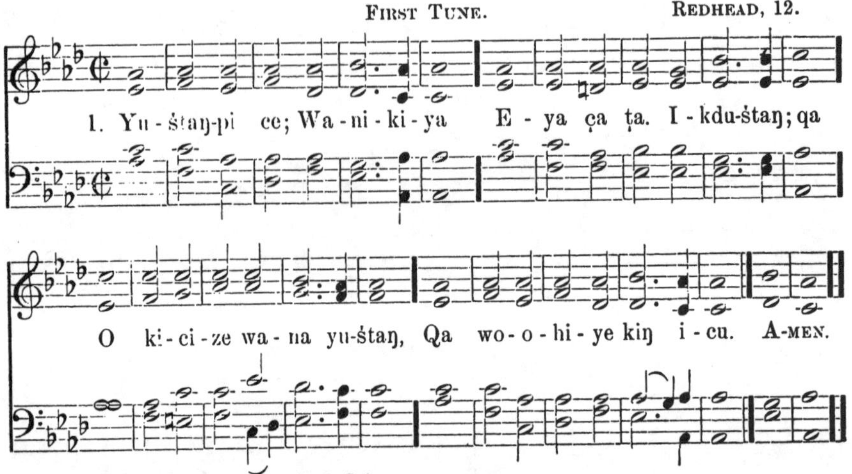

From "Tunes Old and New" by permission of Rev. Dr. Tucker.

2 Yuŝtaŋpi ce; owapi qoŋ
Iyeced; qa waayata
Eyapi qoŋ, Miye ḣca e
Wanikiya mikduŝtaŋ ce.

3 Yuŝtaŋpi ce; qa ozaŋpi
Wakaŋ kiŋ he yuḣdecapi,
Qa Aaron he wayuŝna qoŋ
Detaŋhaŋ he henana kta.

4 Yuŝtaŋpi ce; maṭiŋ kta e
Wahowaye ciŋ dee e
Oŋ woaḣtani kiŋ wakte,
Qa oŋ wicota nipi kta.

5 Yuŝtaŋpi ce; Wakaŋŝica
Ihaŋgwaye, ça oŋ maka
Ed wowiyuŝkiŋ kiŋ u kta,
Qa wowaŝte yukiŋ kta ce.

6 Yuŝtaŋpi ce; oyaka po;
Makata qa maḣpiyata,
Wakaŋŝica ti qed nakuŋ,
Yuŝtaŋpi kiŋ oyaka po. AMEN.

Good Friday.

39 "'Tis Finished; So the Saviour Cried." L. M.

"Wana yuśtaŋpi ce, eya; hehaŋd pa makata iyeye ça taniya kiŋ hiyuya."—St. John xix: 30.

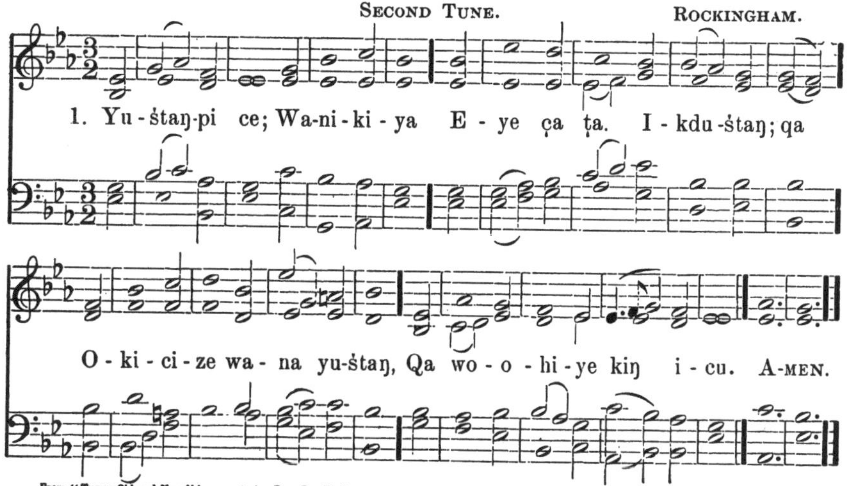

From "Tunes Old and New," by permission Rev. Dr. Tucker.

2 Yuśtaŋpi ce; owapi qoŋ
Iyeced; qa waayata
Eyapi qoŋ, Miye ȟca e
Wanikiya mikduśtaŋ ce.

3 Yuśtaŋpi ce; qa ozaŋpi
Wakaŋ kiŋ he yuȟdecapi,
Qa Aaron he wayuśna qoŋ
Detaŋhaŋ he henana kta.

4 Yuśtaŋpi ce; maṭiŋ kta e
Wahowaye ciŋ dee e
Oŋ woaȟtani kiŋ wakte,
Qa oŋ wicota nipi kta.

5 Yuśtaŋpi ce; Wakaŋśica
Ihaŋgwaye, ça oŋ maka
Ed wowiyuśkiŋ kiŋ u kta,
Qa wowaśte yukiŋ kta çe.

6 Yuśtaŋpi ce; oyaka po;
Makata qa maȟpiyata,
Wakaŋśica ti qed nakuŋ,
Yuśtaŋpi kiŋ oyaka po. AMEN.

The Christian Year.

40 "Bound Upon the Accursed Tree." Ten 7s.

"Awicakehaŋ wicaśa kiŋ de Wakaŋtaŋka ciŋhiŋtku kiŋ Hee."—St. Mark xv: 39.

From "Tunes Old and New" by permission of Rev. Dr. Tucker.

2 Caŋ kiŋ ed okataŋpi,
Wokokipe qa wakaŋ,
Hehehe, tuwe kta he?
Wicokaya ḣca eṡa,
Wi kiŋ he aokpaza,
Qa maka kiŋ he ṡkaŋṡkaŋ,
Ṭapi kiŋ kinipi, qa
Iŋyaŋ kiŋ nabdebdeca;
Oŋ iyeuŋkiyapi;
Jesus, Christ kiŋ, de Niye!

3 Caŋ kiŋ ed okataŋpi,
Oŋṡike ça ṭa nuŋ se,
Hehehe, tuwe kta he?
Ṭiŋ kta uŋkaŋ he ehaŋd
Ed howaye ḣce ciŋ oŋ,
Qa taŋcaŋ kiŋ ḣapi ed
Iŋyaŋ oŋ natakapi,
Qa hed ceya hipi qoŋ,
Oŋ iyeuŋkiyapi;
Jesus, Christ kiŋ, de Niye!

4 Caŋ kiŋ ed okataŋpi,
Wokokipe qa wakaŋ,
Hehehe, tuwe kta he?
Ktepi kiŋ oŋ cekiya,
Qa kini, nakuŋ he oŋ,
Ṭe ciŋ oŋ niwicaya,
Woohiye kiŋ yuha,
Qa wakaŋpi ob yaŋka;
Oŋ iyeuŋkiyapi;
Jesus, Christ kiŋ, de Niye! Amen.

Easter Eve. — Kini Itokab Ḣtayetu kiŋ.

41 Vienna. 7s.

"Owotaŋna uŋyawapi kte ciŋ oŋ ake najiŋkiyapi." — Rom. iv: 25.

[*Monkland, Hymn* 107, *may be used.*]

From "Tunes Old and New" by permission of Rev. Dr. Tucker.

2 Taku wokipajiŋ kiŋ,
Taku wokakije kiŋ
Ko owas akipe ça
Caŋ kiŋ ed okataŋpi.

3 Yamni caŋ ehaŋd, iho!
He kini waŋyakapi;
Qa Atkuku Ti kiŋ ed
Wowitaŋ kduha yaŋka.

4 Toie nauŋḣoŋpi,
Toḣaŋ kiŋ uŋkopapi;
Qa uŋṭapi kiŋ hehaŋd,
Heciya uŋyaŋpi kta.

5 Qa Ateyapi wakaŋ,
Qa Ciŋhiŋtku kiŋ wakaŋ,
Woniya Wakaŋ kiŋ ko,
Wowitaŋ yuha nuŋwe. Amen.

The Christian Year.

Easter. — Kini Aŋpetu kiŋ.

42 St. Martin's. C. M.

"Tona iśtiŋmapi qoŋ hena ed taku tokaheya icaġe ciŋ Hee." — 1 Cor. xv: 20.

FIRST TUNE.

By permission of A. S. Barnes & Co.

2 Waskuyeca tokaheya
Wicaṭe ciŋ etaŋ
Icaġe ciŋ he Ee ce,
Piya inajiŋ oŋ.

3 Eciŋ wicaśa kiŋ etaŋ
Wicaṭe ciŋ he u;
Iyeced he etaŋhaŋ oŋ
Wicani teca ce.

4 Wicaśa Adam he etaŋ
Ihaŋgwicayapi;
Iyeced Christ kiŋ ed piya
Owasiŋ nipi kta.

5 Wakaŋtaŋka etapa kiŋ
Ekta Jesus yaŋka;
Aŋpetu waŋ ehake qed
Wayasu u kta ce. AMEN.

Easter. — Kini Aŋpetu kiŋ.

42 Passover. C. M.

"Tona iștiŋmapi qoŋ hena ed taku tokaheya icaġe ciŋ Hee." — 1 Cor. xv: 20.

SECOND TUNE.

2 Waskuyeca tokaheya
Wicaṭe ciŋ etaŋ
Icaġe ciŋ he Ee ce,
Piya inajiŋ oŋ.

3 Eciŋ wicaṡa kiŋ etaŋ
Wicaṭe ciŋ he u;
Iyeced he etaŋhaŋ oŋ
Wicani teca ce.

4 Wicaṡa Adam he etaŋ
Ihaŋgwicayapi;
Iyeced Christ kiŋ ed piya
Owasiŋ nipi kta.

5 Wakaŋtaŋka etapa kiŋ
Ekta Jesus yaŋka;
Aŋpetu waŋ ehake qed
Wayasu u kta ce. AMEN.

43 "Jesus Christ is Risen To-day." 7s.

"Ded uŋ ṡni; wana ikduekicetu, ḣeye ciqoŋ iyececa."—St. Matt. xxviii: 6.

First Tune. Easter Hymn.

From "Tunes Old and New" by permission of Rev. Dr. Tucker.

2 Christ waŋkaŋd Itaŋcaŋ kiŋ,
Aliluya!
Oŋ yataŋ idowaŋ po,
Aliluya!
Qa waḣtanipisa kiŋ,
Aliluya!
Haŋ, niwicayiŋ kta ciŋ;
Aliluya!

3 Ho, Wanikiya kini,
Aliluya!
Iyakiṡ'a po dehaŋd,
Aliluya!
Wopida waṡte yuha,
Aliluya!
Oŋ Iye yataŋpi ye,
Aliluya!

4 Haŋ, Ate, Niciŋkṡi qa,
Aliluya!
Woniya Wakaŋ nakuŋ,
Aliluya!
Wowitaŋ odowaŋ de,
Aliluya!
Ohiŋni niçupi kta,
Aliluya! Amen.

Easter.

43 "Jesus Christ is Risen To-day." 7s.

"Ded uŋ śni; wana ikduekicetu, heye ciqoŋ iyececa." — St. Matt. xxviii: 6.

SECOND TUNE. WORGAN.

1. Je-sus Christ wa-na ki-ni, A-li-lu-ya! Wo-o-hi-ye taŋka ḣca, A-li-lu-ya! Waŋca-na caŋ a-kaŋd ṭa, A-li-lu-ya! Haŋ, uŋ-ni-pi kta e oŋ. A-li-lu-ya! A-MEN.

From "Tunes Old and New" by permission of Rev. Dr. Tucker.

2 Christ waŋkaŋd Itaŋcaŋ kiŋ,
Aliluya!
Oŋ yataŋ idowaŋ po,
Aliluya!
Qa waḣtanipisa kiŋ,
Aliluya!
Haŋ, niwicayiŋ kta ciŋ;
Aliluya!

3 Ho, Wanikiya kini,
Aliluya!
Iyakiś'a po dehaŋd,
Aliluya!
Wopida waśte yuha,
Aliluya!
Oŋ Iye yataŋpi ye,
Aliluya!

4 Haŋ, Ate, Niciŋkśi qa,
Aliluya!
Woniya Wakaŋ nakuŋ,
Aliluya!
Wowitaŋ odowaŋ de,
Aliluya!
Ohiŋni niçupi kta,
Aliluya! AMEN.

44 "Awake, ye Saints, Awake." 6s. 8s.

"Itaŋcaŋ aŋpetu kaġe ciŋ he dee, he ed uŋkiyuśkiŋpi qa caŋte uŋwaśtepi kta." — Ps. cxviii: 24.

Lenox.

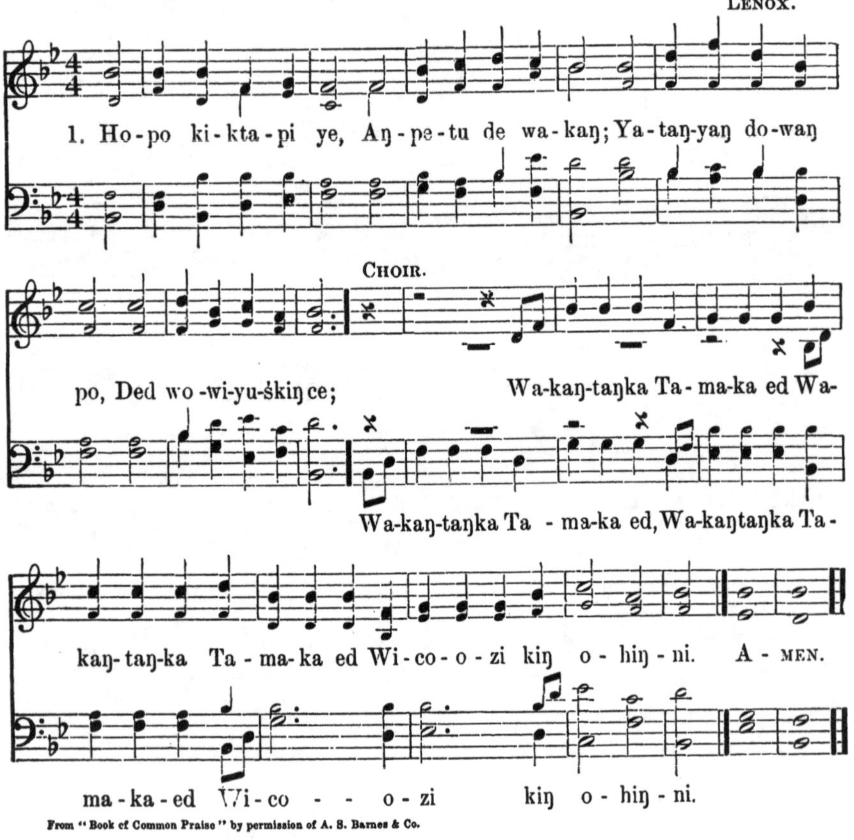

From "Book of Common Praise" by permission of A. S. Barnes & Co.

2 Aŋpetu de wakaŋ,
Ed Christ kini kiŋ oŋ;
Wicoŋṭe ktena qa
Niuŋkiyapi ce:
Maħpiyata uŋyaŋpi kta
Iye wakaŋyaŋ ti kiŋ ed.

3 Itaŋcaŋ kiŋ kini,
Yataŋ idowaŋ po:
Maħpiya qa maka
Yaonihaŋpi ye:
Christ waŋcana ħciŋ ktepi qoŋ
Wana Itaŋcaŋ ħca yaŋka.

4 Itaŋcaŋ taŋka kiŋ,
Niś miwakaŋ duha,
Qa wowicake kiŋ,
Wiconi kiŋ nakuŋ:
Nioie uŋqupi ye,
Wiconi ħca caŋku kiŋ he. Amen.

Easter.

45 "The Strife is O'er, the Battle Done." P. M.

'Odowaŋ teca waŋ Itaŋcaŋ kiŋ kahiyayapi ye, He taku wowinihaŋ ecoŋ kiŋ heoŋ." —Ps. xcviii: 1.

VICTORY.

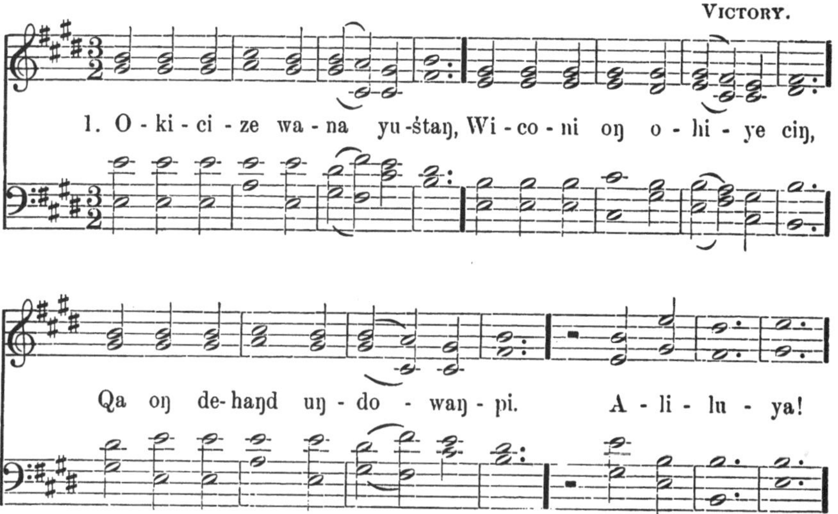

From "Tunes Old and New" by permission of Rev. Dr. Tucker.

2 Wicoŋṭe towaśake kiŋ
Christ ataya ihaŋgya ce:
Oŋ nina iyakiś'a po,
Aliluya!

3 Aŋpetu yamni ṭa waŋke
Ciqoŋ ctuŋ inajiŋ ce:
Oŋ wowitaŋ yuha nuŋwe!
Aliluya!

4 Nakuŋ wakaŋśica ti kiŋ
Tiyopa kiŋ nataka ce,
Maḣpiya kiŋ yuzamni ce;
Aliluya!

5 Nicakije teḣike ciŋ
He oŋ niuŋkiyapi ye,
Uŋkinidowaŋpi kta ce:
Aliluya!

AMEN.

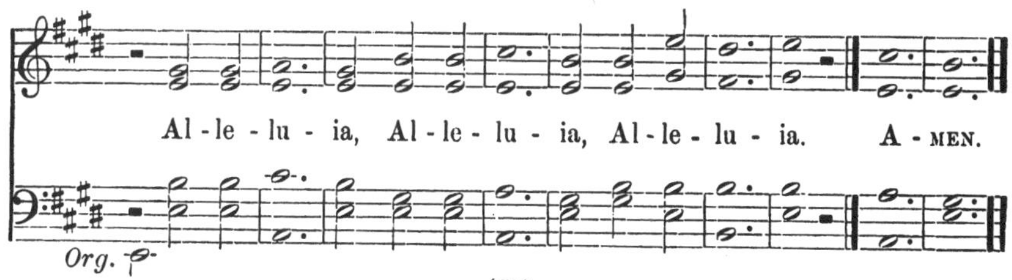

46 Coronæ. 8s. 7s. 4.

"Wana Christ wicoŋṭe etaŋhaŋ piya ikicaġa." — 1 Cor. xv: 20.

[*Saxe Weimer. Hymn* 167, *may be used.*]

From "Tunes Old and New" by permission of Rev. Dr. Tucker.

2 Aliluya! Aliluya!
Wocaŋteṡice ḣce ciŋ,
He wana hekicinana,
Oŋ ikiciyuṡkiŋ po.

3 Aliluya! Aliluya!
Woteḣi wicoŋṭe kiŋ,
Ataya akipa unkaŋ
Sataŋ kiŋ ihaŋgya ce.

4 Aliluya! Aliluya!
Haŋ, maka sitomniyaŋ,
Wiyuṡkiŋye ḣciŋ dowaŋ po;
Christ dehaŋd inajiŋ ce.

5 Aliluya! Aliluya!
Haŋ, wicoŋṭe kiŋ etaŋ
He uŋkiṡ uŋkiyuṡkapi,
Toekicetu kiŋ oŋ. AMEN.

Easter.

47 "Jesus Lives!" P. M.

"Tuwe ṭe ça ake kini, qa ito owihaŋke waniŋd ni wauŋ; Amen; qa Wakanṡica ti kiŋ wicoŋṭe ko tiyobiyuṡdoke kiŋ yuha maŋka."—Wayuo i: 18.

ST. ALBINUS.

From "Tunes Old and New" by permission of Rev. Dr. Tucker.

2 Jesus ni! Wicoŋṭe he
Ohiŋniyaŋ ħciŋ wiconi
Oŋ tiyopa heca kta,
E uŋkiciyuħdokapi.
Aliluya!

3 Jesus ni! Owas oŋ ṭa;
Heced wakaṡoteṡni ħciŋ
He akna uŋqoŋpi oŋ,
Jesus wowitaŋ yuha kta.
Aliluya!

4 Jesus ni! Qa Christ caŋte
Oŋ teuŋħidapi ħce ciŋ
He wakaŋṡicapi kiŋ,
Tohiŋni uŋkipi kte ṡni.
Aliluya!

5 Jesus ni! Maka akaŋd
He Iṡnana taŋka kta ce;
Qa owihaŋke waniŋd,
He kici uŋqoŋpi kta ce.
Aliluya!
AMEN.

The Christian Year.

48 "He is Risen! He is Risen!" 8s, 7s, 7s.

"Ehaŋqoŋ Itaŋcaŋ kiŋ kini." — St. Luke xxiv : 34.

First Tune. Unser Herrscher.

From "Tunes Old and New" by permission of Rev. Dr. Tucker.

2 Tona woaḣtani ota
Oŋ iyokiṡicapi,
Qa akiḣaŋiçiyapi,
Easter kiŋ yuhapi ce:
Christ dehaŋd uŋyuskapi,
Christ Iye ohiya ce.

3 Najiŋ! najiŋ ce! Iye ḣca —
Oŋ tiyopa kiŋ yuġaŋ;
Woaḣtani tokaṡke kiŋ
He etaŋ uŋyuṡkapi,
Qa uŋyuwakaŋpi, oŋ
Easter kiŋ uŋyuhapi. Amen.

Easter.

48 "He is Risen! He is Risen!" 8s, 7s, 7s.

"Ehaŋqoŋ Itaŋcaŋ kiŋ kini." — St. Luke xxiv : 34.

SECOND TUNE. IRBY.

From "Tunes Old and New" by permission of Rev. Dr. Tucker.

2 Tona woaḣtani ota
Oŋ iyokiṡicapi,
Qa akiḣaŋiçiyapi,
Easter kiŋ yuhapi ce:
Christ dehaŋd uŋyuskapi,
Christ Iye oḣiya ce.

3 Najiŋ! najiŋ ce! Iye ḣca —
Oŋ tiyopa kiŋ yuġaŋ;
Woaḣtani tokaṡke kiŋ
He etaŋ uŋyuṡkapi,
Qa uŋyuwakaŋpi, oŋ
Easter kiŋ uŋyuhapi. AMEN.

The Christian Year.

Ascension. — Waŋkaŋd kikda Aŋpetu kiŋ.

49 "Thou art Gone Up on High." D. S. M.

"Iye kiŋ maḣpiya kiŋ ekta kikda." — 1 Peter iii: 22.

FIRST TUNE. DIADEMATA.

From "Goodrich & Gilbert Hymnal" by permission of E. P. Dutton & Co.

2 Waŋkaŋd idade ciŋ,
Tokaheya Niye
Makata kuya ded yahi,
Qa wokakije waŋ
Iyotaŋ pe ḣce ciŋ
Sdodyaya oŋ, Niye
Wateśdagnicatoŋpi ce,
Waŋkaŋd idade ciŋ.

3 Ecanoŋ kiŋ okne
Ecoŋqoŋpi kta ce,
Uŋkitaŋokśaŋ woteḣi
Qa wokokipe ko
Anauŋtaŋpi śa;
Nitacaŋku kiŋ he
Teḣike śa naŋke ciŋ ḣed
Uŋkaipi nuŋwe.

4 Waŋkaŋd idade ciŋ;
Tuka maḣpiyata
Ouŋyaŋpi owasiŋ ob
Ake yau kta ce.
Nitowaśake oŋ
Niuŋkiyapi ye,
Nietapata ḣeced oŋ
Inauŋjiŋpi kta. AMEN.

Ascension.

49 "Thou art Gone Up on High." S. M.

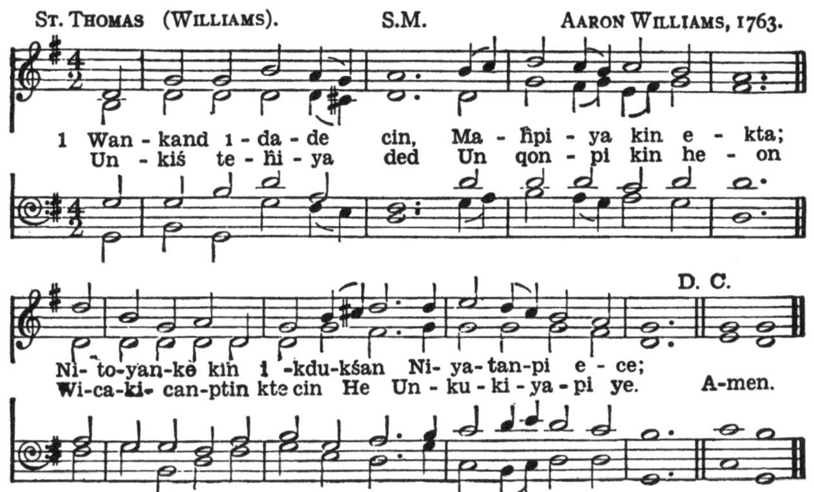

2 Waŋkaŋd idade ciŋ,
Tokaheya Niye
Makata kuya ded yaḣi,
Qa wokakije waŋ
Iyotaŋ pe ḣce ciŋ
Sdodyaya oŋ, Niye
Wateṡdagnicatoŋpi ce,
Waŋkaŋd idade ciŋ.

3 Ecanoŋ kiŋ okna
Ecoŋqoŋpi kta ce,
Uŋkitaŋokṡaŋ woteḣi
Qa wokokipe ko
Anauŋtaŋpi ṡa;
Nitacaŋku kiŋ he
Teḣike ṡa naŋke ciŋ hed
Uŋkaipi nuŋwe.

4 Waŋkaŋd idade ciŋ;
Tuka maḣpiyata
Ouŋyaŋpi owasiŋ ob
Ako yau kta ce.
Nitowaṡake oŋ
Niuŋkiyapi ye,
Nietapata heced oŋ
Inauŋjiŋpi kta. Amen.

The Christian Year.

50 **Hope.** S. M. D.

"Waŋkaŋd yakiyakda." — Ps. lxviii: 18.

[*Cambridge, Hymn 49, may be used.*]

From "Tunes Old and New" by permission of Rev. Dr. Tucker.

2 O Christ, waŋkaŋd yaki;
Eśa tokaheya
Maka akaŋd nicakija,
Qa oŋ Initaŋcaŋ;
Uŋkiyepi nakuŋ
Uŋkakijapi śa
Nihakabya uŋyaŋpi oŋ
Nici uŋqoŋpi kta.

3 O Christ, waŋkaŋd yaki;
Eśa maĥpiya ed
Wicaduha kiŋ ob ake
Hukud yau kta ce;
Qa toked hed uŋkiś
Nietapa ekta
Inauŋjiŋpi kte ciŋ he
Eced uŋnipi nuŋ. AMEN.

51 "Stand Up, my Soul, Shake Off thy Fears." L. M.

"Ate, tona mayaqu kiŋ hena, tokiya wauŋ kiŋ hed miciuŋpi kta waciŋ." —St. John xvii: 24.

[*Wareham, Hymn 23, may be used.*]

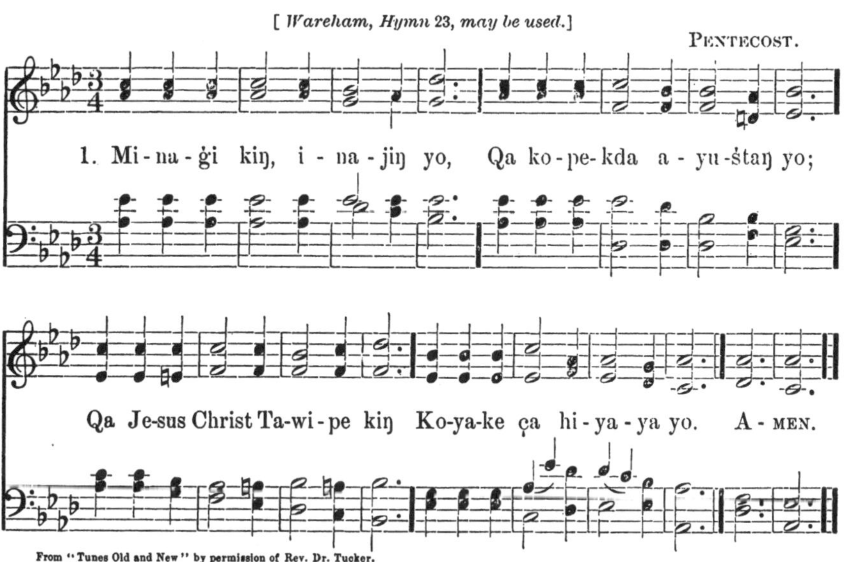

From "Tunes Old and New" by permission of Rev. Dr. Tucker.

2 Bdetaŋhuŋkayaye ciŋ He,
Ihuŋni kiŋ ekta ya yo;
Qa wowiyuśkiŋ ohiŋni
Tiyopa qed yai kta ce.

3 Wakaŋśica kiŋ, toka kiŋ,
Wayaĥtani hena nakuŋ,
Nicipajiŋyaŋ uŋpi qeś
Christ Jesus He waciŋyaŋ yo.

4 He ţa tuka kini kiŋ oŋ
Niś tokaniyaŋpi owas
Ohiniciciyapi ce;
Kowicakipe śni uŋ wo.

5 He oŋ caŋteţiŋsya ya yo,
Maĥpiyata tiyopa qed,
Hed wokoyake ska koyag
Qa wiyuśkiŋyaŋ uŋpi ce. AMEN.

The Christian Year.

Whitsuntide. — Aŋpetu-Wakaŋ-ska kiŋ.

52 St. Alban. 11s.

"Wakaŋtaŋka Taniya śakowiŋ maka owaŋcaya yewicayapi kiŋ."
— Wayuo v: 6.

FIRST TUNE.

From "Tunes Old and New" by permission of Rev. Dr. Tucker.

Whitsuntide.

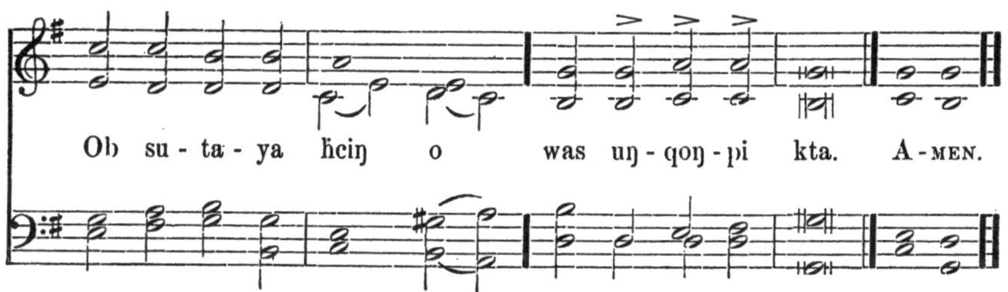

2 Woksape wakaŋ Niśakowiŋpi kiŋ,
Niś Iyoyaŋpa hce ciŋ Niyepi ce;
Oŋśiuŋkidapi ye, aŋpetu de;
Qa uŋkitawaciŋpi caŋkuye ciŋ
Ed iyojaŋjaŋuŋkiciciya po;
Heced oŋ niuŋyakiyapi kta ce.

3 Wookaȟniġe Niśakowiŋpi kiŋ,
Iyakideced waniśakapi ce,
Oŋśiuŋkidapi ye, aŋpetu de,
Qa uŋsihapi caŋkuyiŋ kte ciŋ he,
Ed iyojaŋjaŋuŋkiciciya po,
Heced óŋ Nihakabya uŋyaŋpi kta.

4 Wowaoŋspekiye kiŋ Niśakowiŋ,
Iyakideced wadaotaŋiŋpi,
Oŋśiuŋkidapi ye, aŋpetu de,
Qa uŋkiśtapi caŋkuyiŋ kte ciŋ hc,
Ed iyojaŋjaŋuŋkiciciya po,
Heced oŋ uŋkaniyuśtaŋpi kte śni.

5 Woowotaŋna Niśakowiŋpi kiŋ,
Wokokipe hca wakaŋ henicapi,
Oŋśiuŋkidapi ye, aŋpetu de,
Qa caŋkuuŋyaŋpi kta iyuha hciŋ,
Ed iyojaŋjaŋuŋkiciciya po,
Heced oŋ wiconi ed uŋkipi kta. AMEN.

52-B O Sion, Haste.

2 Oiyokpaza el kaśka unpi qa
Woaĥtani ekna wicota ĥca,
Wanikiya niwicayin kta ṭe cin
Tuweni owicakiyake śni.

Jesus toyuśke, etc.

3 Itancan kin wiconi eĥpeye cin,
Qa tona kakijapi kin owas,
Nipi kta on wateśdagkitonpi kta
Oyagniśipi kin inaĥni yo.

Jesus toyuśke, etc.

4 Oyate iapi obe owasin,
Wakantanka wocantekiye on
Kuniçiya qa maka akan ṭe cin
Heon nipi kte cin oyaka yo.

Jesus toyuśke, etc.

5 De nicincapi oyagwicaśi yo,
Qa woyuha nitawa kiçun wo,
Iyepi on woçekiye eya yo,
Jesus hi kta ca kajuju kta ce.

Jesus toyuśke, etc.

6 O Sion, ake u kta keye cin he,
Towaśte sdonyewicakiya yo,
Kinhan ite kin itkokipapi kta,
Niĥanhi on kuśeyapi kte śni.

Jesus toyuśke,
Wopekiton
Wookiye ko
Dena oyaka yo.

The Christian Year.

53 "Come, Holy Ghost, our Souls Inspire." L. M.

"Mitaniya kiŋ acicaśtaŋpi kta, mioie kiŋ okaȟniȟciciyapi kta."—Wicoie Wakan i: 23.

[*Grace Church, Hymn* 23, II, *may be used.*] MELCOMBE.

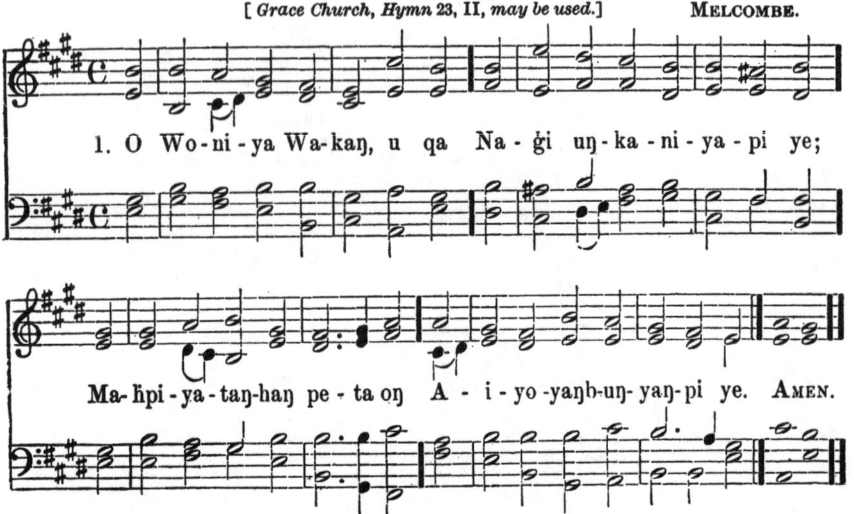

From "Tunes Old and New" by permission of Rev. Dr. Tucker.

2 Qa Woniya Wakaŋ Niye
Sdawicaye ciŋ, He Niye,
Nitowaśte śakowiŋ kiŋ
Hena wicayaqu ece.

3 Qa oŋ sdawicayaye ciŋ
Waŋkaŋtaŋhaŋ dena ee;
Wiconi, wokicaŋpte qa
Wacaŋtkiyapi peta kiŋ.

4 Taŋyaŋ uŋtoŋwaŋpi śni kiŋ,
Iyoyaŋpa waŋ ohiŋni
Kiŋ oŋ, uŋtoŋwaŋpi kta e,
Aiyoyaŋbuŋyaŋpi ye.

5 Nitowaśte kiŋ ota oŋ
Ite uŋśapapi hena
Sdauŋkiciciyapi ye,
Qa wiyuśkiŋuŋyaŋpi ye.

6 Bdetaŋhuŋkaniyaŋpi ca,
Kiyena śice ciŋ u śni:
Oŋ toka niŋd uŋqoŋpi kta,
Nitookiye u nuŋwe.

7 Ateyapi, Ciŋhiŋtku kiŋ,
Nupiŋd etaŋ wicayahi,
Hena Niwaŋjipina kiŋ,
Sdodyeuŋyakiyapi nuŋ.

8 He oŋ ouŋcaġe uya
Owasiŋ cd odowaŋ de
Owihaŋkeśniyaŋ ȟciŋ he
Uŋkahiyayapi kta ce;

9 Ateyapi, Ciŋhiŋtku kiŋ,
Qa Woniya Wakaŋ, Hena,
Nitowaśte kiŋ ohiŋni
Yataŋ idowaŋpi nuŋwe. AMEN.

Whitsuntide.

54 "Our Blest Redeemer, e'er He Breathed." P. M.

"Wakde śni kiŋhaŋ Wicakicaŋpte ciŋ ed nihipi kte śni; tka wakde ciŋhaŋ niyepi ekta uwaśi kta." — St. John xvi: 7.

St. Cuthbert.

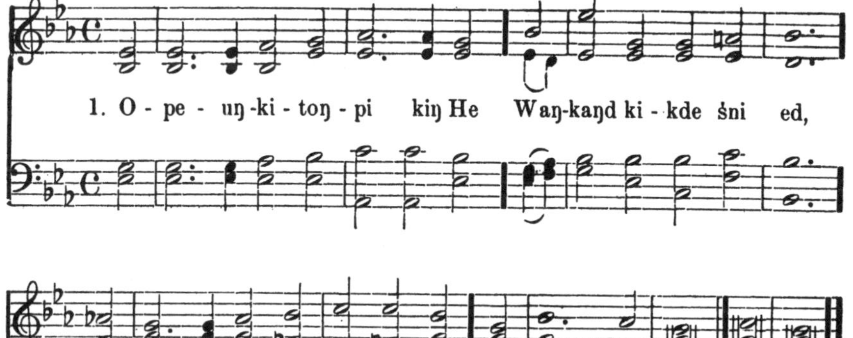

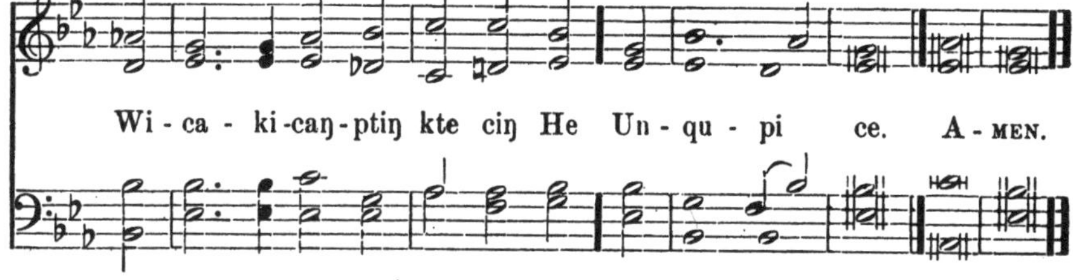

From "Tunes Old and New" by permission of Rev. Dr. Tucker.

2 He tid-wakiŋyena kaḣya,
Wacaŋtkiyapi kiŋ
Qa wookiye kiŋ yuha,
Awicahaŋ.

3 Wicacaŋte waŋ oŋśiḣaŋ
Iyeya caŋ ed i,
Qa Towaśte śakowiŋ oŋ
Hed ti ece.

4 Caŋte mahed wicaho waŋ
Nauŋḣoŋpi ece,
Qa oŋ uŋkicaŋptapi kiŋ,
He Tawa ce.

5 Qa wowaśte uŋyuhapi
Haŋ, woohiye kiŋ
Caŋtoyuze wakaŋ ko, He
Uŋqupi ce.

6 O Woniya Wakaŋ, u ye,
Uŋcaŋtepi kiŋ ed,
Qa ouŋyakiyapi kta
E hed uŋ ye. Amen.

The Christian Year.

Trinity Sunday. — Yamni Taaŋpetu Wakaŋ kiŋ.

55 "The God of Abraham Praise." P. M.

"Micaje kiŋ hee owihaŋke waniŋd, heced Miksuyapi kta." — Kdi. iii: 15.

Onśpa I. LEONI.

From "Tunes Old and New" by permission of Rev. Dr. Tucker.

Trinity Sunday.

2 WAUN kiŋ taŋka kiŋ,
Maka maȟpiya ko
Oyakapi ece kiŋ He
Jehova ce; —
Wakipatuje ça
Caje wakaŋ kiŋ He
Bdawaśte kiŋ, yawaśtepi
Ihaŋke śni.

3 Etapa Tawa kiŋ
Ed wowiyuśkiŋ ce,
Hena awakitiŋ kta e
Ecoŋmaśi
E oŋ, mak'a etaŋ,
Waŋkaŋd bde kta e
He oŋ Abram wakaŋda qoŋ
Yataŋpi ye;

4 Makata woksape,
Makata woyataŋ,
Qa wowaśake tawa ko
Iȟpewaya;
Iye wahacaŋka
Qa coŋkaśke suta,
Qa woyuha mitawa kiŋ
Iwacu kta. AMEN.

55-B Onward, Christian Soldiers.

St. Gertrude. 6.5., 12 lines Arthur S. Sullivan, 1871.

2 Woohiye tanin,
Satan nakipa.
Ya po, Christ wicaśa,
Woohiye en.
Hades wanna cancan
Woyatan nahon;
Ho, mitakuyepi,
Iyakiśa po.

Chorus.

3 Wocekiye opa,
Optaye tanka;
Wakan manipi kin,
Hen maunnipi.
Kiyuśpeya śniyan
Unwanjipi ce;
Woape, wosdonye,
Wowaśtedake.

Chorus.

4 Maka wokiconze,
Ihangyapi śa
Jesus taoptaye,
Ohinniyan kta.
Waihangye cin he
Ohiyin kte śni;
Christ toiwahoye
He sutayan han.

Chorus.

5 Oyate mani po,
Wowiyuśkin en.
Ho, unkiyepi ob
Yatanyan dowan.
Christ Itancan kin he
Ohoda, yatan,
Ohinniyan ekta,
Tuwe kin oyas.

Chorus. Amen.

The Christian Year.

56 Hebron. L. M.

"Iye kiŋ ed wiconi; qa wiconi kiŋ he wicaśa iyoyaŋbwicaye ciŋ Hee." —St. John i: 4.

From "Tunes Old and New" by permission of Rev. Dr. Tucker.

2 Wanikiya, Itaŋcaŋ kiŋ,
Iyuśkiŋyaŋ idowaŋ po;
Maĥpiyata wiconi ed
Iyoyaŋpa wakaŋ, wakaŋ.

3 Itaŋcaŋ kiŋ waniśaka,
Qa Woniya Wakaŋ Niye;
Ouŋyaye ciŋ he mahed
Iyoyaŋpa wakaŋ, wakaŋ.

4 Ateyapi, Ciŋhiŋtku kiŋ,
Qa Woniya Wakaŋ kiŋ He,
Wakaŋtaŋka waŋjina kiŋ,
He wowitaŋ yuha nuŋwe. AMEN.

Concluded from opposite page.

2 O wakaŋ, wakaŋ, wakaŋ, inidowaŋpi,
Qa wateśdake Nitokab iĥpeyapi;
Cherubim qa Seraphim ohonidapi,
Ohiŋni ĥce ciŋ, He Niye ĥca ce.

3 O wakaŋ, wakaŋ, wakaŋ, Iyoyaŋpa ska,
Śicapi kiŋ waŋniyakapi kte śni ce,
Niś owihaŋke waniŋd Niwakaŋ ĥce ciŋ,
Wowaśake, wowaśte duha nuŋwe.

4 O wakaŋ, wakaŋ, wakaŋ, Itaŋcaŋ, ĥce cin!
Niś Niohan kiŋ owas niyataŋpi kta;
O wakaŋ, wakaŋ, wakaŋ, waoŋśida kiŋ,
Yamni tuka Wakaŋtaŋka waŋjina. AMEN.

Trinity Sunday.

57 "Holy, Holy, Holy! Lord God Almighty!" P. M.

"Aŋpetu, haŋhepi ko ayaśtaŋ śni heced eyapi, Wakaŋ, Wakaŋ, Wakaŋ, Itaŋcaŋ Wakaŋtaŋka Iyotaŋ waśaka, Tuwa uŋ, qa uŋ qoŋ, u kte ciŋ Hee ce." — Wayuo iv: 8.

NICÆA.

From "Tunes Old and New" by permission of Rev. Dr. Tucker.

58 Haven. 7s. D.

"Maĥpiya kiŋ ekta yamni wayaotaŋiŋpi ecc, Ateyapi kiŋ, Wicoie kiŋ, qa Woniya Wakaŋ kiŋ; uŋkaŋ hena yamni waŋjipina."— 1 John v: 8.

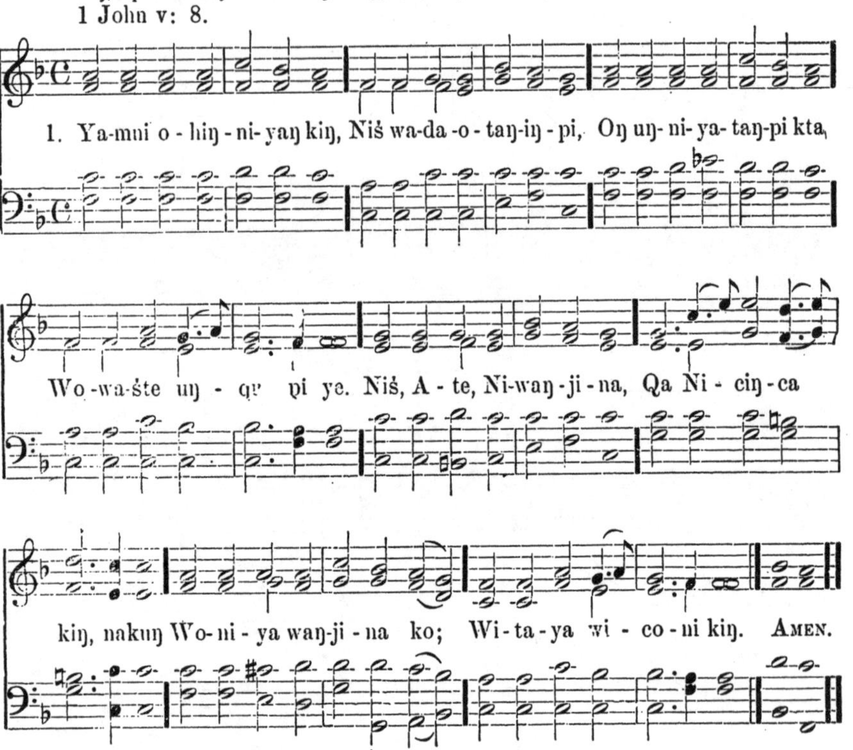

From "Tunes Old and New" by permission of Rev. Dr. Tucker.

2 Qa Itaŋcaŋ kiŋ waŋji,
Qa Wawiciya waŋji,
Wocekiye kiŋ waŋji,
Wowaŝte kiŋ Heepi.
Qa waŋkaŋd wakaŋpi ce,
Qa maka akaŋd nakuŋ,
Woniya kiŋ ed nakuŋ,
Towitaŋpi ohiŋni.

3 Wowaoŋŝida waŋji,
Wokajuju kiŋ waŋji,
Qa wicayuska waŋji,
Wowaŝte kiŋ Heepi.
Qa waŋkaŋd Itaŋcaŋ kiŋ,
Deciya Itaŋcaŋ kiŋ,
Ṭapi ed Itaŋcaŋ kiŋ,
Nipi ed Itaŋcaŋ kiŋ.

4 Qa Wakaŋtaŋka waŋji,
Qa Wanikiya waŋji,
Woniya waŋjina ko,
Wowaŝte kiŋ Heepi.
Okiwaŋjipina ce,
Qa otokahe waniŋd,
Qa owihaŋke waniŋd,
Ohniyaŋ yataŋpi kta. Amen.

Trinity Sunday.

59 "We Give Immortal Praise." 6s. 4s.

"Iye etaŋhaŋ, qa Iye eciyataŋhaŋ, qa Iye okna taku owasin uŋ; owihaŋke waniŋd wowitaŋ kici uŋ uuŋwe." —Rom. xi: 36.

[*Christ Church, Hymn* 156, *may be used.*] DARWELL.

From "Tunes Old and New" by permission of Rev. Dr. Tucker.

2 Wakaŋtaŋka Ate,
Ciŋhiŋtku kiŋ wakaŋ;
He we kpapsoŋ kiŋ oŋ
Niuŋkiyapi ḣca;
Kini, qa oŋ maḣpiya ed
Dehaŋd Itaŋcaŋ taŋka ce.

3 Wakaŋtaŋka Ate,
Taniya kiŋ wakaŋ;
He Jesus Taw[illegible] kiŋ
Owicati kiŋ oŋ
Wicakicaŋpte, ça eced
Nakuŋ niwicaya ece.

5 Wakaŋtaŋka Ate,
Ciŋhiŋtku, Woniya,
Niyamnipi eṡa
Niwaŋjipina ḣca,
Qa he okaḣniḣpica ṡni,
Tka he wicauŋdapi ce. AMEN.

The Christian Year.

The Lord's Day. — Itaŋcaŋ Taaŋpetu kiŋ.

60 **Pearce.** 6s. D.

"Itaŋcaŋ aŋpetu kaġe ciŋ he dee, he ed uŋkiyuśkiŋpi qa caŋteuŋwaśtepi kta." — Ps. cxviii: 24.

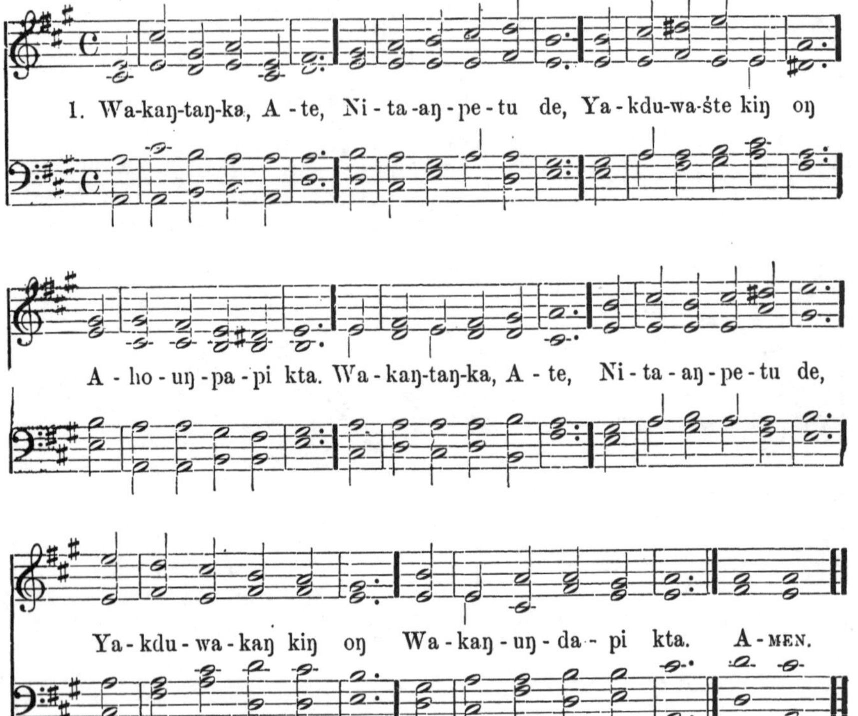

From "Tunes Old and New" by permission of Rev. Dr. Tucker.

3 Wakaŋtaŋka, Ate,
Taaŋpetu waśte;
Oŋ wiyuśkiŋyaŋ ħciŋ
Uŋdowaŋpi kta ce.

4 Wakaŋtaŋka, Ate,
Taaŋpetu wakaŋ;
Aŋpetu taŋka kiŋ
Uŋkiyuśkiŋpi kta.

5 Wakaŋtaŋka. Ate,
Oyate kiŋ owas
Ob woyataŋ waśte
Uŋniçupi kta ce. Amen.

Ember Days. — Wicaśa Wakaŋ wicakaġapi kta itokab aŋpetu kiŋ.

61 Pax Dei. 10s.

"Tuwena oyake śni kiŋhaŋ toked naḣoŋpi kta he?" —Rom. x: 14.

First Tune.

From "Tunes Old and New" by permission of Rev. Dr. Tucker.

2 Tuweni He oyake śni kiŋhaŋ,
Eciŋ He toked oŋ naḣoŋpi kta?
Ekta yewicaśipi śni kiŋhaŋ,
Toked eciŋ oyakapi kta he?

3 "Odakota waśte oyakapi,
Qa Wotaŋiŋ waśte kiŋ he nakuŋ
Oyakapi, siha waśtepi ce;"
Eya owapi kiŋ wicakapi.

4 Uŋkiś sdoduŋyaŋpi henakeca,
Nauŋḣoŋpi kiŋ ko oyake śni
Uŋqoŋpi kta uŋkokiḣipi śni.
Itaŋcaŋ, Niś kici uŋqoŋpi ye.

5 Qa tuwe tokeca etaŋhaŋ oŋ
Wanikiyapi kta yuke śni ce;
Wicacaje kiŋ tokeca waŋji
Niuŋyaŋpi kte ciŋ, wanica ce. Amen.

Ember Days. — Wicaśa Wakaŋ wicakaǧapi kta itokab aŋpetu kiŋ.

61 St. Austin. 10s.

"Tuwena oyake śni kiŋhaŋ toked naȟ'oŋpi kta he?" — Rom. x: 14.

Second Tune.

2 Tuweni He oyake śni kiŋhaŋ,
Eciŋ He toked oŋ naȟoŋpi kta?
Ekta yewicaśipi śni kiŋhaŋ,
Toked eciŋ oyakapi kta he?

3 "Odakota waśte oyakapi,
Qa Wotaŋiŋ waśte kiŋ he nakuŋ
Oyakapi, siha waśtepi ce;"
Eya owapi kiŋ wicakapi.

4 Uŋkiś sdoduŋyaŋpi henakeca,
Nauŋȟoŋpi kiŋ ko, oyake śni
Uŋqoŋpi kta uŋkokihipi śni.
Itaŋcaŋ, Niś kici uŋqoŋpi ye.

5 Qa tuwe tokeca etaŋhaŋ oŋ
Wanikiyapi kta yuke śni ce;
Wicacaje kiŋ tokeca waŋji
Niuŋyaŋpi kte ciŋ, wanica ce. Amen.

Ember Days.

62 "Go Forth, ye Heralds, in My Name." L. M.

"Ikcewicaŝa kiŋ ekta Christ Tawoyuha Okaĥniĥpica ŝni kiŋ he obdakiŋ kta."—Ephes. iii: 8.

[*Federal Street, Hymn* 110, *may be used.*]

MISSIONARY CHANT.

From "Tunes Old and New" by permission of Rev. Dr. Tucker.

2 Iyokipiya Wotaŋiŋ,
Owas naĥoŋwicaya po,
Tukted wiconi kiŋ yukaŋ
Oŋspewicakiya ya po.

3 Caŋte kicaksapi hena
Taŋyaŋ wicayuwiwi po;
Qa ceya uŋpi kiŋ, iŝta
Wicakicipakiŋta po.

4 Tukted kaŝa yaipi kiŋ,
Wabduŝka se ksabya uŋ po;
Wakiŋyena kiŋ waĥbana
Iyeced waĥbana uŋ po.

5 Wakaŋtaŋka yeniŝipi,
Nioĥaŋpi maĥpiyataŋ
Oŋspeniciyapi kiŋ, he
Oyate ed kdutaŋiŋ po.

6 Iyuwiŋ cona ĥciŋ Miye
Etaŋ iyacupi ece,
Oŋ wowaŝtedake okna
Ituya saŋb wicaqu po.

7 He oŋ nitawooŋspepi,
Wicakenicidapi kta;
Qa ŝkiŋniciyapi kiŋ oŋ
Waĥtanipis'a nipi kta. AMEN.

The Christian Year.

Other Holy Days. — Wokiksuye Aŋpetu kiŋ.

63 Paradise. 8s. 6s.

" Itaŋcaŋ wowitaŋ qa woyuonihaŋ qa wowaśake iyacukta iyeniceca."
— Wayuo iv: 10.

[*Hopkins, Hymn 64, may be used.*]

From " Goodrich and Gilbert Hymnal " by permission of E. P. Dutton.

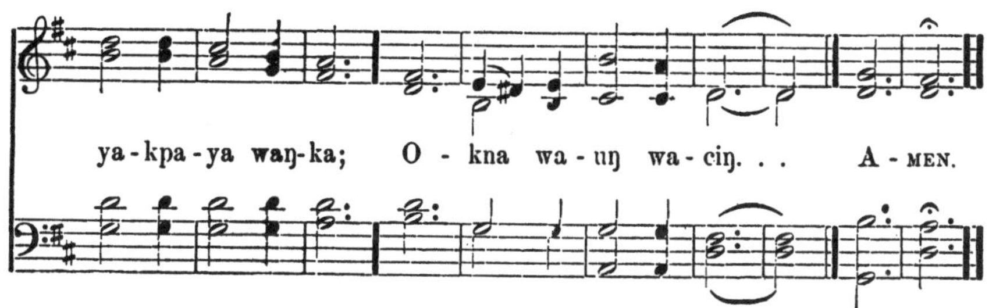

2 Wakaŋtaŋka, maĥpiyata
Nitaoyate kiŋ
Hed wiyuśkiŋ dowaŋpi ce:
Wiconi waŋ waśte
Hed ska koyakapi;
Tiowiyakpakpa
Qa coŋkaśke suta;
Okna wauŋ waciŋ.

3 Wakaŋtaŋka, maĥpiyata
Oyate kiŋ owas
Nitowaśte yataŋpi ce;
Wiconi taŋka waŋ
Hed ska koyakapi;
Ate Wakaŋ Ti ed
Iyoyaŋpa ska kiŋ;
Okna wauŋ waciŋ.

4 Wakaŋtaŋka, maĥpiyata
Nitotoŋwe kiŋ ed,
Ohiyapi dowaŋpi ce;
Wiconi aŋpa kiŋ
Hed ska koyakapi;
Wicocaŋte waśte,
Makoce ko waśte;
Okna wauŋ waciŋ. AMEN.

64 "O Paradise! O Paradise!" P. M.

"Ekta bde ça Christ kici wauŋ kte ȟciŋ."—Phil. i: 23.

[*Paradise, Hymn* 63, *may be used.*] HOPKINS.

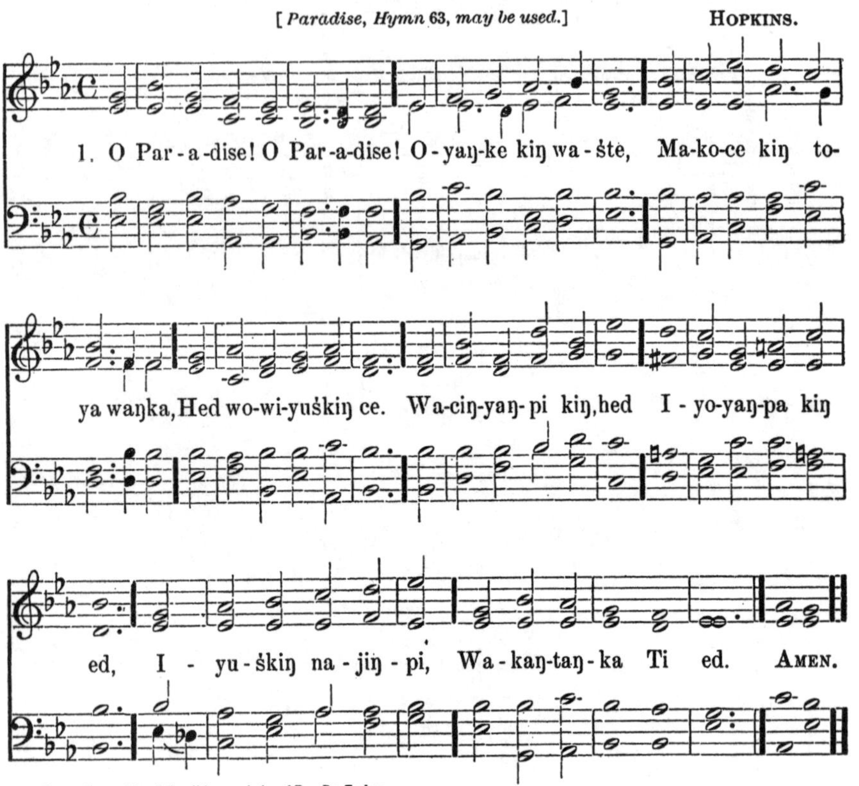

From "Tunes Old and New" by permission of Rev. Dr. Tucker.

2 O Paradise! O Paradise!
Wakaŋtaŋka Ti ed,
Ozikiyapi waŋ waśte;
Tuwe he ciŋ kte śni?

3 O Paradise! O Paradise!
Wiconi haŋske ciŋ
Hed Jesus Ti wakaŋ kiŋ ed
Wauŋ waciŋ ȟca ce.

4 O Paradise! O Paradise!
Pidapi taŋka waŋ;
Wiconi kiŋ ţepica śni
Maȟpiyata yaŋka. AMEN.

Other Holy Days.

65 Sarum. P. M.

"Wakaŋtaŋka Taoyate kiŋ okiħpapi waŋ wicakicihaŋ."— Heb. iv: 9.

1. Wa - kaŋ-taŋ - ka Ta - ma - ko - ce wa - kaŋ, He ed o - zi - i - çi - ya - pi wa - śte; Wa - śte-śte - pi kiŋ hed o - uŋ-yaŋ - pi; A - li - lu - ya, A - li - lu - ya. A - MEN.

From "Tunes Old and New" by permission of Rev. Dr. Tucker.

2 Wakaŋtaŋka Tamakoce wakaŋ,
He ed wicowaśte wiconi kiŋ;
Waayatapi kiŋ hed uŋpi ce;
Aliluya.

3 Wakaŋtaŋka Tamakoce wakaŋ,
Hed wi owas waskuyeca sutoŋ;
Wicaśa ksapa hed ouŋyaŋpi;
Aliluya.

4 Wakaŋtaŋka Tamakoce wakaŋ,
He ed waħca toya waŋka ece;
Wicaśa waħbana hed uŋpi ce;
Aliluya.

5 Wakaŋtaŋka Tamakoce wakaŋ,
Hed ohiŋni wiconi mni yukaŋ;
Wicaśa hed wiyakpakpapi ce;
Aliluya.

6 Wakaŋtaŋka Tamakoce wakaŋ,
Hed ohiŋni iyoyaŋpa yukaŋ;
Wicaśa hed zaniyaŋ uŋpi ce;
Aliluya.
AMEN.

II. The Communion of Saints.

WAKANPI ODAKODKICIYAPI KIN.

66 Medfield. C. M.

"Awicakehaŋ Ateyapi kiŋ kici okiciciya uŋqoŋpi." —1 John i: 3.

First Tune.

From "Book of Common Praise" by permission of A. S. Barnes & Co.

2 Wicouŋ kiŋ owotaŋna,
Wakaŋtaŋka yuśtaŋ,
Qa He etaŋ wiconi ce,
Otakuye waśte.

3 Wicowazi wakaŋ kiŋ he
Wakaŋtaŋka uya,
Qa He etaŋhaŋ wowaśte,
Otakuye waśte.

4 Odakodkiciyapi kiŋ,
Wakaŋtaŋka yuśtaŋ,
Hetaŋhaŋ wookiye u,
Otakuye waśte.

5 Qa wowahokiciye kiŋ,
Wakaŋtaŋka etaŋ,
Oŋ He kiksuya uŋpi ye,
Otakuye waśte.

6 Wakaŋtaŋka Ateyapi,
Nakuŋ Ciŋhiŋtku kiŋ,
Qa Woniya Wakaŋ kiŋ He,
Otakuye waśte. Amen.

The Communion of Saints.

66 St. Ann's. C. M

"Awicakehan Ateyapi kin kici okiciciya unqonpi." — 1 John i: 3.

SECOND TUNE.

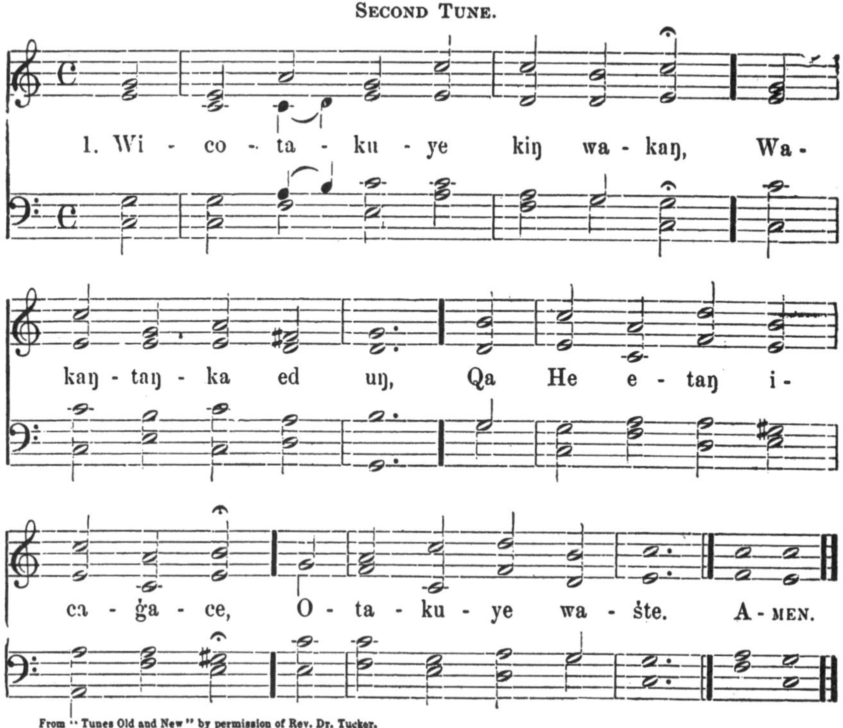

From "Tunes Old and New" by permission of Rev. Dr. Tucker.

2 Wicouŋ kiŋ owotaŋna,
Wakaŋtaŋka yuśtaŋ,
Qa He etaŋ wiconi ce,
Otakuye waśte.

3 Wicowazi wakaŋ kiŋ he
Wakaŋtaŋka uya,
Qa He etaŋhaŋ wowaśte,
Otakuye waśte.

4 Odakodkiciyapi kiŋ,
Wakaŋtaŋka yuśtaŋ,
Hetaŋhaŋ wookiye u,
Otakuye waśte.

5 Qa wowahokiciye kiŋ
Wakaŋtaŋka etaŋ,
Oŋ He kiksuya uŋpi ye,
Otakuye waśte.

6 Wakaŋtaŋka Ateyapi,
Nakuŋ Ciŋhiŋtku kiŋ,
Qa Woniya Wakaŋ kiŋ He,
Otakuye waśte. AMEN.

III. The Church.

OKODAKICIYE WAKAN KIN.

67 "I Love Thy Kingdom, Lord." S. M.

"Tona waštenidakapi kiŋ hena wapipi kta." — Ps. cxxii: 6.

LEIGHTON.

By permission of Oliver Ditson & Co., owners of Copyright.

2 Opeuŋkitoŋpi
Wašte kiŋ he Iye
Okodakiciye wakaŋ
We oŋ opekitoŋ.

3 Okodakiciye
Waštewadake ciŋ;
Tacoŋkaške nitokab haŋ,
Wakaŋtaŋka wašte.

4 He oŋ waceyiŋ kta,
Oŋ ceciciyiŋ kta,
Tohaŋyaŋ ni wauŋ kiŋhaŋ
He oŋ ȟtawani kta.

5 He toȟaŋ kiŋ wakaŋ,
Mitowiyuškiŋ kiŋ,
Hena owasiŋ isaŋpa
Tewaȟida ece.

6 Wakicoŋzapi kiŋ
Qa wowaštedake,
Qa woyataŋ odowaŋ kiŋ
Waštewadaka ce.

7 Jesus, Koda wakaŋ,
Wicašayatapi,
Wanikiya wašte, wakaŋ
Uŋkitawapi kiŋ,

8 Oŋ-kmuŋkapi etaŋ,
Qa toka kiŋ owas,
Ninape kiŋ waekdaku
Niwicayiŋ kta ce.

9 Nitowicake kiŋ
Sutaya hiŋ kte ciŋ,
Iyeced wowitaŋ Zioŋ
Sutaya qupi kta. AMEN.

The Church.

68 Palmyra. P. M.

"Wakaŋtaŋka Zion nikiyiŋ kta." — Ps. lxix: 36.

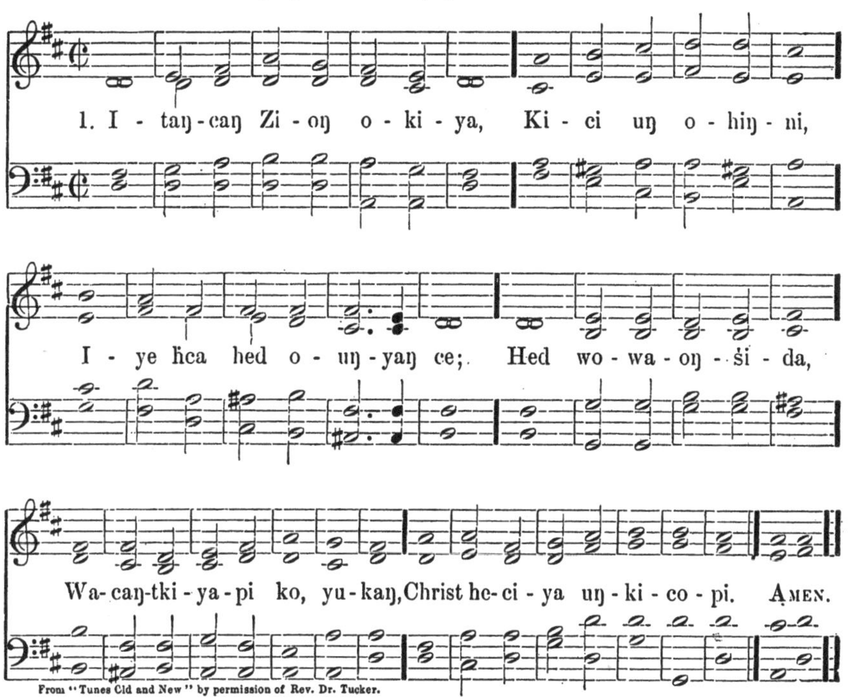

From "Tunes Old and New" by permission of Rev. Dr. Tucker.

2 Itaŋcaŋ kiŋ yataŋpi ye,
Wicaciŋca owas;
"Tohaŋd ake wau kta ce,"
Taŋiŋyaŋ ħçiŋ eya,
Nakuŋ akeś oyakiŋ kta.
Christ heciya uŋkicopi.

3 Tehaŋwaŋkaŋd Itaŋcaŋ kiŋ
Waoŋśida ħca ce;
Itaŋcaŋ Ti kiŋ he ekta
Makoce kiŋ waśte,
Wiconi ħce ciŋ hetu ce;
Christ heciya uŋkicopi.

4 Qa heci Zioŋ ed uŋ kiŋ
He wowaśake toŋ,
Qa Totoŋwe wakaŋ kiŋ ed,
Itaŋcaŋ kiŋ Caje
Yataŋ dowaŋpi ħca yukaŋ;
Christ heciya uŋkicopi. Amen.

The Church.

69 "Glorious Things of Thee are Spoken." 8s. 7s. D.

"O Wakaŋtaŋka otoŋwe tawa kiŋ, taku waŝte ĥca oŋ oniyakapi."
—Ps. lxxxvii: 2.

FIRST TUNE. WITIMA.

1. Zi - oŋ, wo - wi - taŋ kiŋ o - ta Oŋ ca - je - ni - ya - ta - pi;

To - i - e ka - kse - pi - ca ŝni, He o - ni - ti kta he oŋ,

Qa Wi - co - i - ca - ġe Iŋ - yaŋ He a - kaŋd i - caĥ - ni - yaŋ,

He oŋ niŝ pa - ho - ho - ŝni - yaŋ, To - ka kiŋ i - ya - ĥa kta. A - MEN.

From "Tunes Old and New" by permission of Rev. Dr. Tucker.

2 Wocaŋtekiye mniyowe,
He etaŋ iwakpa kiŋ
Ko hena waŋyakapi ye;
Qa wakpa kiŋ hececa
Oŋ tuwe e mni ciŋ kta he?
Towaŝte kiŋ ohiŋni,
He Tuwa wicaqu kiŋ He
Towaŝte iyececa.

3 Tipi kiŋ owasiŋ eded
Peta qa maħpiya kiŋ
Ko aokdutewicaya,
Hed Itaŋcaŋ Ti kiŋ oŋ,
Zioŋ ed taŋyaŋ uŋpi kiŋ!
Jesus we oŋ skapi kiŋ!
Jesus He waciŋyaŋpi kiŋ,
Oŋ iye wakaŋpi ce. Amen

69 Austria. 8s. 7s. D.

"O Wakaŋtaŋka otoŋwe tawa kiŋ, taku waŝte ħca oŋ oniyakapi."
—Ps. lxxxvii: 2.

Second Tune.

From "Tunes Old and New" by permission of Rev. Dr. Tucker.

2 Wocaŋtekiye mniyowe,
He etaŋ iwakpa kiŋ
Ko hena waŋyakapi ye;
Qa wakpa kiŋ hececa
Oŋ tuwe e mni ciŋ kta he?
Towaŝte kiŋ ohiŋni,
He Tuwa wicaqu kiŋ He
Towaŝte iyececa.

3 Tipi kiŋ owasiŋ eded
Peta qa maħpiya kiŋ
Ko aokdutewicaya,
Hed Itaŋcaŋ Ti kiŋ oŋ,
Zioŋ ed taŋyaŋ uŋpi kiŋ!
Jesus we oŋ skapi kiŋ!
Jesus He waciŋyaŋpi kiŋ,
Oŋ iye wakaŋpi ce. Amen.

70 "The Church's One Foundation." 7s. 6s. D.

"Zioŋ ed iŋyaŋ waŋ oise pa ȟca ewakde, kaȟnigapi, teȟika; uŋkaŋ tuwa he waciŋye ciŋhaŋ wiśteciŋ kte śni ce." — 1 Peter ii: 6.

AURELIA.

From "Tunes Old and New" by permission of Rev. Dr. Tucker.

The Church.

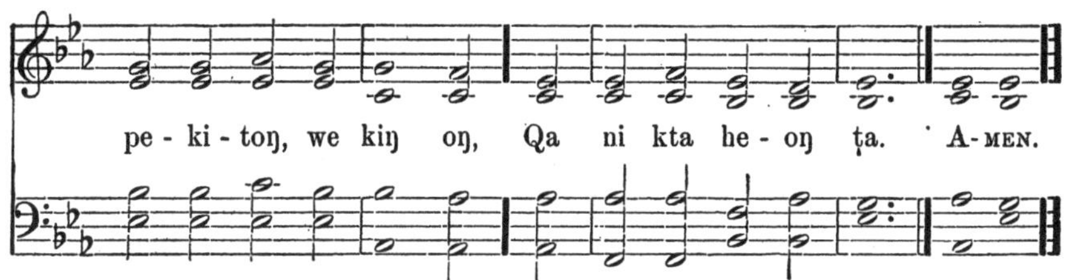

2 Maka kiŋ owaŋcaya,
Tka okiwaŋjina;
Itaŋcaŋ, wowaciŋye,
Baptisma ko yuha,
Christ Jesus He yawaŝte,
Qa Woyute Wakaŋ,
Qa woape waŋjina
Yuha tokata ya.

3 Okodakiciye kiŋ
Yuŝkiŝkapis'a e,
Qa wowicada ota
He oŋ kakija ŝa;
Maħpiyata wakaŋpi
Awaŋyag uŋpi, qa
Ded ceya heckiya
Odowaŋ qupi kta.

4 Ḣtani qa wicakiŝ, qa
Kicis ko uŋ eŝa,
Odakodkiciyapi
Owihaŋke cona
Yuŝtaŋpi kta ape uŋ,
Hehaŋd ohiye ciŋ,
Qa wowaŋyake ħce ciŋ
Waŋyag okiħpiŋ kta.

5 Eŝa maka kiŋ de ed
Wakaŋtaŋka kici,
Wakaŋpi kiŋ hena ob,
Hė okiwaŋjina:
Uŋkiŝ nakuŋ, Itaŋcaŋ,
Maħpiya kiŋ ekta
Obe wakaŋpi kiŋ ob
Uŋniyataŋpi nuŋ. AMEN.

IV. The Sacraments.

WOICICONZE WAKAN KIN.

The Lord's Supper. — Itaŋcaŋ Ḣtayetu Wotapi kiŋ.

71 Kirke. L. M.

"Aġuyapi wiconi kiŋ he Miye ce." — St. John vi: 35.

[*Rockingham, Hymn 39, and Hamburg, Hymn 73, may be used.*]

2 Jesus Nitowaoŋśida,
Dehaŋd uŋkiksuyapi ce;
Uŋnipi kta yaciŋ kiŋ oŋ
Niwe kiŋ he yakpapsoŋ ce.

3 Jesus, waŋkaŋd maḣpiya kiŋ
Hed wowitaŋ duha, tka he
Yakpaġaŋ qa niktepi oŋ
Wawaḣtani yakajuju.

4 Jesus, haŋyed aġuyapi
Dawaŝte uŋkaŋ he ehaŋd:
"Mitaŋcaŋ kiŋ he dee ce,
Owasiŋ yuta po," eha.

5 Qa wiyatke dawaŝte, qa
"Mawe papsoŋpi dee ce,
Wicouŋ teca tawa kiŋ,
Etaŋ yatkaŋ po," hed eha.

6 Wanikiya, niwe kiŋ oŋ
Taŋyeḣ uŋyuwaŝtepi ye,
He oŋ ake yahi kiŋhaŋ,
Uŋkinidowaŋpi kta ce. AMEN.

The Sacraments.

72 Mear. C. M.

"Tuwa Micehpi yute ça Mawe yatke ciŋ he Mici uŋ, qa Miś kici wauŋ." — St. John vi: 56.

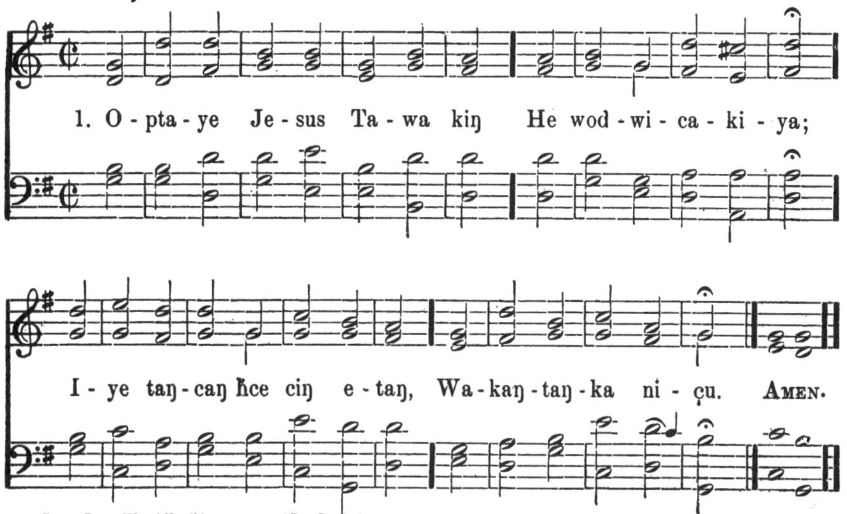

From "Tunes Old and New" by permission of Rev. Dr. Tucker.

2 Caje wicadapi hena
Wicayuska ece;
He wowiyuśkiŋ taŋka hca,
Wakaŋtaŋka niçu.

3 Deuicanapi kiŋ hena
Owasiŋ upi ye,
"Haŋ, haŋ," cya ayupta po,
Iye niniyaŋpi.

4 Niyaśicapi kiŋ hena
Wicayawaśte po;
He Christ ecoŋniśipi ce,
Iye niniyaŋpi.

5 Itaŋcaŋ kiŋ itokabya
Wateśdake waśte,
Iye owas niçupi kta,
Wiconi kiŋ ekta. Amen.

The Sacraments.

73 "My God, and is Thy Table Spread." L. M.

"U po, wana taku owasiŋ wiyeya hiyeya ce." — St. Luke xiv: 17.

[*Duke Street, Hymn* 126, *may be used.*]

HAMBURG.

From "Tunes Old and New" by permission of Rev. Dr. Tucker.

2 Wakaŋyaŋ wodwicayapi,
Christ Jesus We, cehpi kiŋ ko,
Tuwa hena icu kiŋhaŋ
Yawaŝtepi kiŋ taŋka ce.

3 Qa Wotapi Wakaŋ kiŋ de
Wicota iyuŝkiŋyaŋ hciŋ
Ed upi niŋ, qa oŋ etaŋ
Wiconi opapi nuŋwe.

4 Qa Wotaŋiŋ Waŝte kiŋ he
Maka sitomniyaŋ i nuŋ;
Eced Aġuyapi kiŋ de
Oyate yutapi nuŋwe.

5 Ateyapi, Ciŋhiŋtku kiŋ,
Qa Woniya Wakaŋ kiŋ He,
Wakaŋtaŋka waŋjina kiŋ.
He wowitaŋ yuha nuŋwe. AMEN.

The Lord's Supper.

74 "Bread of the World, in Mercy Broken." P. M.

"Jesus hewicakiya; Aġuyapi wiconi kiŋ He Miye ce." — St. John vi: 36.

From "Tunes Old and New" by permission of Rev. Dr. Tucker.

2 Wicani kta wicoie kiŋ
  Oyake ciŋ Niye ħca ce,
Niṭe ciŋ he oŋ woaħtani
  Uŋkiciṭapi kiŋ Niye.

3 Caŋte iyokiśica uŋ kiŋ,
  Waħtanipis'a ko owas
Iśtamnihaŋpe tawapi kiŋ
  Awicakicitoŋwaŋ ye;

4 Qa wowaśte Nitawa kiŋ, oŋ
  Naġi kiŋ woduŋyayapi;
He Wotapi Wakaŋ kiŋ de ed
  Sdodkiyeuŋkiyapi ye. AMEN.

The Sacraments.

75 "According to Thy Gracious Word. C. M.

"Deced Miksuya ecoŋ po."—St. Luke xxii: 19.

St. John, Westm.

From "Tunes Old and New," by permission of Rev. Dr. Tucker.

2 Nitaŋcaŋ kiŋ yuśpuśpupi
Aġuyapiwaya,
Qa We yakpasoŋ qoŋ bdatkaŋ
Oŋ ciksuyiŋ kta ce.

3 Gethsem'ne ed yauŋ qoŋhaŋ
We oŋ tenimni, qa
Iyoniciśice ciqoŋ,
Oŋ ciksuyiŋ kta ce.

4 Qa caŋicipaweġa ed
Ahiwatoŋwaŋ caŋ,
O Wośnapi mitawa kiŋ,
Oŋ ciksuyiŋ kta ce.

5 Nicakija eśa, miye
Temayaḣida kiŋ,
Haŋ, niwauŋ ihuŋniyaŋ
Oŋ ciksuyiŋ kta ce.

6 Waśakeśniyaŋ ţekiniŋd
Wauŋ, qa wowitaŋ
Kduha ake yaḣi kiŋhaŋ,
Christ, miksuya uŋ ye. Amen.

76 Mendon. L. M.

" Hokšiçopa ed Maupi kta iyowiŋwicakiya po." —St. Mark x: 14.

[*Federal Street, Hymn* 110, *may be used.*]

From "Tunes Old and New" by permission of Rev. Dr. Tucker.

2 Wakaŋheja waŋji tohaŋd
Waciŋyaŋ Jesus cekiya
Eca taŋyaŋ nakicihon,
Qa Towašte etaŋhaŋ qu.

3 Šiceca ciscipina kiŋ,
Iye kodaniyaŋpi ce,
Qa taku šice ciŋ owas
Etaŋ inicupi kta ce.

4 Šiceca kiŋ mahpiya ed
Koktopawiŋge ota hcin,
Iye kici hed uŋpi qa
Yataŋ idowaŋpi kta ce.

5 Mahpiya kiŋ akotaŋhaŋ
Makoce waŋ wašte waŋka;
Wakaŋtaŋka ciŋca hena
Hed wiyuškiŋyaŋ uŋpi kta. AMEN.

77 Mount Nebo. C. M.

"Tiyopa kiŋ ciqana qa caŋku kiŋ nakuŋ ocisciyena e wiconi iyakde."
—St. Matt. vii: 14.

[*Arlington, Hymn* 165, *may be used.*]

3 Nioie wakaŋ kiŋ He,
Sutaya hiŋ kta ce,
Iyoyaŋpa Nitawa oŋ,
Sataŋ hiŋḣpayiŋ kta.

4 Caŋku wiconi kiŋ waŝte,
Caŋku kiŋ ciscina;
Oknayaŋ yapi kiŋ owas,
Iyuŝkiŋpi kta ce.

5 Uŋkiyepi nakuŋ He ed
Uŋkiyuŝkiŋpi kta;
Maḣpiyata wiconi ed,
Uŋptayapi kta ce.

6 Wanikiyauŋyaŋpi kiŋ,
Waoŋŝida ḣca ce;
Waŋkaŋd maḣpiyata yaŋka,
Wiconi kiŋ yuha.

7 Wiconi taŋka ḣce ciŋ he
Ed woŝice waniŋd;
Wicaŝa ska hed uŋpi ce,
Christ Jesus He kici. AMEN.

Baptism.

78 "Soldiers of Christ, Arise." S. M

"Itaŋcaŋ kiŋ ed waśagya uŋ po, Iye Towaśake wicookihi kiŋ oŋ."
—Ephes. vi: 10.

FIRST TUNE. SILVER STREET.

From "Tunes Old and New" by permission of Rev. Dr. Tucker.

2 Wakaŋtaŋka Iye
Waśagniyaŋpi ce,
Ciŋhiŋtku kiŋ waciŋyaŋpi
Oŋ woohiye ce.

3 He Towaśake kiŋ
Owas koyagya po;
Okicize waŋ taŋka kiŋ
Oŋ wiyeya uŋ po.

4 He oŋ tohaŋd taŋyaŋ
Nikduśtaŋpi kiŋhaŋ,
Waŋkaŋta woohiye kiŋ
Iyekcupi kta ce.

5 Wakaŋtaŋka Ate,
Ciŋhiŋtku kiŋ nakuŋ,
Qa Woniya Wakaŋ kiŋ He
Wakaŋtaŋka Niye. AMEN.

78 "Soldiers of Christ, Arise." S. M.

"Itaŋcaŋ kiŋ ed waśagya uŋ po, Iye Towaśake wicookihi kiŋ oŋ."
—Ephes. vi; 10.

SECOND TUNE.

LABAN. L. MASON.

By permission of Rev. Dr. Hutchins.

2 Wakaŋtaŋka Iye
Waśagniyaŋpi ce,
Ciŋhiŋtku kiŋ waciŋyaŋpi
Oŋ woohiye ce.

3 He Towaśake kiŋ
Owas koyagya po;
Okicize waŋ taŋka kiŋ
Oŋ wiyeya uŋ po.

4 He oŋ tohaŋd taŋyaŋ
Nikduśtaŋpi kiŋhaŋ,
Waŋkaŋta woohiye kiŋ
Iyekcupi kta ce.

5 Wakaŋtaŋka Ate,
Ciŋhiŋtku kiŋ nakuŋ,
Qa Woniya Wakaŋ kiŋ He
Wakaŋtaŋka Niye. AMEN.

79 "The Gentle Saviour Calls." S. M.

"Hokšiçopa ed mahipi kta iyowiŋwicakiya po."—St. Matt. xix: 14.

[*Boylston, Hymn 116, may be used.*]

From "Tunes Old and New" by permission of Rev. Dr. Tucker.

2 Isto waoŋšida
Okna iwicacu,
Nape awicaknake ça
Wicayawašte ce.

3 "Awicanicapi
Šni po, mahpiyata
Ouŋyaŋpi kiŋ decapi
He oŋ etaŋ," eya.

4 He oŋ iyuškiŋyaŋ
Uŋnicaupi kta,
Uŋyaduhapi kiŋ okna
Wicaduha nuŋwe.

5 Wakaŋtaŋka Ate,
Ciŋhiŋtku kiŋ nakuŋ,
Qa Woniya Wakaŋ kiŋ He
Wakaŋtaŋka Niye. AMEN.

The Sacraments.

80 Waterbury, No. 10. 6s. 5s.

"Sicaya ecoŋpi ayuśtaŋ po, taku waśte ecoŋpi oŋspeiçiciya po." — Isa. i: 16, 17.

[*Saint Lucian, Hymn* 160, *may be used.*]

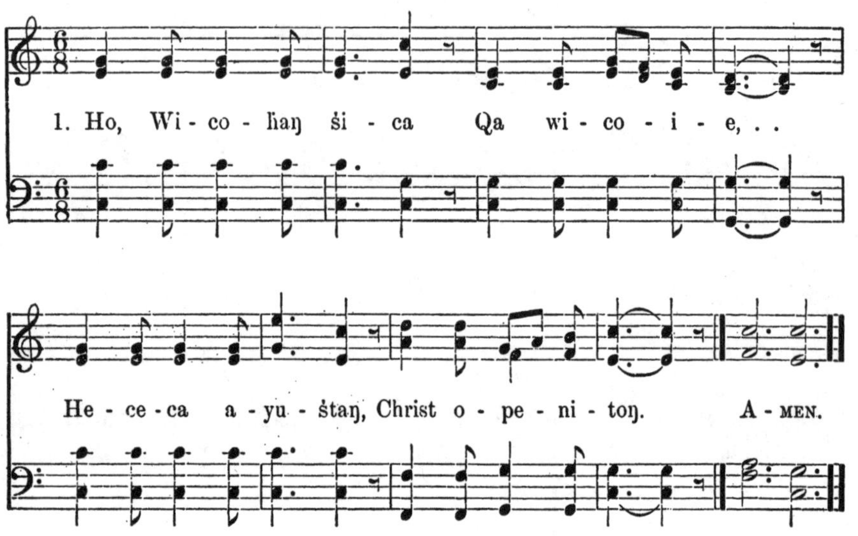

2 Jesus He waśte ce,
Jesus He wakaŋ;
Qa śiceca tawa
Iś wakaŋpi ce.

3 Tka wakaŋśica kiŋ
He nicuwapi;
Taku śice ciŋ he
Oŋ niknayaŋpi.

4 Tka naȟoŋpi śni po,
He niktepi ciŋ;
Śice ciŋ kipajiŋ,
Wowaśte ecoŋ.

5 Haŋ, wahoŋiyaŋpi,
Tobaptisma ed;
Hed niçicoŋzapi
He kiksuya po.

6 He ehaŋ nitoŋpi,
Jesus Christ he ed,
Śice ciŋ kipajiŋ,
Wowaśte ecoŋ.

7 Jesus He Itaŋcaŋ;
Jesus He wakaŋ,
Qa śiceca Tawa
Iś wakaŋpi ce. AMEN.

V Offices of the Church.

OKODAKICIYE WAKAN TAWOECON KIN.

Catechism. — Wiwicawaŋġapi.

81 Caswell. 6s. 5s.

"Ceyakiyapi kiŋhaŋ kaked eya po."—St. Luke xi: 2.

[*St. John, Hymn* 35, *may be used.*]

From "Tunes Old and New" by permission of Rev. Dr. Tucker.

2 Hed Nitawaciŋ kiŋ
He ecoŋpi kiŋ,
He iyeced deci
He ecoŋpi nuŋ.
Qa oaŋpetu caŋ
Woyute kiŋ he,
De aŋpetu kiŋ ed
He uŋqupi ye.

3 Qa tuwa miye kiŋ
Toħaŋ śice ciŋ,
He aweciktoŋja,
Heced miksuya.
Wowiyutaŋ kiŋ he
Ed amaye śni;
Wośice etaŋhaŋ
Emakdaku ye.

4 Wokicoŋze kiŋ he,
Wowaśake kiŋ,
Wowitaŋ kiŋ he ko,
Haŋ, Nitawa nuŋ.
Qa Ate, Ciŋhiŋtku,
Woniya nakuŋ,
He Wakaŋtaŋka kiŋ,
Ohiŋniyaŋ ce. AMEN.

Offices of the Church.

82 Protection. 8s. 7s.

"Caŋku owihaŋke wanice ciŋ okna amayaŋ ye." Ps. cxxix: 34.

By permission of the Biglow & Main Co., owners of Copyright.

2 Christ, Koda wanišake ciŋ,
Niš caŋku wašte ȟce ciŋ,
Woaȟtani niŋd okna ȟciŋ
Yus amayaŋ ye, O Christ.

3 Haŋ, mioȟaŋ šica ota,
Qa mawaȟpanica ce;
Tka nitowaoŋšida kiŋ
He imajica kta ce.

4 Haŋ, ocide qa Nioȟaŋ
Waŋcag owapa kta ce,
O Wanikiya wašte kiŋ,
Wowašte mayaqu nuŋ. AMEN.

83 Redhead, 48. 7s.

"Taȟcašuŋka tipi tiyopa kiŋ He Niye ce."—St. John x: 7.

2 Wowaciŋye taŋka kiŋ,
Nitehaŋ wanuni, qa
Taȟcaska waŋ nuni kiŋ
He iyeced miš wauŋ.

3 Jesus Christ, Wawiciya,
Coŋkaške Nitawa ed,
Taȟcaska Nitawa kiŋ
Opeya wauŋ waciŋ.

4 Christ Waawaŋkdake ciŋ,
Taȟcaska Tiyopa kiŋ,
Miš tiyopaciyiŋ kta
E, ioŋšimada ye.

5 Qa Ateyapi Wakaŋ,
Qa Ciŋhiŋtku kiŋ wakaŋ,
Woniya Wakaŋ kiŋ ko,
Wowitaŋ yuha nuŋwe. AMEN.

84 St. Constantine. 6s. 5s.

"Wakaŋtaŋka Nitowacaŋtkiye waŝte kiŋ oŋ oŋŝimada ye."—Ps. li: 1.

[*St. Lucian, Hymn* 160, *may be used.*]

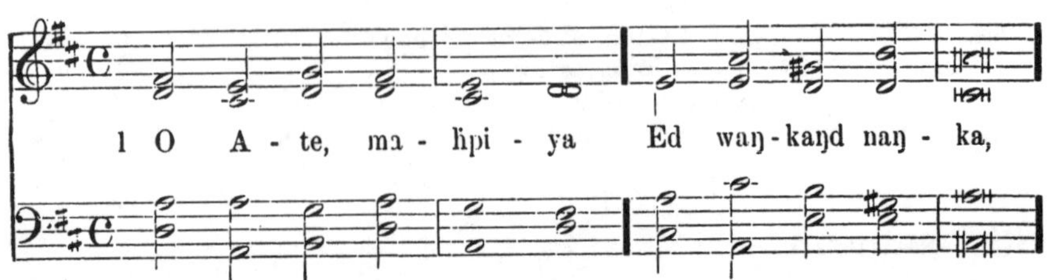

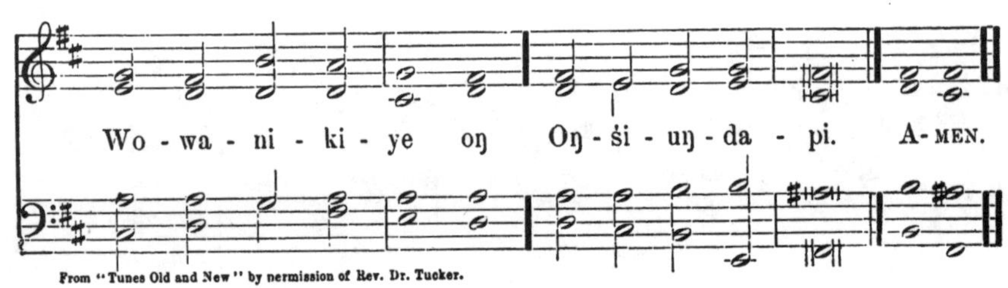

From "Tunes Old and New" by permission of Rev. Dr. Tucker.

2 Qa Nicaje taŋka
He yataŋpi kta;
Wowaŝake kiŋ oŋ
Oŋŝiuŋdapi.

3 Woniya Wakaŋ kiŋ,
Tecauŋyaŋpi,
Oŋ uŋnaġipi kiŋ
Oŋŝiuŋdapi.

4 Woŝkaŋŝkaŋ Nitawa
He ecana kta;
Oŋ Nitoyaŋke oŋ
Oŋŝiuŋdapi.

5 Ded wiconi qeyaŝ,
He teĥika ce;
Yus uŋkayadapi,
Oŋŝiuŋdapi.

6 Ded maka akaŋtu,
Okpaza ece;
Aŋpa teca kiŋ oŋ
Oŋŝiuŋdapi.

7 De aŋpetu kiŋ oŋ
Woyute kiŋ he,
Wokoyake ko, oŋ
Oŋŝiuŋdapi.

8 Wokicoŋze kiŋ he,
Wowitaŋ kiŋ ko,
Ohiŋniyaŋ ĥiŋca,
Niŝ Nitawa nuŋ. AMEN.

85 Brightest and Best. 11s. 10s.

"Niyate qa nihuŋ wicakduonihaŋ yo." —Kdi. xx: 12.

From "Goodrich S. S. Hymnal" by permission of E. P. Dutton & Co.

2 Heced hokśiçopapi kiŋ waśteśte,
Tuwa Wakaŋ kiŋ waśtedapi kiŋ,
Hena atkukupi huŋkupi koya,
He oŋ ohowicakidapi kta.

3 Heced hena ded maka kiŋ akaŋta,
Wowaśte ohni sdodyapi kta ce;
Uŋkaŋ tokata wiconi kte ciŋ ed,
Ohiŋniyaŋ hciŋ niuŋpi kta ce.

4 Heced maĥpiya kiŋ wowaśte kiŋ ed,
Wowiyuśkiŋ hca waŋ taŋka yuha,
Heci odowaŋ waŋ teca waśte oŋ
Jesus yataŋyaŋ idowaŋpi kta. AMEN.

Offices of the Church.

86 Palmyra. P. M.

" Adam ed owasiŋ ṭapi kiŋ he iyeced Christ ed owasiŋ piya niyapi kta." — 1 Cor. xv: 22.

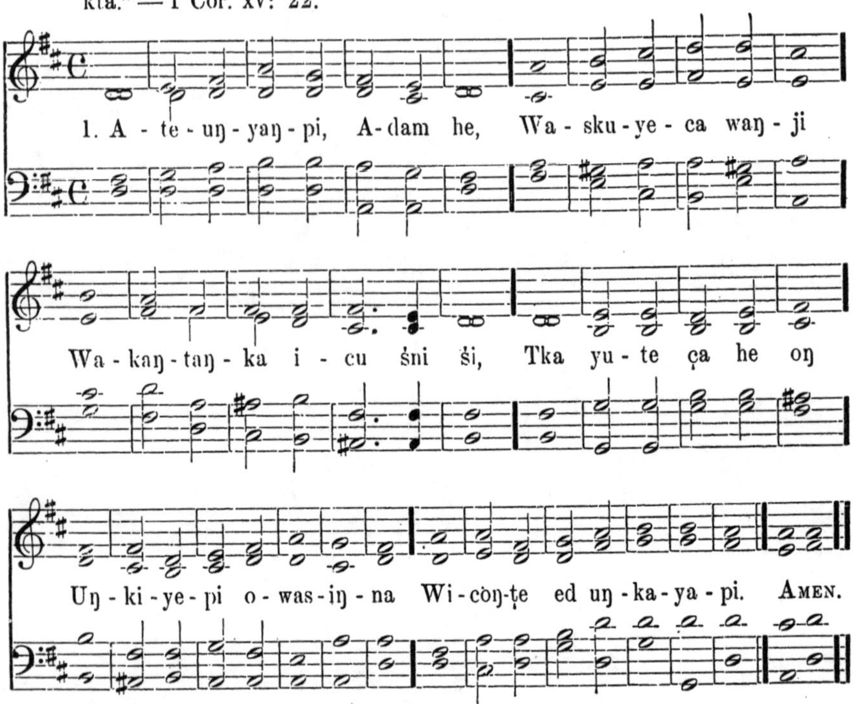

From "Tunes Old and New" by permission of Rev. Dr. Tucker.

2 Wakaŋtaŋka yawaśte po;
Ciŋhiŋtku, Jesus Christ,
Wicaceḣpi, wicawe ko
Ed opa kta u śi;
He woaḣtani nica, tka
Opeuŋkitoŋpi kta ṭa.

3 Atkuku Toahope kiŋ
Nauŋḣoŋpi śni s'a,
Tka Iś iyuha ḣciŋ ecoŋ,
Hehaŋd waŋkaŋd kikda;
Tuwa Iye waciŋye ciŋ
He tohiŋni ḣciŋ ṭiŋ kte śni. AMEN.

Catechism.

87 Clapham. Six 7s.

"Wacaŋtkiyapi kiŋ he Woahope kiŋ yuecetupi kiŋ hee."—Rom. xiii: 10.

[*Dix, Hymn 143, may be used.*]

From "Tunes Old and New" by permission of Rev. Dr. Tucker.

2 Mazayaḣotoŋpi waŋ,
Qa nakuŋ wakiŋyaŋ kiŋ
Nina ḣciŋ ḣotoŋ icaŋd
Peta se, wakaŋkdi kiŋ
He kiŋ okśaŋyaŋ taŋiŋ,
Owaŋcaya śod uya.

3 Peta taŋka waŋ okna
He akaŋd Itaŋcaŋ i,
Uŋkaŋ hotaŋkakiya
Toahope kiŋ hena
Opewicaśi kiŋ he
Israel nakiḣoŋpi.

4 Tka oḣakab Jesus hi,
Woope Wikcemna kiŋ
Israel wicaqupi
Ptaya He yuptecena;
Woope waŋ teca ka,
Uŋkaŋ kakeḣciŋ eya;

5 "Decetu; Wakaŋtaŋka
He caŋte kiŋ ataya
Oŋ waśteyadakiŋ kta;
Qa nikiyena ti kiŋ,
Niye ḣca iyececa,
He waśteyadakiŋ kta." Amen.

Offices of the Church.

88 Tallis' Ordinal. C. M.

"Mitokab taku wakaŋ tokeca duhe kte śni." —Kdi. xx: 3.

From "Tunes Old and New," by permission of Rev. Dr. Tucker.

2 Waśteuŋdakapi ħce ciŋ
He taku ħca eśa,
Ohouŋdapi kiŋ hee,
Wakaŋ śni ħca tuka.

3 Hayake, woiyokipi,
Wahececa owas,
Wakaŋtaŋkawaya, hena
Imayutaŋ kiŋhaŋ.

4 Nakuŋ wicaśa ota ħciŋ,
Itaŋcaŋ Hee śni
Tuka, makata woyuha
Iyotaŋdapis'a.

5 Iyouŋkiśicapi qa
Uŋţapi kta eca,
Hena niuŋyaŋpi kta e
Okihipi kta he?

6 Wakaŋtaŋka, Niśnana ħciŋ
Caŋte mayuha ye;
Waśtewadaka ota śa
Waŋjina E Wakaŋ. AMEN.

89 Holy Days. 7s. 6s. D.

"Mitokab taku wakaŋ tokeca duha kte śni." — Kdi. xx: 3.

FIRST TUNE.

From "Tunes Old and New," by permission of Rev. Dr. Tucker.

2 Iye nape makaġa,
Qa Towaśake oŋ
Waŋkaŋd mayuza, uŋkaŋ
Tawaciŋ kiŋ eced
Ecoŋmayaŋ okihi;
Christ, yusamayaŋ ye,
Mioḣaŋ qa tawaciŋ
Waśte makaġa ye.

3 Wana sdodniyaŋpi kiŋ
Wicotapi eśa,
Nahaŋḣciŋ tokedciŋciŋ
Wacekiyapis'a:
Uŋcaŋtepi taŋmahed,
Uŋkabdezapi qeś,
Wakaġapi waŋ ti se,
Waŋyakapi kta tka.

4 Tuwa Wicakaġe ciŋ
Naḣma caŋteoze,
Qa Toyaŋke ed uŋ kiŋ
Owas waŋyaka ce:
Wakaŋtaŋka Nitokab
Iḣpemiçiyiŋ kta;
Niśna ohocida kta
Oŋspemakiya ye. AMEN.

Offices of the Church.

89 "Just a Word for Jesus.', 7s. 6s. Double.

"Mitokab taku wakaŋ tokeca duha kte ṡni." — Kdi. xx: 3.

2 Iye nape makaġa,
  Qa Towaṡake oŋ
Waŋkaŋd mayuza, uŋkaŋ
  Tawaciŋ kiŋ eced
Ecoŋmayaŋ okihi;
  Christ, yusamayaŋ ye;
Mioḣaŋ qa tawaciŋ
  Waṡte makaġa ye.

3 Wana sdoduiyaŋpi kiŋ
  Wicotapi eṡa,
Nahaŋḣciŋ tokedciŋciŋ
  Wacekiyapis'a:
Uŋcaŋtepi taŋmahed,
  Uŋkabdezapi qeṡ,
Wakaġapi waŋ ti se,
  Waŋyakapi kta tka.

4 Tuwa Wicakaġe ciŋ
  Naḣma caŋteoze,
Qa Toyaŋke ed uŋ kiŋ
  Owas waŋyaka ce:
Wakaŋtaŋka Nitokab
  Iḣpemiçiyiŋ kta;
Niṡna ohocida kta
  Oŋspemakiya ye. Amen.

Confirmation. — Wicayusutapi.

90 "O Happy Day, that Stays my Choice." L. M.

"Micante kin sutaya han; wadowan qa dowanwakiyin kta." — Ps. lvii: 8.

[*Rockingham, Hymn 39, may be used without the chorus.*]

2 Aŋpetu de miçicaśka,
Qa Towaśte waśtewada,
Iye Ti kiŋ waŋkaŋd, wakaŋ,
Qa heciya wadowaŋ kta.

3 Micaŋte kiŋ wana bduśtaŋ,
Itaŋcaŋ kiŋ mayaduha,
Niyakna ħciŋ wauŋ waciŋ,
Niho anawaġoptaŋ kta.

4 Dehaŋd iyozimiçiya,
Wanikiya Wakaŋtaŋka
Yati kiŋ owapa kiŋ oŋ
Maka tewaħida śni ce.

5 Maħpiya kiŋ maho naħoŋ,
Sutaya ħciŋ miçiconza,
Tohaŋ wani hehaŋyaŋ ħciŋ
Wakaŋtaŋka mayaduha. AMEN.

Offices of the Church.

91 "Witness, ye Men and Angels; Now." C. M.

"Jehovah Taku Wakaŋ yada kiŋ Hẹe . . . nakaha eyakiya."—Woope Ita. xxvi: 17.

FIRST TUNE. DUNDEE.

From "Tunes Old and New" by permission of Rev. Dr. Tucker.

2 Uŋnipi kiŋ hehaŋye hciŋ,
Itaŋcaŋ Jesus Christ
He ed uŋkiçiçupi, qa
Kici uŋqoŋpi kta.

3 Nakuŋ, wauŋśagśakapi
Uŋkeciŋpi kte śni,
Tuka Itaŋcaŋ Towaśte
Waciŋuŋyaŋpi kta.

4 Nacaŋcaŋyaŋ mauŋnipi,
He oŋ uŋsihapi
Owotaŋna hciŋ aya ye,
Nitacaŋku okna.

5 Ateyapi, Ciŋhiŋtku kiŋ,
Qa Woniya Wakaŋ
Wakaŋtaŋka waŋjina kiŋ,
Owihaŋke wanind. AMEN.

Confirmation.

91 "Witness, ye Men and Angels; Now." C. M.

"Jehovah Taku Wakaŋ yada kiŋ Hee . . . nakaha eyakiya." — Woope Ita. xxvi: 17.

From "Tunes Old and New" by permission of Rev. Dr. Tucker.

2 Uŋnipi kiŋ hehaŋye ȟciŋ,
Itaŋcaŋ Jesus Christ
He ed uŋkiçiçupi, qa
Kici uŋqoŋpi kta.

3 Nakuŋ, wauŋśagśakapi
Uŋkeciŋpi kte śni,
Tuka Itaŋcaŋ Towaśte
Waciŋuŋyaŋpi kta.

4 Nacaŋcaŋyaŋ mauŋnipi,
He oŋ uŋsihapi
Owotaŋna ȟciŋ aya ye,
Nitacaŋku okna.

5 Ateyapi, Ciŋhiŋtku kiŋ,
Qa Woniya Wakaŋ
Wakaŋtaŋka waŋjina kiŋ,
Owihaŋke wauiŋd. AMEN.

Offices of the Church.

Visitation of the Sick. — Wayazaŋkapi waŋwicayag ipi kiŋ.

92 St. Thomas. S. M.

"O Itaŋcaŋ, Nitoope caŋku kiŋ oŋspemakiya ye." — Ps. cxix.

From "Tunes Old and New" by permission of Rev. Dr. Tucker.

2 Jesus, micaŋte kiŋ
De miciyuska ye;
Kiŋhaŋ caŋku yakaġe ciŋ
Okna mawani kta.

3 Jesus, mitawaciŋ
Yuowotaŋna ye;
Kiŋhaŋ Yati wakaŋ kiŋ hed
Okna wauŋ kta ce.

4 Jesus, maṭiŋ kte ciŋ
Ed oŋṡimada ye;
Nape wakaŋ Nitawa oŋ
Waŋkaŋd imacu ye.

5 Wakaŋtaŋka Ate,
Ciŋhiŋtku kiŋ nakuŋ,
Qa Woniya Wakaŋ kiŋ He
Wakaŋtaŋka Niye. AMEN.

Visitation of the Sick.

93 "Nearer, my God, to Thee." P. M.

"Oyate waŋ Iye ikiyena uŋpi kiŋ." — Ps. cxlviii: 13.

2 Wanuni se wauŋ,
  Kopewakda;
Maniŋd amakpaza,
  Imuŋka, tka
Wiwahaŋbde waśte;
  Kici ciuŋ epca,
    Nikiyena.

3 Caŋku miyecaġa,
  Waŋkaŋd ekta,
Qa wokoyake ska
  Mayaqu ce;
Wakaŋpi micopi,
  Qa hed wauŋ waciŋ
    Nikiyena.

4 Wana iyoyaŋpa,
  Ciyataŋ kta;
Caŋtemaśice ciŋ
  Wana waniŋd,
Zani wauŋ kta ce,
Mita Wakaŋtaŋka
  Nikiyena. AMEN

Offices of the Church.

Burial of the Dead. — Wicaȟapi kiŋ.

94 "Asleep in Jesus! Blessed Sleep." L. M.

"Tona Jesus ed iśtiŋmapi kiŋ hena Iye kici Wakaŋtaŋka uwicakiyiŋ kta." — 1 Thess. iv: 14.

Rest.

2 Christ Jesus ed iśtiŋmapi,
Hed woiyokipi kta ce;
Wicoŋte pe waniŋdya hed,
Wanikiya waŋyakapi.

3 Christ Jesus ed iśtiŋmapi,
Iś wookiye kiŋ yuha,
Qa wokokipe cona ȟiciŋ,
Wanikiya waŋyakapi.

4 Christ Jesus ed iśtiŋmapi,
Hena wicayuwakaŋpi;
He ho waśte naȟoŋpi qa
Wanikiya waŋyakapi.

5 Christ Jesus ed iśtiŋmapi,
Wicayuonihaŋpi ce;
Iye Taoyatepi kiŋ,
Wanikiya waŋyakapi.

6 Christ Jesus ed iśtiŋmapi,
Hed wowaciŋye taŋka ce;
Wakaŋtaŋka Taoyate,
Wanikiya waŋyakapi. Amen.

Burial of the Dead.

95 Ortonville. C. M.

"Taku šica waŋjina kowakipiŋ kte šni, Niye mici yauŋ kiŋ heoŋ."
—Ps. xxiii: 4.

2 Haŋ, okpaza wicoḣaŋ kiŋ
Ekta wauŋ eša,
Dehaŋd iyoyaŋpa ekta,
Jesus kici wauŋ.

3 Iyoyaŋpa wiyakpa kiŋ
He Jesus Ee ce;
Wiconi kiŋ wašte e ed,
Jesus kici wauŋ.

4 Iyokišid wauŋ eša,
Iye ḣca micaŋpta:
"Nicakijapi kta," eya,
Jesus kici wauŋ.

5 Jesus kici wauŋ kiŋhaŋ,
Owihaŋkešniyaŋ,
Hayake ska ḣca waŋ koyag,
Jesus kici wauŋ.

6 Wakaŋtaŋka itokabya
Wauŋ kta, ohiŋni;
Iyuškiŋyaŋ ḣciŋ, ohiŋni,
Jesus kici wauŋ. Amen.

Offices of the Church.

96 St. Mary. C. M.

"O Itaŋcaŋ, omawihaŋke kiŋ sdodyemakiya ye, qa mitaaŋpetu kiŋ tohaŋyaŋ ktaheciŋhaŋ." — Ps. xxxix: 5.

FIRST TUNE.

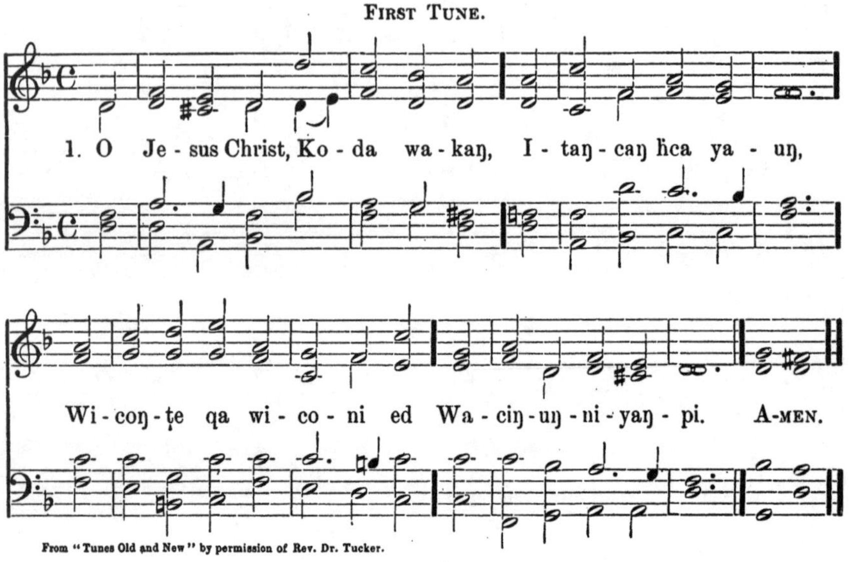

From "Tunes Old and New" by permission of Rev. Dr. Tucker.

2 Tohaŋd yaciŋ eca nakuŋ
Uŋyecopi ece;
He oŋ iwiyeya ȟciŋ, qa
Wakta uŋqoŋpi ce.

3 Waciŋniye ȟca ṭapi kiŋ
Caŋicipaweġa
Nitawa kiŋ ihukuya
Ape niwaŋkapi.

4 O Jesus Christ, Koda wakaŋ,
Maka kiŋ de akaŋd
Ptedyena ȟciŋ uŋskaŋpi, qa
Hehaŋd uŋkupi kta.

5 Wicanaġi tacaŋku kiŋ,
Christ Jesus, He Niye,
Caŋku wiconi kiŋ hee
Okna uŋkupi kta. AMEN.

Burial of the Dead.

96 Winchester (New.) C. M.

"O Itaŋcaŋ, omawihaŋke kiŋ sdodyemakiya ye, qa mitaaŋpetu kiŋ tok̇aŋyaŋ kta heciŋhaŋ." — Ps. xxxix: 5.

SECOND TUNE.

From "Tunes Old and New" by permission of Rev. Dr. Tucker.

2 Tohaŋd yaciŋ eca nakuŋ
  Uŋyecopi ece;
He oŋ iwiẏeya ḣciŋ, qa
  Wakta uŋqoŋpi ce.

3 Waciŋniye ḣca ṭapi kiŋ
  Caŋicipaweġa
Nitawa kiŋ ihukuya
  Ape niwaŋkapi.

4 O Jesus Christ, Koda wakaŋ,
  Maka kiŋ de akaŋd
Ptedyena ḣciŋ uŋṡkaŋpi, qa
  Hehaŋd uŋkupi kta.

5 Wicanaġi tacaŋku kiŋ,
  Christ Jesus, He Niye,
Caŋku wiconi kiŋ hee
  Okna uŋkupi kta. AMEN.

Offices of the Church.

97 "Sweet Bye and Bye." 9s. 6s.

"Tka nakaha makoce waŋji iyotaŋ waŝte maĥpiya ekta waŋke ciŋ hee akitapi." — Heb. xi: 16.

By permission of Oliver Ditson Company.

Burial of the Dead.

2 Qa caŋku kiŋ ihaŋke kiŋ hed,
Christ Jesus He uŋkakipepi;
He ouŋye waŋ heci waŝte
E piuŋkiciciyapi kta.

3 He makoce waŝte qa wakaŋ,
Qa wicayawaŝtepi kiŋ ob,
Hed odowaŋ onaȟoŋ waŝte
Waŋ uŋkahiyayapi kta ce.

4 Qa uŋnaġipi tohiŋna ȟciŋ
Hed iyokiŝicapi kte ŝni,
Qa ozikiyapi waŋ waŝte
E owasiŋ uŋkicupi kta.

5 Nakuŋ heci Ateuŋyaŋpi,
He waoŋŝida ȟce ciŋ, he oŋ
He ekta nina hoyeya po,
Qa Caje kiŋ idowaŋpi ye. Amen.

98 "Brightest and Best." 10s.

"Wokoyake ska koyakapi kiŋ hena tuwepi he?" — Wayuo vii: 13.

From Goodrich S. S. Hymnal, by permission of E. P. Dutton & Co.

2 Jesus we kiŋ he papsoŋpi kiŋ oŋ
Woaḣtani kiŋ iḣpeyapi ce;
Heced wiconi kiŋ teca e ed,
Jesus itokab inajiŋpi kta.

3 Wokoyake ska, wateśdake ko,
Nina waśte qa wiyakpa koyag,
Haŋ, qa waḣca kiŋ waśte ḣca yuha,
Jesus itokab inajiŋpi kta.

4 Jesus śiceca waśtewicada,
Tokicoŋze kiŋ ed opapi kta;
Heepi tawawicayiŋ kta ce,
Jesus itokab inajiŋpi kta. AMEN.

Burial of the Dead.

99 "As the Sweet Flower that Scents the Morn." L. M.

"Wakaŋtaŋka Tokicoŋze kiŋ dececapi kiŋ etaŋhaŋ kiŋ heoŋ."—St. Mark x: 14.

[*Hamburg, Hymn 73, may also be used.*] INTERCESSION.

From "Tunes Old and New" by permission of Rev. Dr. Tucker.

2 Iyeceḣciŋ, hokṡiçopa
Kiŋ de iṡ tohiŋhaŋna kiŋ
Wiciyokipi; tka wana
Uŋkitokab iyaya ce.

3 Haŋ, tuka woteḣi hena
Sdodye ṡni ḣciŋ iyaya ce,
Iyokiṡicapi ṡni po —
Iye taŋye ḣciŋ uŋ kta ce.

4 Ateyapi, Ciŋhiŋtku kiŋ,
Qa Woniya Wakaŋ kiŋ He,
Wakaŋtaŋka waŋjina kiŋ,
He wowitaŋ yuha nuŋwe. AMEN.

Offices of the Church.

Consecration of Churches. — Owocekiye Tipi yuwakaŋpi kiŋ.

100 "With One Consent Let All the Earth." L. M.

"Tatiyopa kiŋ mahed wopida yuha ya po." — Ps. c: 3.

Old Hundredth.

From "Tunes Old and New" by permission of Rev. Dr. Tucker.

2 Kokipeya iyuśkiŋ po,
Iyuśkiŋyaŋ ohoda po,
Qa woyataŋ odowaŋ kiŋ
Iye kahiyayapi ye.

3 Hecena hciŋ Wakaŋtaŋka
Wicauŋdapi kiŋ Ee,
Uŋkiś, qa taku kiŋ owas,
Iye uŋketaŋhaŋpi ce;

4 Iye uŋkdahniġapi ce,
Optaye wodwicakiya,
Obe waŋ oŋśiwicada
Kiŋ he uŋkiyepi hca ce.

5 Haŋ, coŋkaśke tiyopa kiŋ
Ohodaya mahed ya po,
Tahocoka nakuŋ mahed
Yaonihaŋyaŋ dowaŋ po;

6 Qa wopida odowaŋ kiŋ
Ayaśtaŋ śni dowaŋpi ye,
Iye Caje wakaŋ kiŋ he
Yataŋpi qa yawaśte po.

7 Itaŋcaŋ hce ciŋ Hee ce,
He awicakehaŋ waśte,
Qa Towaoŋśida kiŋ he
Cetuŋkdapica śni ece;

8 Qa wowicake Tawa kiŋ,
Ehaŋtaŋhaŋ sutaya haŋ,
Ihuniyepicaśni haŋ
Eced sutaya hiŋ kta ce. Amen.

Consecration of Churches.

101 Canonbury. L. M.

"Caŋte kduṭiŋza po, tona Itaŋcaŋ ayapepi kiŋ." — Ps. xxxi: 27.

[*Rousseau, Hymn* 37, *may be used.*]

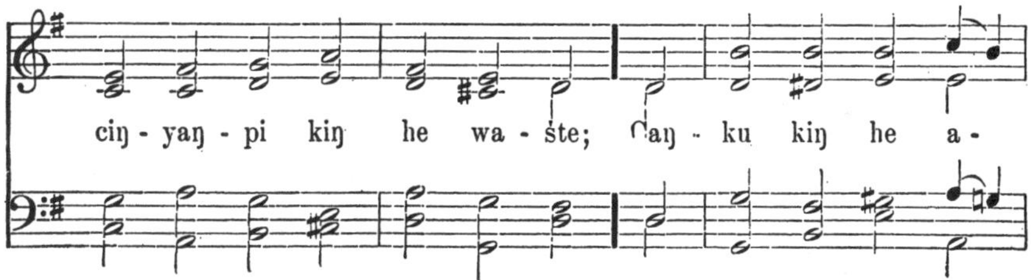

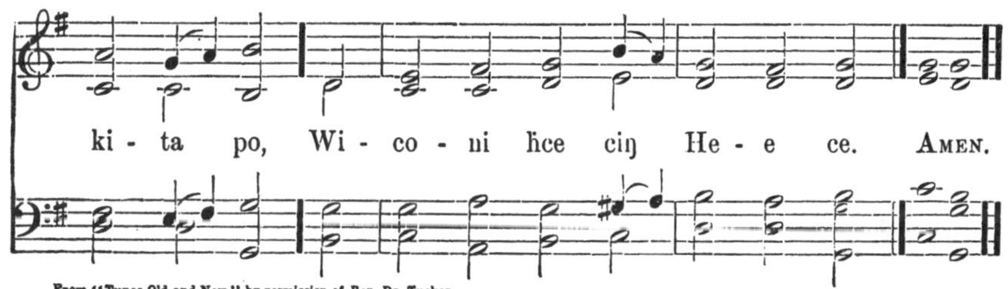

From "Tunes Old and New" by permission of Rev. Dr. Tucker.

2 Wicotawaciŋ taŋka kiŋ
Wiconi kiŋ iyakde kta;
Owihaŋke wanice ciŋ
Wakaŋtaŋka kiŋ Hee ce.

3 Wakaŋtaŋka ohodaya,
Tawaciŋ okiwaŋjina
Ekta, owihaŋke waniŋd
Iyuškiŋyaŋ uŋyaŋpi kta.

4 Owihaŋkiŋ kte ciŋ hehaŋd
Ed wowinihaŋ taŋka kta;
Qa woahope Tawa kiŋ
Ahouŋpapi kta wašte.

5 Ateyapi, Ciŋhiŋtku kiŋ,
Qa Woniya Wakaŋ kiŋ He,
Wakaŋtaŋka waŋjina kiŋ,
He wowitaŋ yuha nuŋwe. AMEN

VI. Missions and Charities.

WOTANIN WASTE AYAPI KIN.

102 "From Greenland's Icy Mountains." 7s. 6s. D.

"U, qa ouŋkiya po." — Ohan. xvi: 9.

MISSIONARY HYMN.

From "Tunes Old and New" by permission of Rev. Dr. Tucker.

2 Hena taŋyeh hiyeya,
Makoce ṡice ṡni;
Qa wita ko waṡteṡte
Ekta yukaŋpi tka
Wicaṡa kiŋ e ṡica,
Nakuŋ iṡtaġoŋġa,
Qa woksape kiŋ nica,
Oŋ iŋyaŋ cekiya.

3 Tuka uŋkiyepi ed
Iyoyaŋpa yukaŋ;
Wicoksape nakuŋ, qa
Wiconi waŋ wakaŋ;
Ito, hena owasiŋ
Wicuŋqupi waṡte;
Qa oŋ maka oyate
Jesus sdodyapi kta.

4 Ho, woyakapi kiŋ he,
Tate, niṡ aya po,
Mini, nakuŋ niyepi
Oyag kaduza po;
Haŋ, Jesus towitaŋ kiŋ
Mniowaŋca hce se
Maka sitomniyaŋ hciŋ
Kaowaŋcaya kta.

5 Eced ouŋcaġe waŋ
Uŋkiciyuskapi
Kiŋ de awaŋyakiŋ kta
E, Tahcaṡuŋkana
Ciŋca, wahtanipi s'a
Niwicayiŋ kta e
Oŋ ktepi qoŋ, Iye hca
Iyuṡkiŋyaŋ kdi kta. AMEN.

Missions and Charities.

103 Ithiel. L. M.

"Okpaza qa wicoŋṭe ohaŋzi kiŋ ed yaŋkapi kiŋ hena iyoyaŋbwicayiŋ kta." — St. Luke i: 79.

[*Mendon, Hymn 76, may be used.*]

From "Book of Common Praise" by permission of A. S. Barnes & Co.

2 Maȟpiya kiŋ ihukuya
Yauŋpi kiŋ, owasiŋ ȟciŋ
Wakaŋtaŋka yataŋpi ye;
Maka yuwaŝte kta e oŋ.

3 Jehovah He Caje waŝte,
Maka kiŋ owaŋcaya ȟciŋ;
Wicaceji owasiŋ He
Yataŋ dowaŋ hiŋkdapi kta.

4 Itaŋcaŋ Towaoŋŝida
Owihaŋke wanica ce;
Oiye kiŋ Iyoyaŋpa
Qa Towicake kiŋ suta.

5 Mniowaŋca kiŋ ohuta
Ed woyataŋ idowaŋ po;
Aŋpetu waŋ hihuni kta,
Qa kud iyaye ŝni nuŋwe.

6 Qa Jesus Toiyoyaŋpa
Maka iyojaŋjaŋyiŋ kta;
Wakaŋŝica kiŋ teȟaŋ kiŋ
Waŋkaŋd inajiŋ ŝni nuŋwe. AMEN.

Missions and Charities.

104 Tallis. L. M.

"Iyoyaŋpa mitawa qa Wanikiya mitawa kiŋ He Itaŋcaŋ kiŋ Hee."
—Ps. xxvii: 1.

From "Tunes Old and New" by permission of Rev. Dr. Tucker.

2 Maka akaŋd Nitacaŋku
  Taŋyaŋ sdodyemakiya ye;
Nitookiye kiŋ wakaŋ
  Nakuŋ hiyohimayaŋ ye.

3 Oyate kiŋ, maka akaŋd,
  Owas niyataŋpi kta ce:
Nawicaȟoŋ ye, O Ate,
  Qa oŋ niwicakiya ye.

4 Nitowiyuŝkiŋ taŋka kiŋ,
  Owas iyuŝkiŋpi kta ce;
Nioȟaŋ kiŋ owasiŋ ȟciŋ
  Ed onicipapi kta ce.

5 Wakaŋtaŋka, Wakaŋtaŋka,
  Uŋkitawapi kiŋ Niye;
Waoŋŝiyada ȟca ece,
  Oŋ oŋŝiuŋkidapi ye. AMEN.

VII. Special Seasons.

WOECON TOKTOKECA.

Thanksgiving. — Wopida Eyapi Aŋpetu kiŋ.

105 Horsley. C. M.

"Taku wicaqupi waśte qa yuśtaŋpi owasiŋ iyoyaŋpa Ateyapi kiŋ eciyataŋhaŋ kud u ece." —St. James i: 17.

From "Tunes Old and New" by permission of Rev. Dr. Tucker.

2 Wakaŋtaŋka kiŋ, Towakaŋ
Maka akaŋd kdohi;
Aŋpetu ohiŋniyaŋ waŋ
Uŋkiyuśtaŋpi ce.

3 Wakaŋtaŋka kiŋ, Toksape
Maka akaŋd kdohi;
Makoce ohiŋniyaŋ waŋ
Uŋkiyuśtaŋpi ce.

4 Wakaŋtaŋka kiŋ, Towitaŋ
Maka akaŋd kdohi;
Ouŋye ohiŋniyaŋ waŋ
Uŋkiyuśtaŋpi ce.

5 Wakaŋtaŋka, Taniya kiŋ
Maka akaŋd kdohi;
Oyaŋke ohiŋniyaŋ waŋ
Uŋkiyuśtaŋpi ce. Amen.

Special Seasons.

106 Jubal. 8s. 7s.

"Wakaŋtaŋka maka kiŋ caŋtewicakiye ciŋ heoŋ Ciŋhiŋtku hecena icaġe ciŋ wicaqu." — St. John iii: 16.

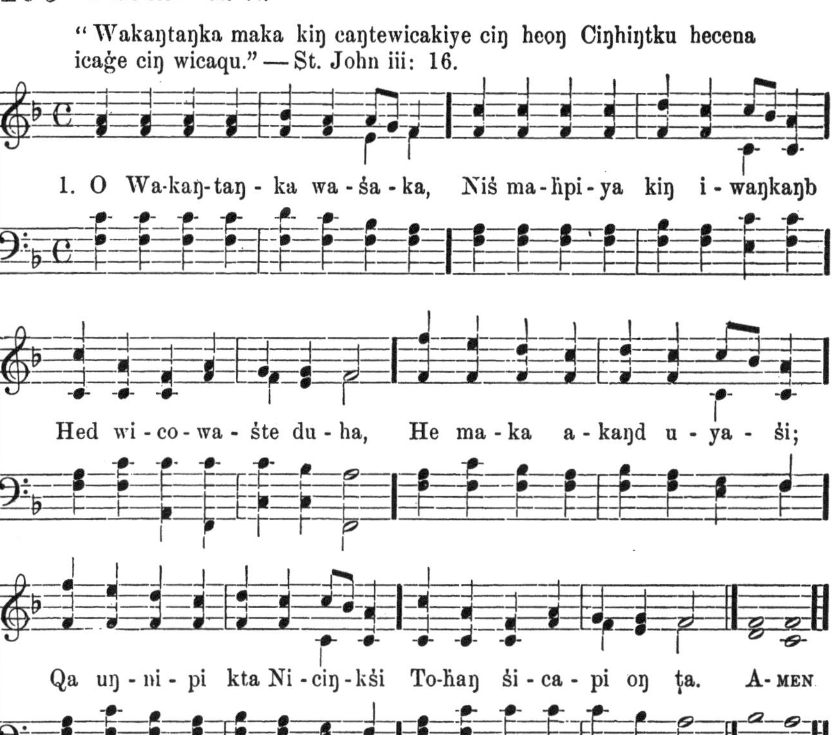

From "Tunes Old and New" by permission of Rev. Dr. Tucker.

2 Qa Wakaŋtaŋka Ti kiŋ ed,
Tona uŋpi kiŋ owasiŋ
Hed waŝtekicidapi;
Uŋkaŋ Jesus Towaŝte kiŋ
He taŋyaŋ yuhapi kta ce;
Heci owapiŋ kte ĥciŋ.

3 Qa Wakaŋtaŋka Iŝnana
Wowaoŋŝida kiŋ Tawa,
Oŋ kapepica ŝni ce;
Towiconi, Towaŝte kiŋ
Toyate wicahiyohi,
Oŋ pidauŋyaŋpi ce.

4 Qa Wakaŋtaŋka waŝte ce;
Taku ĥca eya owasiŋ
Hena wowicake ĥca;
Tona He awaciŋpi kiŋ
Hena e wiconi ĥce ciŋ
Ohiŋni yuhapi kta. Amen.

107 "Praise, O Praise Our God and King." 7s.

"Taku ceḣpitoŋ kiŋ owasiŋ woyute wicaqu; Towaoŋšida kiŋ he owihaŋke wanica."—Ps. cxxxvi: 25.

MONKLAND.

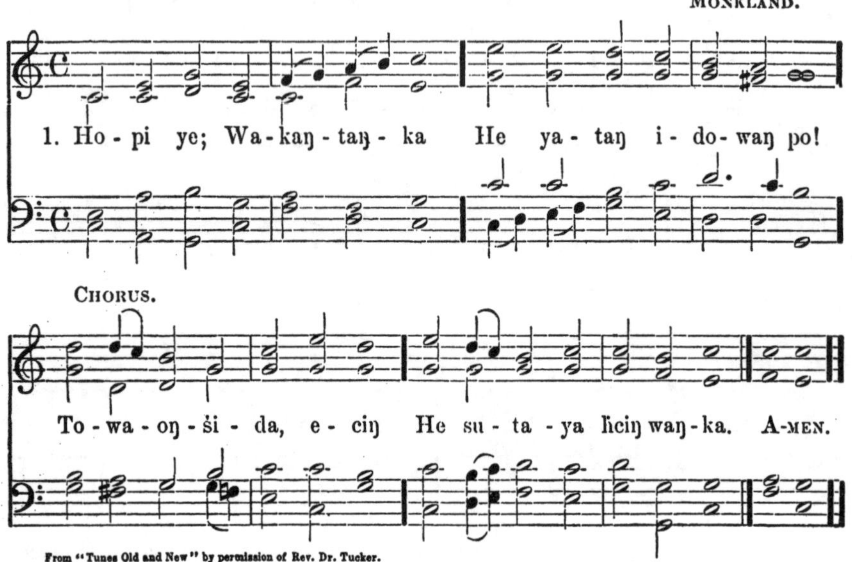

From "Tunes Old and New" by permission of Rev. Dr. Tucker.

2 He aŋpetuwi yuha,
Kaġe ca hinapeya;

3 Qa haŋhepiwi kiŋ he,
He iyeḣyeḣya ece;

4 He maġajuye ciŋ oŋ
Taku yutapi sutoŋ;

5 Maġa kiŋ aġuyapi
Odota icaḣye ši;

6 Woksapi uŋqupi kiŋ
Oŋ caje idowaŋ po;

7 Woyute nakuŋ waŋji,
He ikapeya wašte;

8 Oŋ wicanaġi kiŋ he
Ni uŋ kta uŋqupi ce. AMEN.

108 "God Bless Our Native Land." 6s. 4s.

"Oyate waŋ Itaŋcaŋ kiŋ he Wakaŋtaŋkayapi kiŋ he wowaŝte yuhapi." — Ps. xxxiii: 12.

AMERICA.

From "Goodrich and Gilbert Hymnal" by permission of E. P. Dutton & Co.

2 Tateyaŋpa ȟca ŝa
Tate qa taja ed
Initaŋcaŋ,
Nitowaŝake oŋ
Uŋkitamakapi
Teuŋȟidapi kiŋ,
Taŋyaŋ hiŋ niŋ.

3 Uŋkitamakapi
Oŋ ceuŋkiyapi;
Wakaŋtaŋka
Waŋkaŋd maȟpiya kiŋ
Akotaŋhaŋ yaŋke
Ciŋ He Iye ȟca E
Uŋkapepi.

4 Uŋkikiyena ȟciŋ
Yauŋ kiŋ, ohiŋni,
Awaŋyag uŋ,
Qa ed oyate kiŋ
Niwicayayiŋ kta
Iyonicipi nuŋ,
Wakaŋtaŋka! AMEN.

Special Seasons.

Family Worship.—Tiwahe ed Wacekiyapi.

109 Olmutz. S. M.

"O Itaŋcaŋ Wakaŋtaŋka wowanikiye mitawa towaśake kiŋ He Niye."—Ps. cxl: 7.

FIRST TUNE.

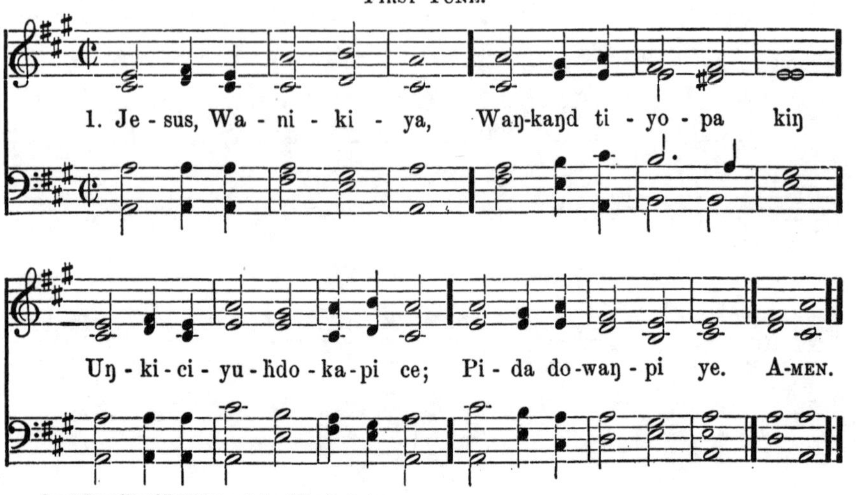

From "Tunes Old and New" by permission of Rev. Dr. Tucker.

2 Jesus, Waoŋśida,
Caŋku wiconi kiŋ
Uŋkiciyuśtaŋpi kiŋ oŋ
Yaonihaŋpi ye.

3 Jesus, Wawiciya,
Wiconi kiŋ yuha,
Qa oŋ uŋnipi kta He e;
Iyuśkiŋyaŋ uŋ po.

4 Jesus, Wacaŋtkiya,
Wicoŋte śice ciŋ
Etaŋ niuŋyaŋpi He e;
Yataŋ dowaŋpi ye.

5 Wakaŋtaŋka Ate,
Ciŋhiŋtku kiŋ nakuŋ,
Qa Woniya Wakaŋ kiŋ He
Wakaŋtaŋka Niye. AMEN.

Family Worship.

109 **Rhoda.** S. M.

"O Itaŋcaŋ Wakaŋtaŋka wowanikive mitawa towaśake kiŋ He Niye." — Ps. cxl: 7.

SECOND TUNE.

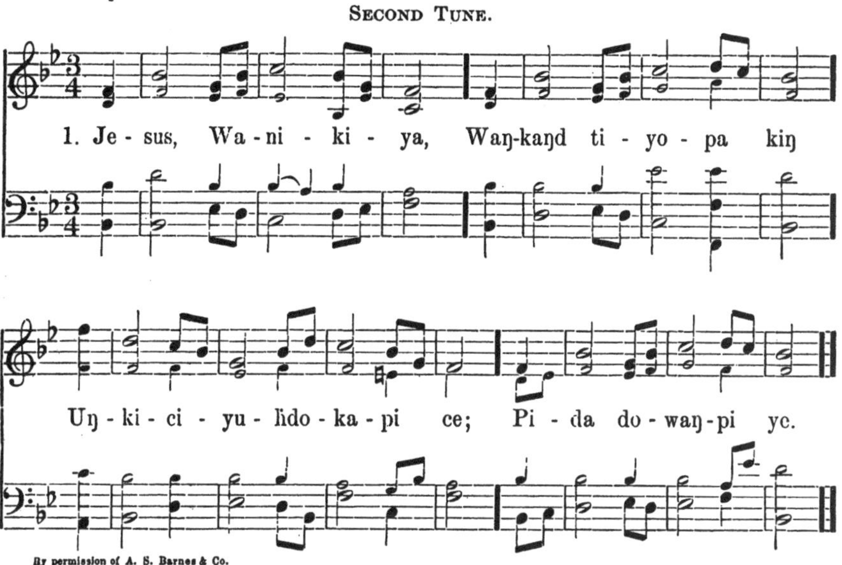

By permission of A. S. Barnes & Co.

2 Jesus, Waoŋśida,
Caŋku wiconi kiŋ
Uŋkiciyuśtaŋpi kiŋ oŋ
Yaonihaŋpi ye.

3 Jesus, Wawiciya,
Wiconi kiŋ yuha,
Qa oŋ uŋnipi kta He e;
Iyuśkiŋyaŋ uŋ po.

4 Jesus, Wacaŋtkiya,
Wicoŋṭe śice ciŋ
Etaŋ niuŋyaŋpi He e;
Yataŋ dowaŋpi ye.

5 Wakaŋtaŋka Ate,
Ciŋhiŋtku kiŋ nakuŋ,
Qa Woniya Wakaŋ kiŋ He
Wakaŋtaŋka Niye. AMEN.

Special Seasons.

110 Federal Street. L. M.

"Hopi ye, Itaŋcaŋ Caje kiŋ uŋyawaŋkaŋtuyapi kta." — Ps. xxxiv: 3.

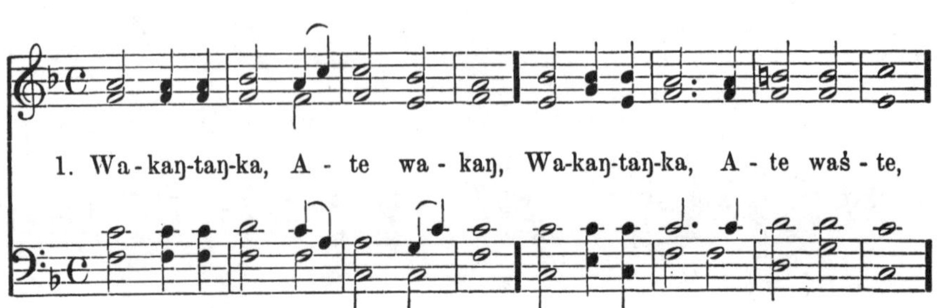

From "Tunes Old and New" by permission of Rev. Dr. Tucker

2 Wakaŋtaŋka waoŋśida,
Oŋ ceuŋkiyapi kta ce;
He oŋśiuŋkidapi kta,
Nakuŋ niuŋkiyapi kta.

3 Christ Jesus woaħtani kiŋ
Kajuju kta waikduśna,
Oŋ wiuŋyuśkiŋpi kte ça
Caje uŋyataŋpi kta ce.

4 Wakaŋtaŋka, Itaŋcaŋ kiŋ,
Uŋyaonihaŋpi kta ce:
Oyate kiŋ owas, u po,
Caje uŋkidowaŋpi kta.

5 Wakaŋtaŋka Taoyate
Jesus waŋyakapi kta ce,
Pidaya ħciŋ yataŋpi kta,
Waŋkaŋd wiconi kiŋ he ed.

6 Oknikde kiŋ wakaŋ, waŋkaŋd,
Wakaŋtaŋka yataŋpi, qa
Wanikiya iyuśkiŋyaŋ,
Ohoda ed patujapi. AMEN.

Family Worship.

111 "Thou Art the Way; to Thee Alone." L. M.

"Caŋku, qa wowicake, wiconi ko he Miye." —St. John xiv: 6.

From "Tunes Old and New" by permission of Rev. Dr. Tucker.

2 Niye kiŋ Wowinicake,
Wicoksape wicayaqu;
Tawaciŋpi idukcaŋ qa
Wicacaŋte duteca ce.

3 Caŋku wiconi kiŋ, Niye
Wicaśa kiŋ wicayeco;
Tuwa anicita kiŋ he
Owihaŋkeśniyaŋ ni kta.

4 Caŋku wiconi kiŋ Niye,
Toŋkiŋ sdoduŋniyaŋpi niŋ;
Waciŋyaŋpi wiconi kiŋ
He wowiyuśkiŋ ohiŋni.

5 Ateyapi, Ciŋhiŋtku kiŋ,
Qa Woniya Wakaŋ kiŋ He,
Wakaŋtaŋka waŋjina kiŋ,
He wowitaŋ yuha nuŋwe. AMEN.

Special Seasons.

Morning. — Hiŋhaŋna.

112 "Christ, Whose Glory Fills the Skies." Six 7s.

"Iyoyaŋpa Nitawa kiŋ ed iyoyaŋpa waŋuŋyakapi kta."— Ps. xxxvi: 9.

[*Dix, Hymn* 143, *may be used.*] HALLETT.

From "Tunes Old and New" by permission of Rev. Dr. Tucker.

2 Aŋpao waŋkaŋtaŋhaŋ,
Micitaŋiŋ ye, dehaŋd,
Qa aŋpe wicaȟpi kiŋ
Miś micaŋte ed u ye
Heced wawabdeze, ça
Oŋ taŋyaŋ mawani kta.

3 Niś yahinape śni caŋ
Hiŋhaŋna kiŋ okpaza;
Qa oiyokiśica,
Miś waŋciyake śŋi ca;
He oŋ micitaŋiŋ ye,
Jesus Christ, Wanikiya. AMEN.

Evening. — Ḣtayetu.

113 "Abide With Me; Fast Falls the Eventide." 10s.

"Uŋkicipi uŋ ye, aŋpetu kiŋ wana owihaŋke kta."—St. Luke xxiv: 29.

EVENTIDE.

From "Goodrich and Gilbert Hymnal" by permission of E. P. Dutton & Co.

2 Wana aŋpetu kiŋ henaŋkeca,
Ded wowiyuŝkiŋ kiŋ sni aya ce,
Qa taku ded owas ţiŋs he ŝni ce;
Niye Niŝnana, mici ħciŋ uŋ ye.

3 Niŝnana ohiŋni waciŋciya;
Nitowaŝte kiŋ he waŝaka ce;
Tuwa nimakiya okihi he?
Niye Niŝnana; mici ħciŋ uŋ ye.

4 Kiyena ħciŋ yauŋ caŋ kope ŝni;
Qa woteħi tke-wada ŝni ece;
Wicoŋţe koya taku ŝni bdawa;
Ohiwayiŋ kta, mici ħciŋ uŋ ye.

5 Nitacaŋicipaweġa waŝte,
Miŝtiŋbe ŝni kiŋ ed, yutaŋiŋ ye;
Omaġoŋġa, hehaŋd maħpiyata
Waŋciyakiŋ kta; mici ħciŋ uŋ ye.

6 Wakaŋtaŋka waŝte, waoŋŝida,
Wanikiya waŝte, wacaŋtkiya,
Qa Woniya waŝte, wayuwakaŋ,
Owihaŋke ŝni wowaŝte yuha. AMEN.

Special Seasons.

114 "Softly Now the Light of Day." 7s.

"Minape kiŋ yuġatapi ħtayetu wośnapi kiŋ ee kta." — Ps. cxli: 2.

WEBER.

From "Tunes Old and New" by permission of Rev. Dr. Tucker.

2 Christ, iśtanibdeze ħca,
Taku keś waŋdaka ce,
Miś wawaħtani hena,
Jesus, miciyuska ye.

3 Aŋpa kiŋ ecana ħciŋ
Miś hemicinana kta;
Woaħtani kiŋ waniŋd,
Jesus Christ, imacu ye.

4 Christ, Niye wicaśa kiŋ
Towaśake śni sdodya,
Woaħtaŋi ko waniŋd,
Ded maka amayani;

5 Tka dehaŋd waŋkaŋd yauŋ,
Qa Nitoyaŋke etaŋ,
Jesus, oŋśidaya ħciŋ
Ed ahimatoŋwaŋ ye.

6 Qa Ateyapi wakaŋ,
Qa Ciŋhiŋtku kiŋ wakaŋ,
Woniya Wakaŋ kiŋ ko,
Wowitaŋ yuha nuŋwe. AMEN.

115 "The Day is Past and Gone." S. M.

"Wookiye yuha imuŋkiŋ kta." — Ps. iv: 9.

SCHUMAN.

From "Tunes Old and New" by permission of Rev. Dr. Tucker.

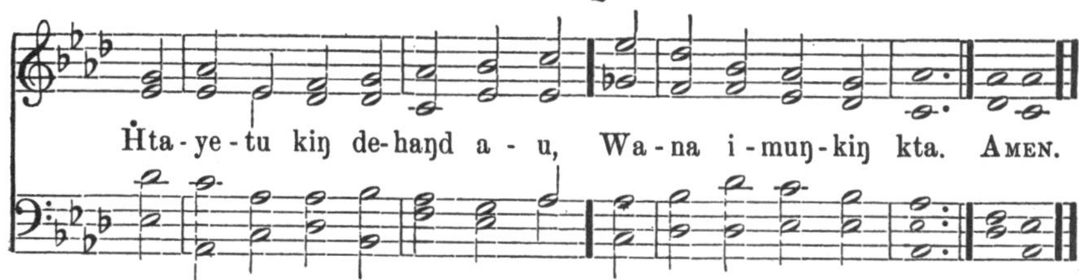

2 Wiconi kiŋ wana
Henanakinica,
Wicoŋṭe kiŋ nakuŋ au
Wakta wauŋ ṡni ce.

3 Ḣtayetu kiŋ de ed,
O Christ, mayuha ye;
Nitoknikde wakaŋ kiŋ oŋ
Awaŋmayaka ye.

4 Wakaŋtaŋka Ate,
Ciŋhiŋtku kiŋ nakuŋ,
Qa Woniya Wakaŋ kiŋ He
Wakaŋtaŋka Niye. AMEN.

116 "The Day is Past and Gone." S. M.

"Itaŋcaŋ Niye niṡnana wikopapi ṡni ed ouŋmayakiya." — Ps. iv: 9.

BOYLSTON.

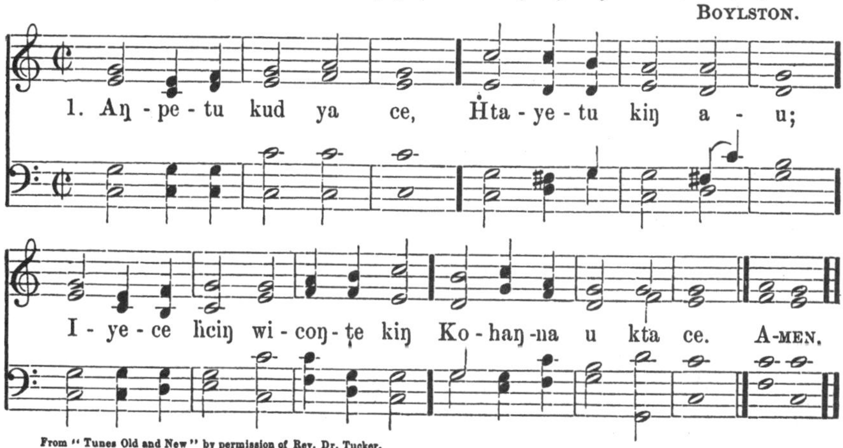

From "Tunes Old and New" by permission of Rev. Dr. Tucker.

2 Hayake tokedked
He ekiknakapi;
Iyece ḣciŋ wicoŋṭe kiŋ
Wawicaki ece.

3 Haŋ, woiṡtiŋbe kiŋ
Ḣtayetu de maqu,
Qa, Jesus, taku ṡice ciŋ
Etaŋ mayuha ye.

4 Wakaŋtaŋka Ate,
Ciŋhiŋtku kiŋ nakuŋ,
Qa Woniya Wakaŋ kiŋ He
Wakaŋtaŋka Niye. AMEN.

Special Seasons.

117 Purleigh. 8s. 6s.

"Wookiye yuha imuŋke ça miśtiŋbiŋ kta."—Ps. iv: 9.

From "Tunes Old and New" by permission of Rev. Dr. Tucker.

2 Wakaŋśica waśake ciŋ
Iyamape uŋ, ohiŋni,
Oŋ mici ħciŋ uŋ ye;
Kiŋhaŋ ohiwayiŋ kta ce.
Haŋhepi wokokipe kiŋ
Ed mici ħciŋ uŋ ye.

3 Tiyoknaka mitawa kiŋ
Haŋhepi de atoŋwaŋ ye,
Taŋyaŋ miśtiŋbiŋ kta;
Nitawipe wakaŋ kiŋ he
Owas koyag miśtiŋbiŋ kta,
Oŋ oŋśimada ye.

4 Minaġi kiŋ, mitaŋcaŋ kiŋ,
Awaŋmiciyaka nuŋwe,
Heua Nitawa ce;
Qa woozikiye waśte
Maqu qa mikdukśaŋyaŋ ħciŋ
Awaŋmayaka ye.

5 Haŋ, heced aŋpao wakaŋ,
Qa wookiye u kiŋhaŋ,
Mayaduħiciŋ kta;
Kiŋhaŋ Nitowaśte kiŋ oŋ
Kici inacijiŋ kta ce,
Qa ceciciyiŋ kta. Amen.

Evening.

118 "Glory to Thee, my God, this Night." L. M.

"Iye ḣupahu kiŋ ihukuya wowinape iyeyayiŋ kta." — Ps. xci: 1.

TALLIS.

From "Tunes Old and New" by permission of Rev. Dr. Tucker.

2 Wakaŋtaŋka ḣtayetu de,
Niḣupahu waśake ciŋ
Ihukuya mayuha ye,
Ciyataŋ kta, Ate waśte.

3 Niciŋkśi Christ waśte kiŋ oŋ
Aŋpetu de wawaḣtani
Owas etaŋ mayuska ye,
Ciyataŋ kta, Ate waśte.

4 Miśtiŋbe śni eced, toŋkiŋ
Maka kiŋ ataya kici
Taŋyaŋ aweciyuta niŋ,
Ciyataŋ kta, Ate waśte.

5 Iwaŋg kowakipe śni kiŋ,
Iyeceḣciŋ maṭiŋ kte ciŋ
Kowakipiŋ kte śni ḣca e,
Owotana amayaŋ ye.

6 Aŋpetu waŋ ehake qed
Taŋyaŋ inawajiŋ kta e,
Iyecedya maṭiŋ kte ciŋ
Dehaŋd oŋspemakiya ye. AMEN.

Special Seasons.

119 "Sun of my Soul, Thou Saviour Dear." L. M.

"Nitaaŋpetuwi ake icimana mahed iyayiŋ kte śni." — Isa. lx. 20.

Hursley.

From "Tunes Old and New" by permission of Rev. Dr. Tucker.

2 Maḣpiya waŋ makataŋhaŋ,
Iśta mitawa kiŋ etaŋ
Ananiḣma au kte śni
E, Jesus, ceciciya ce.

3 Tohaŋd miśtiŋbe kte ciŋhaŋ,
Nitamaku kiŋ ohiŋni
Aokiḣpapi kiŋ waśte
Kiŋ he awacaŋmi nuŋwe.

4 Qa aŋpahaŋ, oḣtayetu
Hehaŋyaŋ mici ḣciŋ uŋ ye;
Niye cona wani kta he
Iyemaccca śni he oŋ.

5 Haŋhepi kiŋ nakuŋ he ed,
Kici mauŋ ye, Jesus Christ,
Niye cona maṭiŋ kta he
Kowakipe ḣce ciŋ he oŋ.

6 Uŋkiktapi kiŋ he ehaŋd,
U, qa uŋyawaśtepi ye;
Kiŋhaŋ nitowacaŋtkiye
Ed ohiŋni uŋqoŋpi kta. Amen.

VIII. Redemption.

OPEUNKITONPI KIN.

120 Heber. C. M.

"Ohiŋniyaŋ Itaŋcaŋ kiŋ ed iyuśkiŋ po."—Phil. iv: 4.

2 Itaŋcaŋ uŋ kiŋ, Jesus Christ,
Ekta uŋyaŋpi, qa
Caje uŋyataŋpi kta ce,
Christ He Wanikiya.

3 Taniya kiŋ icupi ye,
Niyuwakaŋpi kta;
Pidaye ĥciŋ ekta u po
Christ He waoŋśida.

4 Oknikde woyataŋ kiŋ he
Waŋkaŋd yuhapi ce;
Wakaŋtaŋka ed wowitaŋ,
Christ He Wawiciya.

5 Ateyapi, Ciŋhiŋtku kiŋ,
Qa Woniya Wakaŋ,
Wakaŋtaŋka waŋjina kiŋ,
Owihaŋke waniŋd. AMEN.

Redemption.

121 Cambridge. C. M.

"Tuwa ohiye ciŋhaŋ he oiyotaŋke Mitawa kiŋ akaŋd Mici iyotaŋkewakiyiŋ kta." — Wayuo iii: 21.

[*Lambeth, Hymn* 136 II, *may be used.*]

From "Book of Common Praise" by permission of A. S. Barnes & Co.

2 Iye uŋkicopi kiŋ ed,
"U po, u po," eya;
"Wiconi taŋka ded uŋ ce,
U po, u po," eya.

3 Mahpiyata oyate kiŋ
Caŋte skaskapi ce;
Wanikiya Itaŋcaŋ ed
Hena niuŋpi ce.

4 Tuwa ohiye hce ciŋhaŋ,
Wateśdake waśte
Iyehyeġe ciŋ he Iye
Teśdagkiyiŋ kta ce.

5 Ateyapi, Ciŋhiŋtku kiŋ,
Qa Woniya Wakaŋ,
Wakaŋtaŋka waŋjina kiŋ,
Owihaŋke waniŋd. AMEN.

122 Coronation. C. M.

"Jesus heya, Caŋku kiŋ qa Wowicake kiŋ qa Wiconi kiŋ ko He Miye." —St. John xiv: 6.

CORONATION.

From "Tunes Old and New" by permission of Rev. Dr. Tucker.

2 Ho̧ po, caŋte wicaka po,
Śogya waciŋyaŋ po,
Oknayaŋ ȟciŋ uŋyaŋpi kta,
Uŋtecapi kta ce.

3 Atę, Nitowicake kiŋ,
Wicaśa kiŋ owas
Sdodyewicayakiye niŋ;
Ohonidapi kta.

4 Caŋku waŋ teca ni uŋ kiŋ,
Christ Jesus Hee ce;
Tuwa oknayaŋ mani kiŋ
Wiconi ed i kta.

5 Wakaŋtaŋka wacaŋtkiya,
Christ Jesus He uśi;
Uŋnipi ciŋ kiŋ he oŋ ţa,
Qa oŋ wiconi ce.

6 Caje kiŋ taŋka, ohiŋni,
Caŋku waśte yuśtaŋ;
Tuwa oknayaŋ mani kiŋ,
Jesus kici uŋ kta. AMEN.

Redemption.

123 Martyrdom. C. M.

"Micaŋte kiŋ Nitowiconi kiŋ oŋ wiyuśkiŋ nuŋwe." — Ps. xiii: 5.

First Tune.

2 Iye tehaŋwaŋkaŋd yaŋka,
Wiconi kiŋ yuha;
Tka He niuŋyaŋpi kta e
Caŋ ed okataŋpi.

3 Takodaku kiŋ ceyapi,
He ṭe ciqoŋ ehaŋd,
Tuka ake piya kini;
Itaŋcaŋ taŋka kiŋ.

4 He woaȟtani kte kta oŋ
Itoŋiçipe śni;
Atkuku Tokicoŋze kiŋ,
He ataya kduśtaŋ.

5 He Toyawaśte kiŋ he oŋ
Uŋyawaśtepi kta;
Nakuŋ waŋkaŋd uŋkicopi,
He Ti wakaŋ kiŋ ed.

6 Qa wiuŋyuśkiŋpi kta ce,
Wiconi kiŋ he ed:
Hed wookiye taŋka ce,
Itaŋcaŋ Ti kiŋ ed. Amen.

Redemption.

123 Christmas. C. M.

"Micaŋte kiŋ Nitowiconi kiŋ oŋ wiyuśkiŋ nuŋwe."—Ps. xiii: 5.

SECOND TUNE.

From "Tunes Old and New" by permission of Rev. Dr. Tucker.

2 Iye tehaŋwaŋkaŋd yaŋka,
Wiconi kiŋ yuha;
Tka He niuŋyaŋpi kta e
Caŋ ed okataŋpi.

3 Takodaku kiŋ ceyapi,
He ţe ciqoŋ ehaŋd,
Tuka ake piya kini;
Itaŋcaŋ taŋka kiŋ.

4 He woaḣtani kte kta oŋ
Itoŋiçipe śni;
Atkuku Tokicoŋze kiŋ,
He ataya kduśtaŋ.

5 He Toyawaśte kiŋ he oŋ
Uŋyawaśtepi kta;
Nakuŋ waŋkaŋd uŋkicopi,
He Ti wakaŋ kiŋ ed.

6 Qa wiuŋyuśkiŋpi kta ce,
Wiconi kiŋ he ed:
Hed wookiye taŋka ce,
Itaŋcaŋ Ti kiŋ ed. AMEN.

IX. The Christian Life.

CHRISTIAN TOUN KIN.

Faith — Wicadapi.

124 "Jesus, Lover of my Soul." 7s. D.

"Niye ed inawaȟbiŋ kta e nawapa." — Ps. cxliii: 9.

[*Martyn, Hymn 3, may be used.*] HOLLINGSIDE.

From "Tunes Old and New" by permission of Rev. Dr. Tucker.

2 Wowinape tokeca
 Takuna bduhe śni oŋ
Ohiŋni waciŋciya;
 Ataya miśnana ȟciŋ
Ded amayuśtaŋ śni ye.
 Omakiye ciŋ Niye,
Christ, niȟupahu kiŋ oŋ
 Pa amicicaȟpa ye.

3 Wowaśte onijuna,
 Oŋ mayaduska kta e;
Mni niwicayiŋ kte ciŋ
 Oŋ taŋyeȟ mayuha ye;
Mni wiconi kiŋ Niye,
 Imnayaŋ ciyatkiŋ kta
E micaŋte kiŋ mahed
 Ohiŋni hinapa ye. AMEN.

125 "How Firm a Foundation." 11s.

"Mini kiŋ ekna idade ciŋhaŋ cici wauŋ kta; . . . peta ekna ṁayani kiŋhaŋ niġu kte śni." — Isa. xliii: 2.

From "Book of Common Praise" by permission of A. S. Barnes & Co.

2 Wakokipe śni yo; kiciciuŋ, haŋ,
Waśagciye ça nakuŋ ociciya;
Minape waśaka, owotaŋna kiŋ,
He ikduzezeya inajiŋ uŋ wo.

3 Qa mini śma opta yeciśi eśa,
Wicacaŋteśica wakpa kiŋ ekta,
Kici ciuŋ he oŋ ohiyayiŋ kta,
Iyoniciśica bduwaśte kta ce.

4 Qa wotehi peta kiŋ ed yauŋ ca,
Miś oŋśicida oŋ niġu kte śni, tka
Nitośice ṭiŋ kta, nitowaśte kiŋ
He saŋpa waśte kta hecena waciŋ.

5 Wicanaġi Jesus inabya uŋ kiŋ,
He toka wicawaqu kte śŋi; nakuŋ
Wakaŋśica, tona ħca kuwapi śa,
Abduśtaŋ kte śni, tka kici wauŋ kta. AMEN.

The Christian Life.

126 Duke Street. L. M.

"Nicaje kiŋ iyececa, heced niyataŋpi kiŋ maka ihaŋke hehaŋyaŋ!"
— Ps. xlviii: 9.

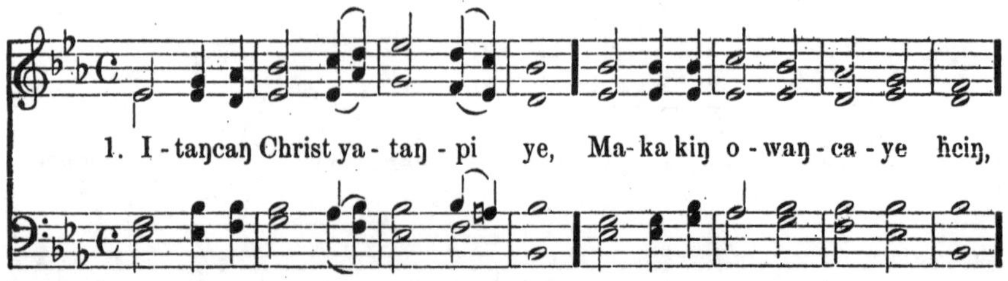

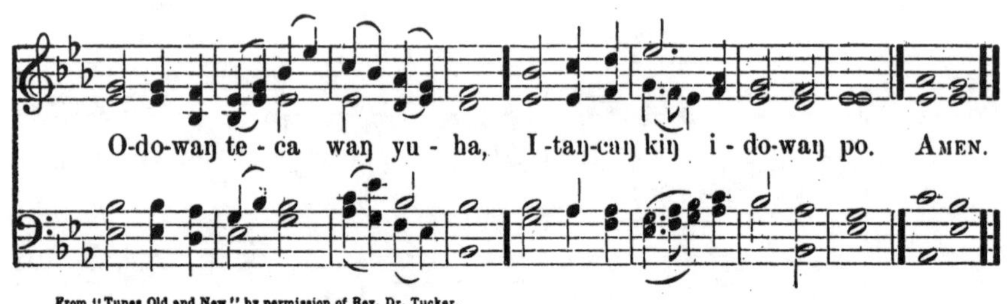

From "Tunes Old and New" by permission of Rev. Dr. Tucker.

2 Wanikiya idowaŋ po,
Caje kiŋ he yawaŝte po;
Qa wowanikiye yuha,
Dehaŋd ieyaŋpaha po.

3 Ikcewicaŝa kiŋ ekta
He towitaŋ oyaka po,
Qa toyuŝ'iŋyaye kiŋ he
Oyate kiŋ owasiŋ ed.

4 Itaŋcaŋ Jesus taŋka ce,
Qa taŋkaya yataŋpi kta;
He, taku kiŋ wakaŋ owas,
Wiciwaŋkaŋb, kokipa po.

5 Ateyapi, Ciŋhiŋtku kiŋ,
Qa Woniya Wakaŋ kiŋ He,
Wakaŋtaŋka waŋjina kiŋ,
He wowitaŋ yuha nuŋwe. Amen.

127 Jesus Calls us o'er the Tumult.

"Nom ihakab yapi qon wanji Andrew ee."

GALILEE (*Second Tune*). 8.7.8.7. WILLIAM H. JUDE, 1887.

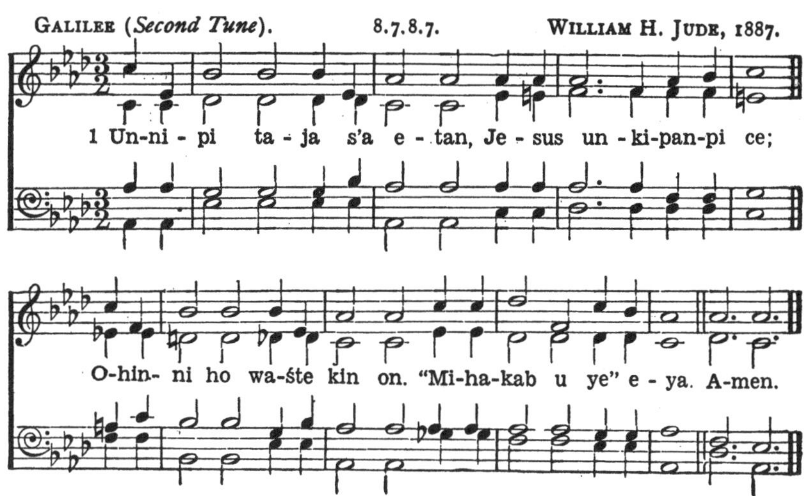

2 Galile bde kin icakda
St. Andrew naĥon qonhan;
Titakuye, wicoĥan ko
Iye on ayuŝtan qon,

3 Makata woohoda, qa
Wakandapi ko etan,
Jesus he unkipanpi qa
"Waŝtemada ye" eya.

4 Wiunyuŝkinpi s'a eŝa,
Oŝiceca ko etan;
Dena owasin isanpa,
"Waŝtemada ye," eya.

5 Jesus unkipanpi kin he
Towaonŝida kin on,
Anaungoptanpi kta e
Canteyus unyan miye
Amen.

The Christian Life.

128 Ellacomb. 7s. 6s. D.

"O, iyutapi ye, qa Itaŋcaŋ kiŋ waŝte e waŋyaka po." — Ps. xxxiv: 8.

2 Wakaŋtaŋka, Iye kiŋ,
Waoŋśida ḣca ce,
He cekiya yaŋka yo;
He oŋśinida kta.
Wakaŋtaŋka, Iye kiŋ,
Waśaka, taŋka ce,
He hoyekiya uŋ wo;
Waśagniyiŋ kta ce.

3 Wakaŋtaŋka, Iye kiŋ,
Wawiciya waśte;
Qa He waciŋyaŋ uŋ wo,
He nicaŋptiŋ kta ce.
Wakaŋtaŋka, Iye kiŋ,
Wicayuska kta ce;
Oŋ He wicada uŋ wo,
Eced niyuska kta.

4 Wakaŋtaŋka, Iye kiŋ,
Wiconi kiŋ yuha;
Waciŋyaŋ he kida yo,
Eced niniyiŋ kta.
Ateyapi, Ciŋca kiŋ,
Qa Woniya Wakaŋ,
Wakaŋtaŋka waŋjina,
Niyataŋpi nuŋwe. AMEN.

129 Montgomery. 7s. 6s.

"Tatiyopa kiŋ mahed wopida yuha ya po." — Ps. c: 2.

From "Book of Common Praise" by permission of A. S. Barnes & Co.

2 Iye makata hi, qa
Oŋ wopida ecoŋ;
Wicataŋcaŋ ed ţe ça
He oŋ wiconi ce.
Qa woaḣtani ota,
Ecoŋqoŋpisa, tka
Wawiciya kiŋ taŋka,
Jesus Christ Hee ce.

3 Wakaŋtaŋka Ciŋhiŋtku,
Christ Jesus He Niye;
Nitaniya wakaŋ oŋ
Uŋkatoŋwaŋpi ye;
Nitokicaŋpte kiŋ oŋ
Uŋkicaŋptapi ye;
Qa wopida yuhaha
Uŋdowaŋpi kta ce.

4 Wanikiya yati ed,
Wiconi ḣca yukaŋ;
Wateśdake wiconi,
Waḣca waśteśte kiŋ
Qa aŋpao wicaḣpi,
Oŋ wopida yuha,
Wakaŋpi wiyuśkiŋyaŋ
He ed dowaŋpi ce. AMEN

The Christian Life.

130 Aurelia. 7s. 6s. D.

"He Iye cantemakiye ça miye on Iye içiçu." —Gal. ii: 20.

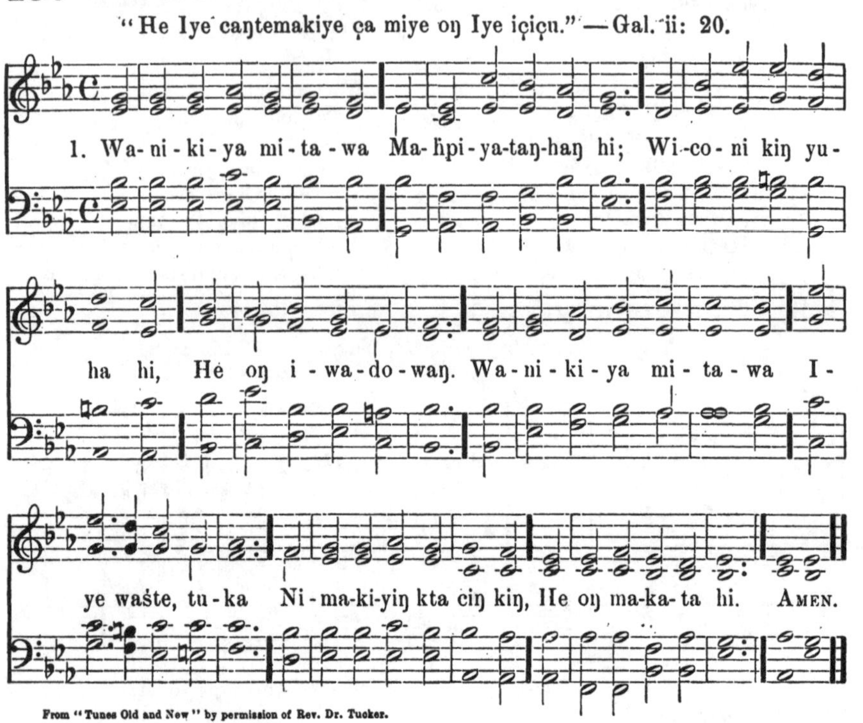

From "Tunes Old and New" by permission of Rev. Dr. Tucker.

2 Wanikiya mitawa
  Iye wakan, tuka
Wawaȟtani kin ota
  He on waŝake ŝni.
Wanikiya mitawa
  Iye wacantkiya,
Qa Towaŝte kin on hca
  Dehanyan ni waun.

3 Wanikiya mitawa
  Teȟi akipe hca,
Qa heon He Iŝnana
  Pidamaye hca ce.
Wanikiya mitawa
  Tacanku kin waŝte,
Tuwe oknayan ye cin,
  Wiconi ed i kta.

4 Wanikiya mitawa
  Iye waonŝida;
Maka oyatepi kin
  Niwicayin kta cin.
Wakantanka mitawa,
  Cinhintku on wani,
Taniya kin amayan,
  Owihanke wanind. Amen.

Praise.

131 8s. 7s.

"Tona caŋte ekta kicaksapi kiŋ Okiziwicaya."— Ps. cxlvii: 3.

First Tune.

2 Qa Jerusalem otoŋwe,
He Iye hca kaġa ce;
Israel kiŋ huŋh nunipi kiŋ,
Tka hena wicakpahi;
Qa caŋtekicaksapi kiŋ
He asniwicaye, ça
Wowayazaŋ tawapi kiŋ
Ko awicayuštaŋya.

3 Qa Itaŋcaŋ uŋyaŋpi kiŋ
Towašake taŋka qa
Toksape kiŋ wopteca šni,
Koya He uŋqupi ce;
Oŋšiiçidaya uŋpi
Kiŋ hena Wakaŋtaŋka
He waŋkaŋd iwicacu ce;
Oŋšiiçiya uŋ po.

4 He aktapi šni owasiŋ,
Kud ihpewicaya ce;
Qa Itaŋcaŋ Tocaŋniye
Oŋ maka yuhuŋhuŋza;
He kipajiŋpica šni ce.
Adam kiŋ ciŋca owas,
Jesus Towašake taŋka
He ihukuya uŋ po. Amen.

The Christian Life.

131 Jubilee Harp. 8s. 7s.

"Tona caŋte ekta kicaksapi kiŋ Okiziwicaya." — Ps. cxlvii: 3.

SECOND TUNE.

CHARLES C. CONVERSE, 1868. By per.

2 Qa Jerusalem otoŋwe,
He Iye ħca kaġa ce;
Israel kiŋ huŋħ nunipi kiŋ,
Tka hena wicakpahi:
Qa caŋtekicaksapi kiŋ
He asniwicaye, ça
Wowayazaŋ tawapi kiŋ
Ko awicayuśtaŋya.

3 Qa Itaŋcaŋuŋyaŋpi kiŋ
Towaśake taŋka qa
Toksape kiŋ wopteca śni,
Koya He uŋqupi ce;
Oŋśiiçidaya uŋpi
Kiŋ hena Wakaŋtaŋka
He waŋkaŋd iwicacu ce;
Oŋśiiçiya uŋ po.

4 He aktapi śni owasiŋ,
Kud iħpewicaya ce;
Qa Itaŋcaŋ Tocaŋniye
Oŋ maka yuhuŋhuŋza;
He kipajiŋpica śni ce.
Adam kiŋ ciŋca owas,
Jesus Towaśake taŋka
He ihukuya uŋ po. Amen.

132 "O Bless the Lord, my Soul." S. M.

"O minaġi kiŋ, Itaŋcaŋ kiŋ yawaśte yo, qa taku mahed mauŋ kiŋ owasiŋ Iye Caje wakaŋ kiŋ."—Ps. ciii: 1.

St. Thomas.

2 Minaġi kiŋ, dehaŋd
Itaŋcaŋ Towaśte
Oŋ oŋśinida kiŋ hena
Kiksuye ħciŋ uŋ wo.

3 Wayaħtani owas
He nicicajuju;
Waniyazaŋ asniniyaŋ,
Qa He niniyaŋ ce.

4 He Tocaŋtekiye
Oŋ wodniyaŋ ece,
Qa Towicake kiŋ he oŋ
Waŋkaŋd niyuza ce.

5 He oŋ, minaġi kiŋ,
He Towacaŋtkiye
Qa Towaśte wicaqu kiŋ
Hena oyaka yo. Amen.

The Christian Life.

133 Park Street. L. M.

"Tohaŋyaŋ wani kiŋ hehaŋyaŋ Itaŋcaŋ kiŋ iwadowaŋ kta." — Ps. civ: 33.

[*Duke Street, Hymn 126, may be used.*]

1. Wa - kaŋ - taŋ - ka, A - te wa - kaŋ, Ni - to - wa -

śa - ke taŋ - ka kiŋ, He oŋ uŋ - ni - ya

taŋ - pi ce, Ni - to - wa - ste uŋ - qu - pi ye

Ni - to - wa - śte uŋ - qu - pi ye. A - MEN.

From "Tunes Old and New" by permission of Rev. Dr. Tucker.

2 Wakaŋtaŋka, Ate waŝte,
Nitowaoŋŝida wakaŋ,
Nakuŋ Nitoiyoyaŋpa,
Hena waciŋuŋyaŋpi kta.

3 Wakaŋtaŋka, Ate wakaŋ,
Wayuwaŝte Nitaŋka kiŋ,
Wiconi kiŋ uŋyaqupi,
He oŋ ohouŋnidapi.

4 Wakaŋtaŋka, Ate waŝte,
Nitowicake taŋka kiŋ,
Niciŋkŝi kiŋ uŋyaqupi,
He oŋ niuŋyayapi ce.

5 Wakaŋtaŋka, Ate wakaŋ,
Wanikiya nitaŋka kiŋ;
Oŋ ceuŋniciyapi kiŋ
Owas taŋyaŋ naħoŋ uŋ ye. AMEN.

134 Redhead, No. 12. (Meditation.) L. M.

"Oŋŝikapi kiŋ Itaŋcaŋ anawicaġoptaŋ." — Ps. lxix: 34.

[*Hebron, Hymn 56, may be used.*]

From "Tunes Old and New" by permission of Rev. Dr. Tucker.

2 Qa oŋŝiiçidapi kiŋ
He ded wicayawaŝte, qa
Wiconi kiŋ wicaqu kta:
Caje kiŋ he yataŋpi ye.

3 Christ Jesus Towaŝake kiŋ,
Qa Towitaŋ kiŋ hena ko,
Oyagpica ŝni ota ce,
Oŋ Jesus Christ ohoda po.

4 Christ Jesus, oŋŝimada ye,
Eced nimayayiŋ kta ce,
Miŝ oŋŝimicida kta ce,
Qa ohiŋni ciyataŋ kta.

5 Ateyapi, Ciŋhiŋtku kiŋ,
Qa Woniya Wakaŋ kiŋ He,
Wakaŋtaŋka waŋjina kiŋ,
He wowitaŋ yuha nuŋwe. AMEN.

The Christian Life.

135 Burlington. C. M.

"O Itaŋcaŋ kiŋ, wopida eciya po." — Ps. cv: 1.

[*Arlington, Hymn* 165, *may be used.*]

From "Tunes Old and New" by permission of Rev. Dr. Tucker.

2 Iye idowaŋpi kta e
  Ciŋwicakiya po,
Qa Towinihaŋ taŋka kiŋ,
  Owas awaciŋ po.

Caje kiŋ he iwiŋkta po:
  Itaŋcaŋ kiŋ, Iye
Akitapi owasina
  Caŋte waštepi nuŋ.

4 Itaŋcaŋ towašake kiŋ
  Owas ikdikda po;
Ite kiŋ he akita po,
  Owihaŋke waniŋd,

5 Wicoȟaŋ wowinihaŋ kiŋ
  Hena kiksuya po,
Tawowapetokeca kiŋ
  Tawoyasu kiŋ ko. AMEN.

Trust. — Wowaciŋye.

136 Warwick. C. M.

"Oyate iyoyaŋbwicaye ciŋ he Miye." —St. John viii: 12.

FIRST TUNE.

From "Book of Common Praise" by permission of A. S. Barnes & Co.

2 Iyoyaŋpa nitawa kiŋ,
Hiyohimayaŋ ye;
Yati wakaŋ kiŋ he okna,
Ciyataŋ ȟciŋ kta ce.

3 Caŋku wakaŋ Nitawa ed
Okna amayaŋ ye;
Iyoyaŋpa wakaŋ kiŋ ed
Inawajiŋ kta ce.

4 Nitaniya Wakaŋ ska kiŋ
Hiyohimayaŋ ye;
Qa wopida waŋ taŋka e
Cicipazo kta ce.

5 Mita-Wanikiya wakaŋ,
Ahimatoŋwaŋ ye;
Niye ed wowaŝte yukaŋ,
Mayaduwaŝte nuŋ.

6 Maȟpiya cu wakaŋ kiŋ he
Ahiŋhemayaŋ ye;
Nitowiconi kiŋ wakaŋ
He ed imacu ye.

7 Wicakicaŋpte ciŋ wakaŋ,
Caŋtomaknaka ye;
Nitowiyuŝkiŋ kiŋ waŝte
He ed mayuha ye. AMEN.

The Christian Life.

136 Lambeth. C. M.

"Oyate iyoyaŋbwicaye ciŋ he Miye."—St. John viii: 12.

By permission of Rev. Dr. Hutchins.

2 Iyoyaŋpa nitawa kiŋ,
Hiyohimayaŋ ye;
Yati wakaŋ kiŋ he okna,
Ciyataŋ ȟciŋ kta ce.

3 Caŋku wakaŋ Nitawa ed
Okna amayaŋ ye;
Iyoyaŋpa wakaŋ kiŋ ed
Inawajiŋ kta ce.

4 Nitaniya Wakaŋ ska kiŋ
Hiyohimayaŋ ye;
Qa wopida waŋ taŋka e
Cicipazo kta ce.

5 Mita-Wanikiya wakaŋ,
Ahimatoŋwaŋ ye;
Niye ed wowašte yukaŋ,
Mayaduwašte nuŋ.

6 Maȟpiya cu wakaŋ kiŋ he
Ahiŋhemayaŋ ye;
Nitowiconi kiŋ wakaŋ
He ed imacu ye.

7 Wicakicaŋpte ciŋ wakaŋ,
Caŋtomaknaka ye;
Nitowiyuškiŋ kiŋ wašte
He ed mayuha ye. AMEN.

Trust.

137 "Father, Whate'er of Earthly Bliss." C. M.

" Itaŋcaŋ Iye taoyate kiŋ wookiye oŋ wicayawaŝte ce."— Ps. xxix: 10.

From "Tunes Old and New" by permission of Rev. Dr. Tucker.

2 Caŋdwoĥiŋyeŝnimaye ça
Caŋdwaŝtemayaŋ ye;
Nitowaŝte mayaqu niŋ
Eciŋ wauŋ kta ce.

3 Tohaŋ wani hehaŋye ĥciŋ,
"Toŋkiŋ ciyuha niŋ,"
Eciŋ ĥciŋ woape kiŋ he
Juha wauŋ nuŋwe.

4 Oikdagya wauŋ kiŋ ed
Iyoyaŋbmayaŋ ye,
Tukted wai kte ciŋ he ed
Taŋyeĥ amai ye.

5 Ateyapi, Ciŋhiŋtku kiŋ,
Qa Woniya Wakaŋ,
Wakaŋtaŋka waŋjina kiŋ
Owihaŋke waniŋd. AMEN.

The Christian Life.

138 Olmutz. S. M.

"Jesus waciŋuŋyaŋpi kiŋ he kaġe ça kduśtaŋ kiŋ He ekta euŋtoŋwaŋpi kta." — Heb. xii: 2.

From "Tunes Old and New" by permission of Rev. Dr. Tucker.

2 Caŋte waŋkaŋdmayaŋ,
Wiconi tipi ed,
Mita Wanikiya kiŋ hed
Waŋbdakiŋ kta waciŋ.

3 Mita Wanikiya
Ed ewatoŋwaŋ ce;
Qa Zion ed wiconi kiŋ
Oŋ ciksuya wauŋ.

4 Waŋkaŋd maḣpiya kiŋ
Ed ewatoŋwaŋ caŋ,
Wiconi mni waŋbdake ça
Caŋtowakpani ce.

5 Niye kiŋ oŋ wau,
Caŋku kiŋ okpaza,
Tka wipe kiŋ mayaqu oŋ
Ohiwayiŋ kta ce.

6 Niye oŋ ni wauŋ,
Amayuśtaŋ śni ye;
Maṭa ed oŋśimada ye,
Waŋkaŋd wai kta ce. Amen.

Trust.

139 Nettleton. 8s. 7s.

"Waawaŋyake mitawa kiŋ, Itaŋcaŋ kiŋ Hee, wimakakijiŋ kte śni."
—Ps. xxiii: 1.

From "Book of Common Praise" by permission of A. S. Barnes & Co.

2 Jesus, Coŋkaśke suta kiŋ,
Mici uŋ ye, ohiŋni;
Heced oŋ pahohośniyaŋ
Cici ħciŋ wauŋ kta ce.
Jesus Christ, He Wowinape,
Mici uŋ ye, ohiŋni;
Heced ohni wiyuśkiŋyaŋ
Cici ħciŋ wauŋ kta ce.

3 Jesus Christ, Waawaŋyake,
Mici uŋ ye, ohiŋni;
Qa wiconi ħca caŋku ed
Ohni yus amayaŋ ye.
Jesus Christ, Wanikiya kiŋ,
Towaśte kiŋ he maqu;
We waśte kiŋ oŋ mayuska,
Oŋ wiconi kiŋ bduha. AMEN.

The Christian Life.

Love — Wacaŋtkiyapi.

140 Manoah. C. M.

"Waŝtemayadaka he?" — St. John xxi. 15.

From "Tunes Old and New" by permission of Rev. Dr. Tucker.

2 Waŝtecidake ŝni kiŋhaŋ,
Owihaŋke waniŋd,
Maṭiŋ kta he sdodwakiya,
Nakuŋ heoŋ ŝni ce.

3 Tka, Jesus, icipaweġa
Akaŋd imayacu.
Maspestona, wahukeza
Qa wowiŝtece ko,

4 Qa woiyokiŝice ciŋ
Qa wokakije ȟca,
Tenimni we, niṭiŋ kta ko.
Tawaṭedyaye ciŋ;

5 Henakeȟciŋ miye kiŋ oŋ
Niye ayakipa,
Miŝ tokaciye ȟca wauŋ
Eŝa he hecanoŋ.

6 Henakeȟ hecanoŋ kiŋ oŋ
Caŋtocikpani kta,
Qa oŋ owihaŋke waniŋd
Icidowaŋ kta ce. Amen.

Love.

141 Pax Dei. 10s.

"Wakaŋtaŋka caŋteuŋkiyapi kiŋ he deciyataŋhaŋ taŋiŋ: Wakaŋtaŋka Iye Ciŋhiŋtku iśnana icaġe ciŋ he makata uśi heciyataŋhaŋ uŋnipi kta e heoŋ." — 1 John iv: 9.

From "Tunes Old and New" by permission of Rev. Dr. Tucker.

2 Wakaŋtaŋka wacaŋtkiyapi kiŋ
Hee; tuwa wacaŋtkiyapi kiŋ
Okna uŋ kiŋ, Wakaŋtaŋka Iye
Kici uŋ kta, owihaŋke waniŋd.

3 Wacaŋtkiyapi kiŋ de oŋ taŋiŋ;
Uŋkiyepi Wakaŋtaŋka Iye
Caŋteuŋkiyapi kiŋ hee śni,
Tka He caŋteuŋkiyapi kiŋ he.

4 Wakaŋtaŋka Ciŋhiŋtku kiŋ waśte,
Waȟtanisa heuŋcapi he oŋ,
Wanikiyiŋ kta e, maka kiŋ ed
Atkuku Towacaŋtkiye oŋ hi.

5 Wakaŋtaŋka caŋteuŋkiyapi;
Uŋkiś iyeceȟciŋ owasina
Caŋteuŋkiciciyapi kta ce —
Wacaŋtkiyapi de yuhapi ye. AMEN.

The Christian Life.

Joy. — Wowiyuśkiŋ.

142 Wilmot. 8s. 7s.

"Waoŋśiwada kiŋ heoŋ, Jehovah eya."—Jer. iii: 12.

From "Book of Common Praise" by permission of A. S. Barnes & Co.

2 Jesus Towaśte kiŋ taŋka,
Hee e mahiyohi;
Towitaŋ kiŋ taŋka kiŋ oŋ
Tokeśa waŋbdakiŋ kta.

3 Jesus Towaśake taŋka
Hee e mahiyohi;
Qa Taĥupahu wakaŋ kiŋ
Oŋ waŋkaŋd mayuziŋ kta.

4 Jesus Christ Wahacaŋka kiŋ
Hee e mahiyohi;
Heced ohiŋni, waśagya,
He kici wauŋ kta ce.

5 O Wakaŋtaŋka Ate kiŋ,
Qa Ciŋhiŋtku kiŋ nakuŋ,
Woniya Wakaŋ Hena ko
Ohniyaŋ yataŋpi ye. Amen.

Courage. — Wocaŋteṭiŋza.

143 Dix. Six 7s.

"Wowaciŋye okicize waŝte kiŋ he ed ecoŋ wo." — 1 Tim. vi: 12.

From "Tunes Old and New" by permission of Rev. Dr. Tucker.

2 Taku ŝica ota ŝa,
Wipe kiŋ bduha kte, ca
Taku woteħi eca,
Niŝ kici mayauŋ kta,
Heced oŋ wani kta ce;
Jesus, yus amayaŋ ye.

3 Okpaza kiŋ ed wauŋ,
Heoŋ Niŝ waciŋciya;
Qa aokpasya wauŋ,
Tka Niye ed aŋpa ħca
Heciya wai kte ħciŋ;
Jesus, yus amayaŋ ye.

4 Qa tohaŋd maṭe ciŋhaŋ,
Abraham wakaŋda kiŋ
He waŋkaŋd waŋbdakiŋ kta,
Uŋkaŋ Isaac, Jacob ko,
Heci ob wauŋ kta ce,
Jesus, yus amayaŋ ye. Amen.

144 Nuremburg. 7s.

"Wicaho waŋ taŋka naḣoŋpi, maḣpiya kiŋ eciyataŋhaŋ hewicakiya; Deciya waŋkaŋd u po, eya." — Wayuo xi: 12.

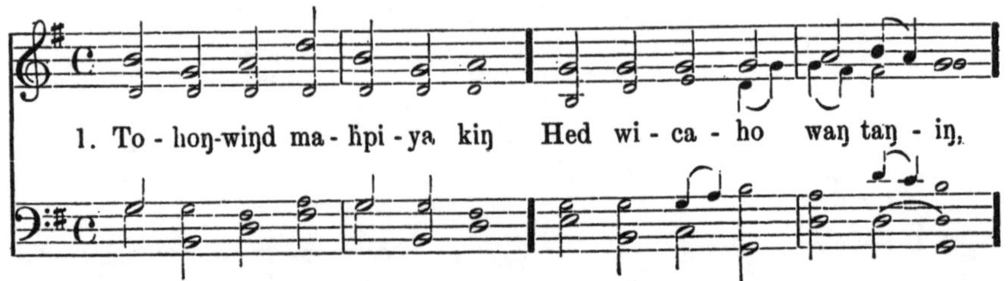

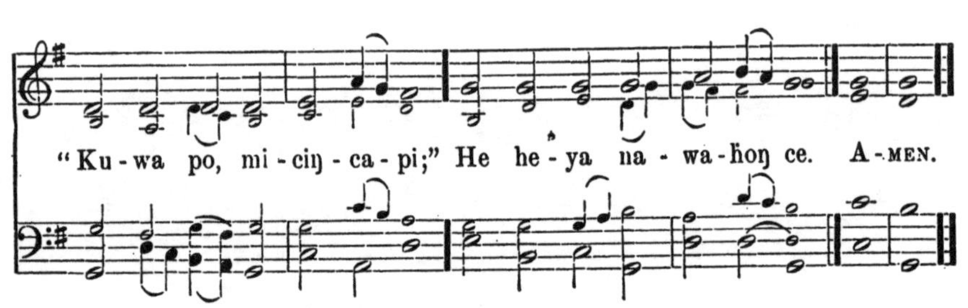

2 Heced oŋ, mitakuye,
Kuwa po, owasiŋna,
Hed maḣpiyata Ate,
Hee ed uŋyaŋpi kta.

3 Ho, owasiŋ upi ye,
Christ Tacaŋku kiŋ okna,
Iŋyaŋg ed uŋyaŋpi kta,
Hed wiconi kiŋ yukaŋ.

4 Qa uŋkicopi kiŋ He,
Ti wakaŋ kiŋ heciya,
Hed wiconi taŋka ce,
Qa owihaŋkiŋ kte śni.

5 Kuwa po, owasiŋna,
Wowaśte wicoḣi ed;
Wopida waŋ taŋka ḣca.
Hed uŋkabdezapi kta.

6 Ed uŋkipi kiŋ hehaŋd
Hed petijaŋjaŋ wakaŋ;
Qa wateśdake waśte
Uŋ uŋdowaŋpi kta ce.

7 Ed uŋkipi kiŋ hehaŋd,
Wokoyake ska ḣce ciŋ
Qa waḣca waśte yuha
Hed uŋkidowaŋpi kta.

8 Heciya Wakaŋpi ob,
Wowiyuśkiŋ taŋka ed,
"O wakaŋ, wakaŋ, wakaŋ,"
Hed heya uŋqoŋpi kta. AMEN.

Courage.

145 Shirland. S. M.

"Wakaŋtaŋka ekta wookiye uŋyuhapi, Jesus Christ Itaŋcaŋuŋkiyap. kiŋ eciyataŋhaŋ." —Rom. v: 1.

2 Okicize waśte
Ecoŋuŋśipi kiŋ,
Owasiŋ Towaśake oŋ
Ecoŋqoŋpi kta ce.

3 Qa Wotaŋiŋ Waśte
Yuha oyaka po;
Jesus ecoŋ niśipi kiŋ,
Eced ecoŋ uŋ po.

4 Jesus Tawipe kiŋ
Owas icupi ye;
Kiŋhaŋ Odakota waśte
Sutaya hiŋ kta ce.

5 Waniśipi kiŋ He
Ohaŋ owotaŋna;
Wakaŋtaŋka waśake ciŋ
Taokiye uŋ po.

6 Odakota waśte,
Okicize waśte,
Qa wowaśake taŋka kiŋ
Koyag uŋqoŋpi kta. AMEN.

The Christian Life.

146 St. Matthias. 6 8s.

"Nihupahu ohaŋzi ihukuya namahma ye." — Ps. xvii: 8.

Onšpa I.

From "Tunes Old and New" by permission of Rev. Dr. Tucker.

2 Wahacaŋka wetoŋ kiŋ oŋ,
Haŋ, wokope kiŋ ota hca,
Tka kopewakda kte šni ce;
Nakuŋ aŋposkaŋtu kiŋ ed,
Waŋhiŋkpe kiŋ kiŋyaŋyaŋ uŋ
He miciyutokaŋ kta ce.

3 Nakuŋ oiyokpaza ed
Makošice kiŋ mani uŋ;
Wicowayazaŋ kiŋ nakuŋ
Aŋpe cokaya kiŋ ehaŋd
Wawihaŋgye ece kiŋ he
Etaŋ awaŋmayakiŋ kta.

4 Koktopawiŋġe micakda,
He oŋ hiŋhpayapi eša,
Nakuŋ mietapa kiŋ ed
Koktopawiŋġe ota ša,
Mikiyenaŋ he u kte šni,
Waŋbdake ciŋ hecena kta.

5 Wakaŋtaŋka ohoda šni,
Iyuwiŋ tawapi kiŋ he,
Išta kiŋ oŋ waŋbdakiŋ kta:
Itaŋcaŋ wowinape kiŋ
Mitawa kiŋ, Niye hca ce,
Kici mauŋ ye, ohiŋni. AMEN.

Courage.

146 Stella. 6. 8s.

"Itaŋcaŋ Niye nišnana wikopapi śni ed ouŋyemayakiya." — Ps. iv: 8.

Onšpa II.

By permission of Rev. Dr. Hutchins.

2 Nita Oknikde kiŋ wakaŋ,
  Aŋpetu qa haŋhepi ko,
Awaŋmayagwicaya ye;
  Nitacaŋku oknaye ȟciŋ
Sutaya yus-amayaŋ ye;
  Misiha kiŋ taŋyaŋ yiŋ kta.

3 Siŋteȟda kiŋ, qa mnaja kiŋ,
  Awicamawani eśa,
Nitowaśake kiŋ he oŋ
  Ohiwicawayiŋ kta ce;
Qa oŋ mita-Wakaŋtaŋka
  Niye kiŋ he sdodyapi kta.

4 Qa ceciciyiŋ kta eca
  Nayaȟoŋ kta kehe cioon,
Qa woiyokiśice ed
  Wauŋ eca, hehaŋd nakuŋ,
Ed omayakiyiŋ kta e,
  Kici mauŋ ye, ohiŋni.

5 Wiconi haŋske ciŋ he ed
  Wauŋ kta, oŋśimada ye;
Nitowanikiye kiŋ He
  Waŋyagmayakiyiŋ kta e,
Aŋpetu haŋske ciŋ he ed,
  Kici mauŋ ye, ohiŋni. AMEN.

The Christian Life.

147 Marlow. C. M.

"Wadinitakapi qoŋ he ayuśtaŋpi śni po, he woyuha taŋka okihi kta."— Heb. x: 35.

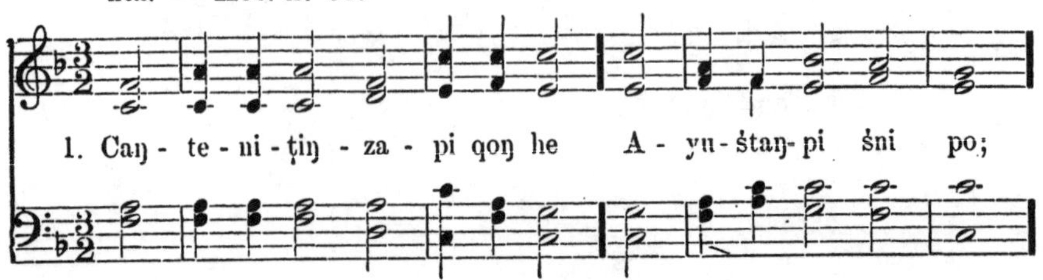

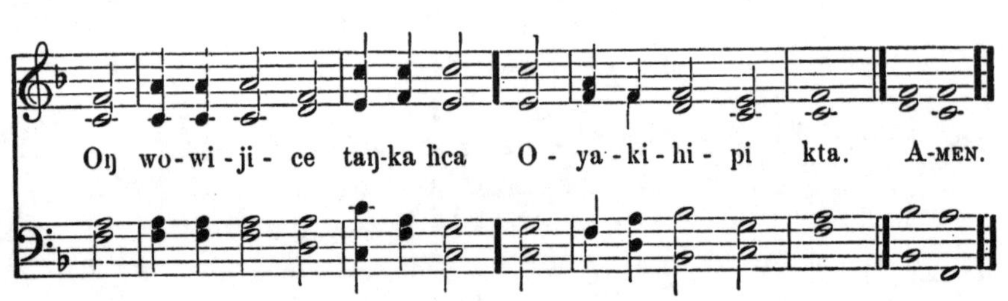

From "Tunes Old and New" by permission of Rev. Dr. Tucker.

2 Eced ecoŋqoŋpi kta ce,
Jesus Caje kiŋ oŋ,
Qa oŋ wahouŋyaŋpi kiŋ
Uŋkicupi kta ce.

3 Tuwa ecana u kte ciŋ,
Wana He hi kta ce;
Yutehaŋ kte śni kiŋ he oŋ,
Iwiyeya uŋ po.

4 Tuwa owotaŋna uŋ kiŋ,
Waciŋyaŋ oŋ ni kta;
Apa namnipi kiŋ, eqeś,
Inihaŋpi kta ce.

5 Apa namnipi kiŋ uŋkiś
Heuŋcapi śni ce;
Wicada oŋ ni uŋ kte ciŋ
Dena heuŋcapi. AMEN.

Action — Wobdiheca.

148 "A Charge to Keep I Have." S. M.

"Wookiĥpe kiŋ he ed uŋkopapi kta e abdiheuŋkiçiyapi kta."—Heb. iv: 11.

DENNIS.

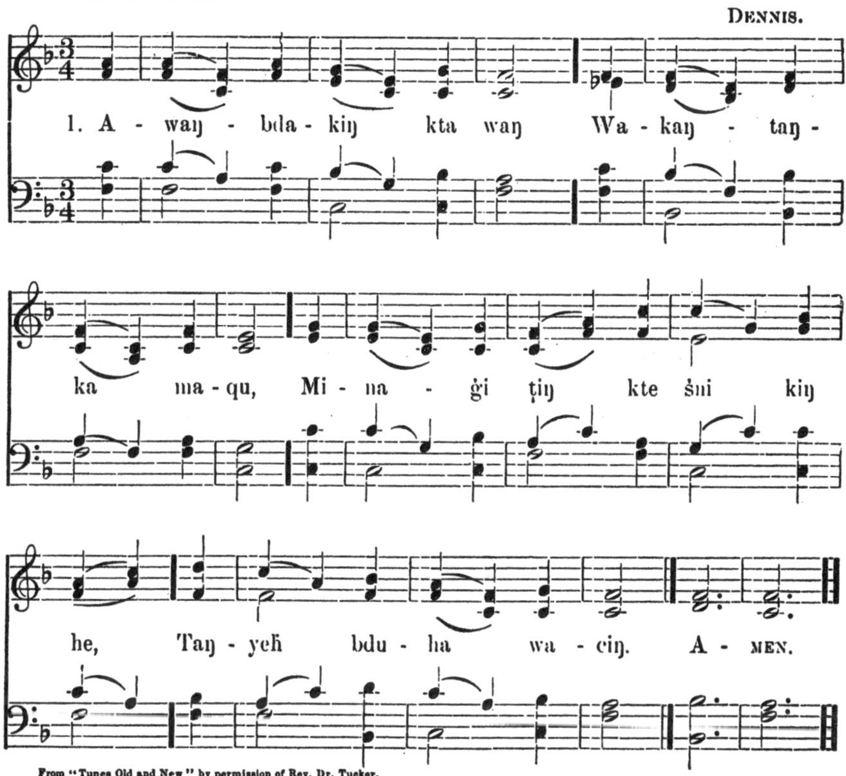

From "Tunes Old and New" by permission of Rev. Dr. Tucker.

2 Maciqana hetaŋ,
Nakuŋ tohaŋ wani,
Mayuhe ciŋ tawaciŋ kiŋ
Ecamoŋ kta waciŋ.

3 Kici ciuŋ kta e
Eced makaġa ye;
Itaŋcaŋ woyasu kiŋ he
Ed omakiya ye.

4 Wakta wauŋ kta e
Iceiciya ce;
Qa Nitokaŋ wauŋ kiŋhaŋ
Maţe ciŋ hee kta.

5 Wakaŋtaŋka Ate,
Ciŋhiŋtku kiŋ nakuŋ,
Qa Woniya Wakaŋ kiŋ He
Wakaŋtaŋka Niye. AMEN.

149 Dulce Carmen. 8s. 7s.

"Wakaŋtaŋka Tawipe kiŋ ocowasiŋ uŋ po." — Ephes. vi: 11.

First Tune.

From "Tunes Old and New" by permission of Rev. Dr. Tucker.

2 We kiŋ qa wicaceȟpi kiŋ
Ob uŋkicizapi śni;
Tka maka kiŋ de akaŋtu
Okpaza itaŋcaŋpi,
Qa wakaŋśica optaye,
Heca ob ecoŋqoŋpi.

3 Ho, Wakaŋtaŋka, Ate kiŋ,
He Tawipe kiŋ owas
Ohiŋni koyagya uŋ po;
Qa ośiceca eśa
Najiŋhaŋ nayajiŋpi kta,
Oŋ nikduśtaŋpi kiŋhaŋ.

4 Wowicake kiŋ nakuŋ he
Oŋ ipiyagkitoŋ po;
Wiyeya, waktaya uŋ po;
Qa wicoowotaŋna
Maza woakaȟpe kiŋ he,
Ohiŋni koyaka po.

5 Qa nisihapi kiŋ koya
Wookiye wotaŋiŋ
He ohe waciŋyaŋ uŋ po;
Akapataŋhaŋ nakuŋ
Wowaciŋye kiŋ kduha po,
He wahacaŋka ee.

6 Heced śice ciŋ waŋhiŋkpe
Tawa kiŋ ideyahaŋ,
Oŋ owas dusnipi kta ce;
Qa mas-wapaha kiŋ he,
Wowanikiye kiŋ hee,
Ohiŋni kiçuŋ uŋ po.

7 Qa Wakaŋtaŋka Oie,
Woniya Tamiwakaŋ,
He nakuŋ iyacupi kta.
Wipe kiŋ dena uŋ kiŋ
Wowiyuśkiŋ ohiŋni ed,
Christ kici ouŋyiŋ kta. Amen.

Action.

149 Regent Square. 8s. 7s.

"Wakaŋtaŋka Tawipe kiŋ ocowasiŋ uŋ po." — Ephes. vi: 11.

Second Tune. Henry Smart.

By permission of Rev. Dr. Hutchins.

2 We kiŋ qa wicaceḣpi kiŋ
Ob uŋkicizapi śni;
Tka maka kiŋ de akaŋtu
Okpaza itaŋcaŋpi,
Qa wakaŋśica optaye,
Heca ob ecoŋqoŋpi.

3 Ho, Wakaŋtaŋka, Ate kiŋ,
He Tawipe kiŋ owas
Ohiŋni koyagya uŋ po;
Qa ośiceca eśa
Najiŋḣaŋ nayajiŋpi kta,
Oŋ nikduśṫaŋpi kiŋḣaŋ.

4 Wowicake kiŋ nakuŋ he
Oŋ ipiyagkitoŋ po;
Wiyeya, waktaya uŋ po;
Qa wicoowotaŋna
Maza woakaḣpe kiŋ he,
Ohiŋni koyaka po.

5 Qa nisiḣapi kiŋ koya
Wookiye wotaŋiŋ,
He ohe waciŋyaŋ uŋ po;
Akapataŋḣaŋ nakuŋ
Wowaciŋye kiŋ kduha po,
He wahacaŋka ee.

6 Heced śice ciŋ waŋḣiŋkpe
Tawa kiŋ ideyaḣaŋ,
Oŋ owas dusnipi kta ce;
Qa mas-wapaha kiŋ he,
Wowanikiye kiŋ hee,
Ohiŋni kiçuŋ uŋ po.

7 Qa Wakaŋtaŋka Oie,
Woniya Tamiwakaŋ,
He nakuŋ iyacupi kta.
Wipe kiŋ dena uŋ kiŋ
Wowiyuśkiŋ ohiŋni ed,
Christ kici ouŋyiŋ kta. Amen.

X. The Judgment.

WOYASU KIN.

150 Uxbridge. L. M.

"Uŋkiyepi Jehovah Wakaŋuŋdapi kiŋ ouŋkiyapi kta." — 11 Aŋpetu Oyak. xxxii: 8.

2 Ocaŋku waŋ toya waŋka,
Wiconi mni kiŋ he okna,
Oyaḣe ṡni kaduza ce,
Wakaŋtaŋka waŋkaŋd Ti ed.

3 Waŋkaŋd otoŋwe kiŋ wakaŋ,
He ed wauŋ waciŋ ḣca ce,
He tawa kiŋ waṡte, wakaŋ;
Wakaŋtaŋka ahopa po.

4 Jesus Wanikiya hed uŋ,
Qa wowitaŋ ohiye ça
Wateṡdake waṡte waŋ uŋ;
Wakaŋtaŋka ohoda po.

5 Miohaŋ ṡica ota kiŋ
Hena e oŋ Iye ḣca ṭa;
He oŋ Iye waciŋyaŋ po:
Wakaŋtaŋka waoŋṡida.

6 Ateyapi, Ciŋhiŋtku kiŋ,
Qa Woniya Wakaŋ kiŋ He,
Wakaŋtaŋka waŋjina kiŋ,
He wowitaŋ yuha nuŋwe. AMEN.

The Judgment.

151 St. Bride. S. M.

"Dena owihaŋke waniŋd wokakije kiŋ ed yapi kta; tka wicaśa owotaŋna kiŋ hena owihaŋke waniŋd wiconi kiŋ ed yapi kta." — St. Matt. xxv: 46.

[*Olmutz, Hymn* 138, *may be used.*]

From "Tunes Old and New" by permission of Rev. Dr. Tucker.

2 Nakuŋ oyaŋke waŋ
  Iś wokokipe ĥca,
Owotaŋpina śni kiŋ hed
  Teĥi sdodyapi kta.

3 Maṭe ciŋhaŋ hehaŋd
  Ake wani kta ce,
Tukte wiconi uŋma ed,
  Okna wauŋ kta he?

4 Hehe! wahuŋke śni,
  Wawaĥtanis'a oŋ
Oyaŋke śice ciŋ etaŋ
  Nimapica kta he?

5 Haŋ, icipaweġa
  Ehaŋna waŋ he ciŋ
Inabya hed maŋke ciŋhaŋ
  We oŋ mayuska kta.

6 Qa ed waciŋyaŋpi,
  Otoŋwe yeġe ciŋ,
Ĥed Jesus Christ idowaŋpi
  Owihaŋkeśniyaŋ. AMEN.

The Judgment.

152 Old 148th. 6s. 8s.

"Maȟpiya qa maka nakaha uŋ kiŋ hena peta oŋ ayuhapi." — 2 Peter iii: 7.

FIRST TUNE.

From "Tunes Old and New" by permission of Rev. Dr. Tucker.

2 Ake tokatata,
 Wicaṡa ṡica oŋ
Itaŋcaŋ, ciŋ kiŋhaŋ,
 Maka ȟuȟnaȟyiŋ kta:
Oqo okokipe e ed
Ihaŋgyapi kta, peta oŋ.

3 Maka sitomniyaŋ
 Ehaŋna mni kiŋ ṡma,
Tka wata waŋ okna
 Wicaṡa nipi qoŋ:
Miṡ Christ Taŋcaŋ kiŋ owapa;
He oŋ Iye nimayiŋ kta. AMEN.

The Judgment.

152 Zebulon. 6s. 8s.

"Maĥpiya qa maka nakaha uŋ kiŋ hena peta oŋ ayuhapi."—2 Peter iii: 7.

SECOND TUNE. L. MASON.

By permission of Rev. Dr. Hutchins.

2 Ake tokatata,
Wicaśa śica oŋ
Itaŋcaŋ, ciŋ kiŋhaŋ,
Maka ĥuĥnaĥyiŋ kta:
Oqo okokipe c ed
Ihaŋgyapi kta, peta oŋ

3 Maka sitomniyaŋ
Ehaŋna mni kiŋ śma,
Tka wata waŋ okna
Wicaśa nipi qoŋ:
Miś Christ Taŋcaŋ kiŋ owapa;
He oŋ Iye nimayiŋ kta. AMEN

XI. Heaven.

MAḢPIYA.

153 "O Mother Dear, Jerusalem!" 8s. 7s.

"Otoŋwe taŋka kiŋ, Jerusalem wakaŋ kiŋ he."—Wayuo xxi: 10.

[*Trust, Hymn 172, may be used.*] AUTUMN.

1. O Je - ru - sa-lem Waŋ-kaŋ - tu, Wo - wi - yu-ṡkiŋ ti - pi kiŋ,

He ca - je te - wa - ḣi - da ce; He - ci - ya Waŋ - ji Wa - kaŋ. FINE.

Qa ti - yo - pa kiŋ ska - ska ḣca Wi i - ye - ced yeḣ - ye - ġa.

Coŋ-ka - ṡke he- na o - was - iŋ Wo- i - yo - ki.- pi - ya haŋ, D.S.

From "Book of Common Praise" by permission of A. S. Barnes & Co.

2 Wojupi nitawa kiŋ he
Ed omanipi waṡte,
Qa waḣca owas icaġa,
Ohiŋni toya waŋka.
Qa nitacaŋku owasiŋ
Iṡ ayucoya waŋka;
Jesus Christ Taokiyepi
Hed omani uŋpi ce.

3 Qa Caŋku anoŋkatahaŋ
Hed wiconi caŋ kiŋ haŋ,
Qa caŋku kiŋ ed wiconi
Mni kadusya hed waŋka.
Caŋ kiŋ wi otoiyohi
Ed waskuyeca yukaŋ,
Qa maḣpiyata zitkana
Ohiŋni dowaŋpi ce.

4 O Jerusalem waŋkaŋtu,
Hed tohaŋd wai kta he?
Haŋ, tohaŋd niye ḣca ed bda
Wowiyuṡkiŋ taŋka kta.
O Jerusalem waŋkaŋtu,
Wowiyuṡkiŋ tipi kiŋ
He caje tewaḣida ce;
Heciya Waŋji Wakaŋ. AMEN.

154 Hendon. 7s.

" Wakaŋtaŋka ticaǧe ciŋ tipi wicanape oŋ kaǧapi ṡni. — 2 Cor. v: 1.

From "Book of Common Praise" by permission of A. S. Barnes & Co.

2 A! wicaho waŋ taŋiŋ:
" Ded waciŋyaŋ ṭe ciŋ he,
Awicakehaŋ ni kta,
He naḣoŋpi ye," eya.

3 Jesus He uŋkipaŋpi:
Ho, wiconi opa po,
Qa nakuŋ iyoyaŋpa
Wipe kiŋ icupi ye.

4 Jesus Christ taoyate,
Heciya maḣpiya kiŋ
Ed wiyakpakpapi, qa
Jesus hed yataŋpi ce.

5 Woyasu aŋpetu kiŋ,
He tohaŋd taŋiŋ kiŋhaŋ,
Woiṡtiŋbe kiŋ etaŋ
Hed inauŋjiŋpi kta. AMEN.

155 Beautiful River. 8s. 7s.

"Wakpa waŋ wiconi mini ska kiŋ he makipazo." —Wayuo xxii: 1.

By permission of the author, Rev. R. Lowry.

2 Haŋ, wakpa waśte hutata
Wowiyuśkiŋ ota ce,
Ed inauŋjiŋpi kta ce,
Qa ohouŋdapi kta.

3 Hed unkipi kiŋ itokab,
Woqiŋ kiŋ uŋkpaȟpapi
Qa Wanikiya Iye ȟca
Wowaśte uŋqupi kta.

4 Hed Wanikiya kiŋ uŋ ce,
He waŋuŋyakapi kta,
Qa yataŋ uŋdowaŋpi kta,
Ohiŋni, wakaŋpi ob. AMEN.

156 Christchurch. 6s. 8s.

"Otoŋwe taŋka kiŋ, Jerusalem wakaŋ kiŋ he." — Wayuo xxi: 10.

From "Tunes Old and New" by permission of Rev. Dr. Tucker.

2 Itaŋcaŋ, Jesus Christ,
Nakuŋ Iye hed ti;
Oknikde kiŋ owas
Iye yataŋpi ce.

3 Atewicuŋyaŋpi
Qoŋ hed ouŋyaŋpi;
Waayatapi ko
Hed Christ waŋyakapi.

4 Wahoŝiyepi hed
Waŋwicabdakiŋ kta,
Dowaŋpi kiŋ nakuŋ
Nawicawaḣoŋ kta.

5 Waciŋyaŋ ṭapi qoŋ
Hed ska koyakapi,
Qa mazaskazi ḣca
Wateŝdagyapi ce. AMEN.

Heaven.

157 St. Cecelia. 6s.

"Makoce iyotaŋ waŝte maĥpiya ekta waŋke ciŋ hee akitapi." — Heb. xi: 16.

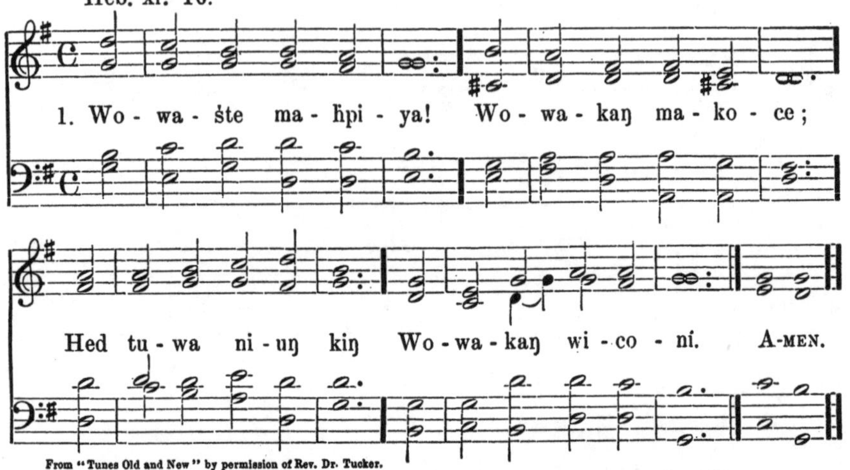

From "Tunes Old and New" by permission of Rev. Dr. Tucker.

2 Wowaŝte maĥpiya!
Wowaŝte makoce;
Hed tuwa niuŋ kiŋ
Wowiyuŝkiŋ taŋka.

3 Wowaŝte maĥpiya!
Woozi makoce
Hed tuwa niuŋ kiŋ
Wowaŝte owiĥaŋ.

4 Wowaŝte maĥpiya!
Christ Tamakoce kiŋ;
Toyaŋke wakaŋ kiŋ
Hed wateŝdagtoŋpi.

5 Wowaŝte maĥpiya!
He makoce to ĥca,
Qa iyoyaŋpa ĥca;
Wowitaŋ kiŋ taŋka.

6 Wowaŝte maĥpiya!
Wodowaŋ makoce;
Heciya wakaŋpi
Woyataŋ dowaŋpi. AMEN.

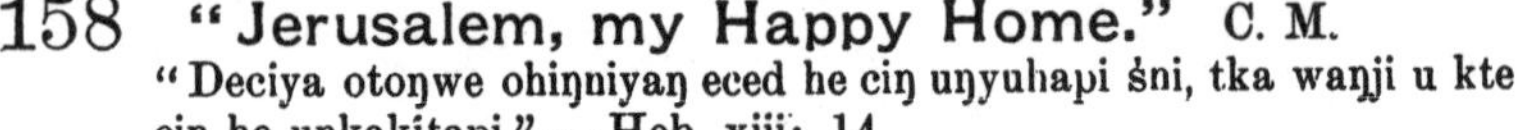

158 "Jerusalem, my Happy Home." C. M.

"Deciya otoŋwe ohiŋniyaŋ eced he ciŋ uŋyuhapi ŝni, tka waŋji u kte ciŋ he uŋkakitapi." — Heb. xiii: 14.

FIRST TUNE. NORTON.

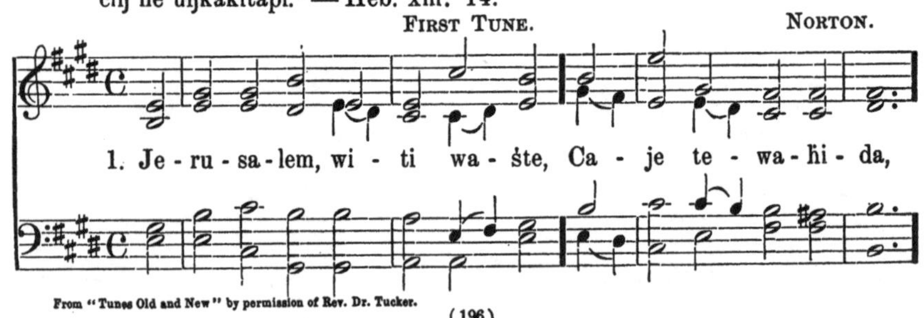

From "Tunes Old and New" by permission of Rev. Dr. Tucker.

2 Maȟpiya kiŋ ed coŋkaśke
Tiyopa ska kiŋ ko,
Hena miiśta kiŋ tohaŋd
Waŋyakapi kta he?

3 Qa mazaskazi oŋ caŋku
Wiyakpakpa waśte,
Hena tohaŋd waŋbdake ça
Omawani kta he?

4 Wahośiyepi, martyr kiŋ,
Waayatapi ko,
Hed Jesus ikdukśaŋ au,
Qa wiyuśkiŋpi ce.

5 Christ ed tewicawaȟida
Hena iyuśkiŋyaŋ
Ecana opapi kta ce,
Obe wakaŋ kiŋ hed.

6 Jerusalem wati waśte,
Waŋciyakiŋ kte ȟciŋ,
Ḣtàwani kiŋ abduśtaŋ kta,
Waŋciyake ciŋhaŋ. AMEN.

158 "Jerusalem, my Happy Home." C. M.

"Deciya otoŋwe ohiŋniyaŋ eced he ciŋ uŋyuhapi śni, tka waŋji u kte ciŋ he uŋkakitapi." — Heb. xiii: 14.

SECOND TUNE. JERUSALEM.

From "Tunes Old and New" by permission of Rev. Dr. Tucker.

Heaven.

159 “Jerusalem, the Golden.” 7s. 6s. D.

“Otoŋwe taŋka kiŋ, Jerusalem wakaŋ, mahpiya kiŋ etaŋhaŋ Wakaŋtaŋka eciyataŋhan kutkiya u kiŋ he makipazo.” — Wayuo xxi: 10.

Ewing.

From “Tunes Old and New” by permission of Rev. Dr. Tucker.

2 Hed wowiyuśkiŋ taŋka
Uŋkiciyaŋkapi,
Qa wowitaŋ wiyakpa,
Okaĥniĥpica śni,
Haŋ, Zion tipi tawa
Oknikde qa nakuŋ
Yataŋ dowaŋpi kiŋ oŋ
Ayucoya hed haŋ.

3 Hed martyr kiŋ wicota,
Qa wiyuśkiŋpi ce,
Itaŋcaŋ Christ hed ohni
Iyoyaŋbwicaya;
Iyoyaŋpa kiŋ ska qa
Abdakena ĥca ce;
Ouŋyaŋpi kiŋ hena
Yupiye ĥciŋ waŋka.

4 David he toyaŋke; qa
Ohiyapi owas,
Iyokiśice śni ĥciŋ
Hed iyakiś'api,
Wicakicopi kiŋ ko,
Haŋ, wiyuśkiŋye ĥciŋ,
Hed heci wotapi, qa
Dowaŋ hiŋkdapi ce.

5 Makoce kiŋ waśte ĥca!
Oiyokipi ĥca!
Wakaŋtaŋka He tona
Wicakaĥniġe ciŋ
Makoce tawapi kiŋ!
Christ oŋśiuŋdapi
Qa oŋ Niyate Ti qed
Uŋkihuŋnipi nuŋ. Amen.

160 St. Lucian. 6s. 5s.

"Taku waŋyakapi kiŋ hena ekta uŋketoŋwaŋpi śni, tka taku tona waŋyakapi śni kiŋ ekta."—2 Cor. iv: 18.

From "Tunes Old and New" by permission of Rev. Dr. Tucker.

2 Qa wiconi ĥce ciŋ
Hed ihaŋke śni,
He maĥpiya etu,
Iś kduha yaŋka.

3 Qa Ciŋhiŋtku, Jesus,
He nakuŋ hed uŋ,
Qa Atkuku kiŋ he
Towitaŋ yuha.

4 Qa wiconi kiŋ ed
Iś waŋkaŋd yaŋka;
Toyaŋke nakuŋ, he
Hed wakaŋ ĥca ce.

5 Woniya Wakaŋ kiŋ
He nakuŋ hed uŋ,
Qa Wanikiya kiŋ
He kici uŋ ce.

6 Ho, ḍena wakaŋpi,
Qa waŋjipina,
Hed wicayataŋpi
Ohiŋniyaŋ ĥciŋ. Amen.

Heaven.

161 Lilly Dale. 10s. 8s.

"Wicaceya, wicokakije ko wanicin kta."—Wayuo xxi: 4.

Heaven.

1 O Wakaŋpi kiŋ iś tamakapi
He waśte qa wiyakpa ce;
He ded ohiŋni ḣciŋ nauŋḣoŋpi,
O, toŋkiŋ he waŋbdakiŋ niŋ!
Cho. Maḣpiya! Maḣpiya! wowiyuśkin,
Haŋ, Wakaŋtaŋka He tamaka kiŋ
Hed, Christ, Nici wauŋ nuŋwe.

2 Haŋ, hed mazaskazi caŋku waśte,
Haŋ, hed iŋyaŋ ska coŋkaśke,
Qa hed wowiyuśkiŋ iyotaŋ kiŋ,
O toŋkiŋ hed wauŋ ḣca niŋ!

3 Haŋ, hed oiyokpaziŋ kte śni ce,
Qa hed ceyapi śni, ṇakuŋ,
Qa hed woiyokiśice uŋ śni
Tka iyoyaŋpa ohiŋni.

4 Haŋ, makata wowiyuśkiŋ śni ce,
Oŋ waŋkaŋta uŋyaŋpi kta,
Qa wiconi taŋka kiŋ, Christ kici,
He ed ohni uŋqoŋpi kta. Amen.

162 "Sweet Hour of Prayer." L. M.

"Minaġi kiŋ Itaŋcaŋ Tahocoka kiŋ oŋ caŋtokpani."—Ps. lxxxiv: 2.

Rev. W. W. Walford. Wm. B. Bradbury.

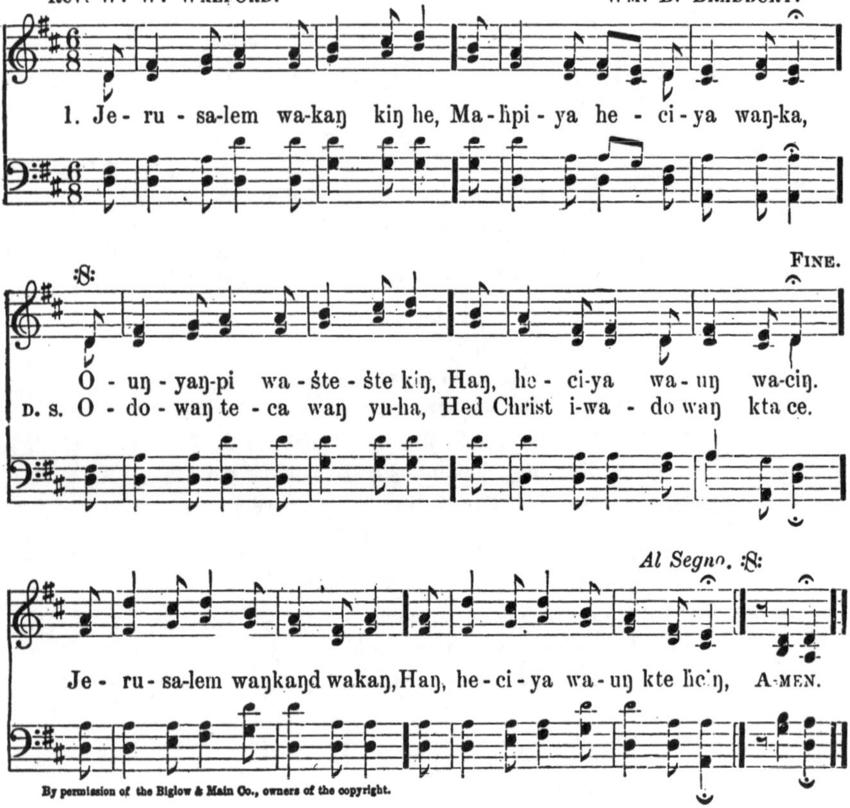

1. Je- ru - sa-lem wa-kaŋ kiŋ he, Ma-ḣpi - ya he - ci - ya waŋ-ka,
O - uŋ - yaŋ-pi wa - ṡte - ṡte kiŋ, Haŋ, he - ci-ya wa - uŋ wa-ciŋ.
D. S. O - do - waŋ te - ca waŋ yu-ha, Hed Christ i-wa - do waŋ kta ce.
Je - ru - sa-lem waŋkaŋd wakaŋ, Haŋ, he - ci - ya wa - uŋ kte ḣeciŋ, A-men.

Fine. Al Segno.

2 Maka abduṡtaŋ ḣce ciŋhaŋ,
Jerusalem waŋkaŋta kiŋ
Ekta wai waciŋ ḣca ce,
O Jesus, omak'ya ye.
Ateyapi, Ciŋhiŋtku kiŋ,
Qa Woniya Wakaŋ kiŋ He,
Wakaŋtaŋka waŋjina kiŋ,
He wowitaŋ yuha nuŋwe. Amen.

163 "Hark! Hark my Soul! Angelic Songs." P. M.

"Haŋhepi kiŋ wana ecanaŋ uŋkihunipi kta, aŋpetu kiŋ kohaŋna u kta." —Rom. xiii: 12.

FIRST TUNE. PILGRIMS.

From "Tunes Old and New" by permission of Rev. Dr. Tucker.

2 "Watuka kiŋ u po, Christ He heya ce;"
Eyapi oŋ uŋkiś uŋyaŋpi kta;
Qa okpaza śa Wotaŋiŋ-waśte kiŋ
Tiyatakiya yusuŋkayapi.

3 Teĥike ça otehaŋtu kte, çeyaś
Owihaŋketa woozikiye
Waśte waŋ ed uŋkihuŋnipi kta ce,
Waŋkaŋd Wakaŋtaŋka Ti kiŋ he ed.

4 Ayaśtaŋ śni dowaŋpi ye, owasiŋ,
Nakuŋ waawaŋdakapi kiŋ he
Enakiyapi śni ye, heced Jesus
Iye kici uŋdowaŋpi kta ce. AMEN.

Heaven.

163 "Hark! Hark my Soul, Angelic Songs." P. M.

"Haŋhepi kiŋ wana ecanaŋ uŋkihunipi kta, aŋpetu kiŋ kohaŋna u kta." — Rom. xiii: 12.

From "Tunes Old and New" by permission of Rev. Dr. Tucker.

Heaven.

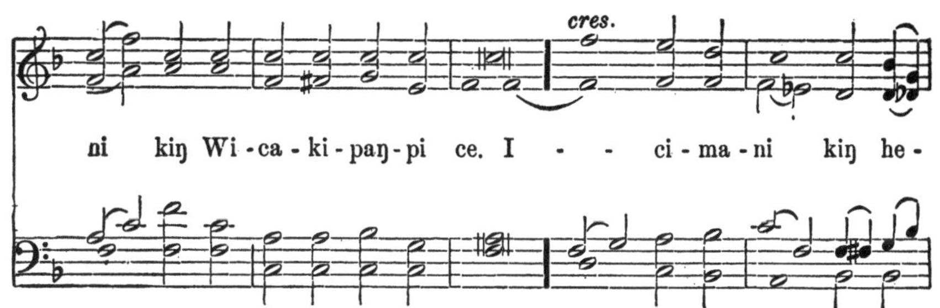

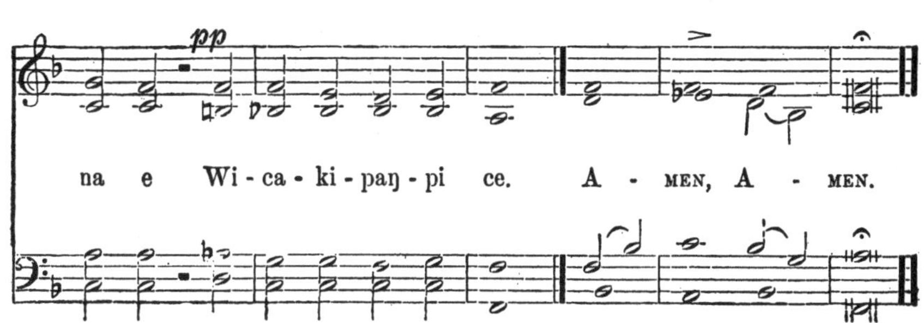

2 "Watuka kiŋ u po, Christ He heya ce;"
Eyapi oŋ uŋkiś uŋyaŋpi kta;
Qa okpaza śa Wotaŋiŋ-waśte kiŋ
Tiyatakiya yusuŋkayapi.

3 Teĥike ça oteĥaŋtu kte çevaś
Owihaŋketa woozikiye
Waśte waŋ ed uŋkihuŋnipi kta ce,
Waŋkaŋd Wakaŋtaŋka Ti kiŋ he ed

4 Ayaśtaŋ śni dowaŋpi ye, owasiŋ,
Nakuŋ waawaŋdakapi kiŋ he
Enakiyapi śni ye, heced Jesus
Iye kici uŋdowaŋpi kta ce. AMEN.

XII. Miscellaneous.

TOKTOKECA.

164 Guardian. 8s.

"Hehaŋd wakpa waŋ wiconi mini ska, caĥtowata iyeced ska, kiŋ he makipazo; he Wakaŋtaŋka qa Taciŋcana oiyotaŋke Tawa kiŋ etaŋhaŋ kaduza."—Wayuo xxii: 1.

From "Book of Common Praise" by permission of A. S. Barnes & Co.

2 Wicaša waŋ ed mahi kiŋ
 Inoŋpa ipuziŋ kte šni;
Niye h̓ca hehe ciqoŋ oŋ,
 O Jesus, mini maqu ye.
Tuwe kaša he ciŋ kiŋhaŋ,
 Išicona ed hi eša,
Wiconi mni qupi kta ce,
 O Jesus, mini maqu ye. AMEN.

165 Arlington. C. M.

"Uŋkaŋ oyate ota upi qa heyapi kta; Upi ye, Jehovah Paha Tawa kiŋ ekta uŋyaŋpi kta, Jacob ta-Wakaŋtaŋka Ti kiŋ ekta." —Isa. ii: 3.

From "Tunes Old and New" by permission of Rev. Dr. Tucker.

2 Mah̓piyataŋhaŋ cu u kiŋ,
 Uŋkahiŋhaŋpi kta,
Kiŋhaŋ uŋcaŋtepi kiŋ ed
 Wah̓ca icaġiŋ kta.

3 Qa taku hed icaġiŋ kta,
 He He Wakaŋ ekta,
Mah̓piya cu hiyakde kta,
 Micaŋte hed uŋ ce.

4 Jehovah He Wakaŋ ekta,
 Taokiye kico,
Qa woope wakaŋ kiŋ qu,
 Wiconi kiŋ he e.

5 Nitah̓e Sinai kiŋ etaŋ
 Niš omakiya ye,
Kiŋhaŋ Nitoope wakaŋ
 Okna waun kta ce. AMEN.

Miscellaneous

166 The Precious Name. 8s. 7s.

" Wicacaje tokeça maḣpiya kiŋ iḣukuya wicaśa wicaqupi oŋ uŋnipi kte ciŋ wanica ce."— Oḣan. iv: 12.

FANNY J. CROSBY. W. H. DOANE.

2 "Jesus" He awaciŋ uŋ wo;
He wahacaŋkaya yo,
Ṡice ciŋ ayakipa caŋ
Cekiya yo, ḣe okna.

3 "Jesus" He awaciŋ uŋ wo;
Wocaŋtewaṡte kiŋ he,
Oŋ waṡaguŋyaŋpi kta ce,
He uŋkicupi eca.

4 "Jesus" He awaciŋ uŋ wo;
He kipatuṡya uŋ wo;
He waŋkaŋd Itaŋcaŋ ḣca e
Wowitaŋ uŋqupi kta. AMEN.

167 "Guide me, O Thou Great Jehovah." 8s. 7s. 4.

"Maka akaŋd oyate tokeca qa ikdaka uŋpi kiŋ ḣeca ikdaotaŋiŋpi."
—Heb. xi: 13.

FIRST TUNE. SAXE-WEIMAR.

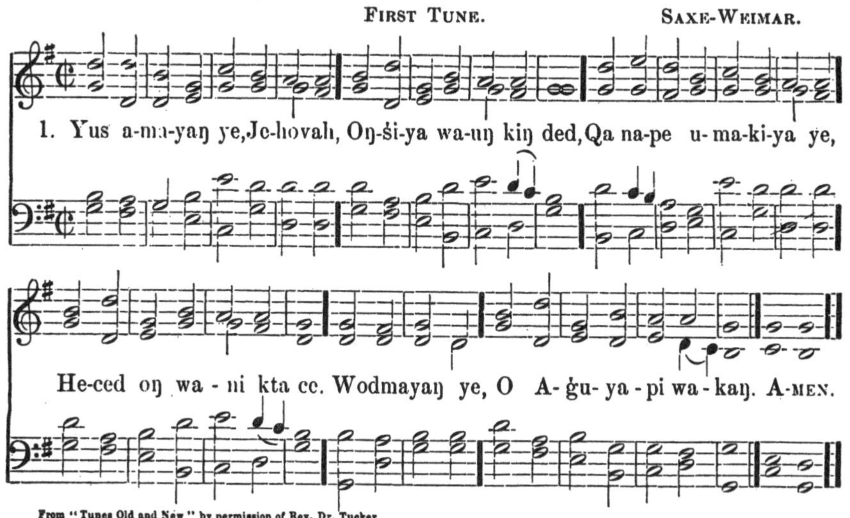

From "Tunes Old and New" by permission of Rev. Dr. Tucker.

2 Mui wiconi kiŋ etaŋhaŋ
U kiŋ he yuḣdoka ye;
Qa maṭiŋ kte ciŋ hehaŋyaŋ
Christ iyoyaŋbmayaŋ ye:
O Itaŋcaŋ,
Woekdaku he Niye.

3 Ded ḣewoskaŋd ḣciŋ wauŋ kiŋ,
Manna kiŋ yudmayaŋ ye;
Qa wahacaŋka mitawa
He Niye kiŋ ee kta:
Ohiŋniyaŋ,
Christ, icidowaŋ kta ce.

4 Jordan ohuta kiŋ he ed,
Wikopeṡnimayaŋ ye;
Qa wicoŋṭe kiŋ ohiya
Canaan ed wai kta ce:
Hed wiconi,
Ed ciyataŋ kta, O Christ. AMEN.

167 "Guide Me, O Thou Great Jehovah." 8s. 7s. 4s.

'Maka akaŋd oyate tokeca qa ikdaka uŋpi kiŋ ĥeca ikdaotaŋiŋpi."—Heb. xi: 13.

ZION. SECOND TUNE. THOMAS HASTINGS, 1830.

2 Mni wiconi kiŋ etaŋhaŋ
U kiŋ he yuĥdoka ye;
Qa matiŋ kte ciŋ heĥaŋyaŋ
Christ iyoyaŋbmayaŋ ye:
O Itaŋcaŋ,
Woekdaku he Niye.

3 Ded ĥewoskaŋd ĥciŋ wauŋ kiŋ,
Manna kiŋ yudmayaŋ ye;
Qa wahacaŋka mitawa
He Niye kiŋ ee kta:
Ohiŋniyaŋ,
Christ, icidowaŋ kta ce.

4 Jordan ohuta kiŋ he ed,
Wikopeśnimayaŋ ye;
Qa wicoŋte kiŋ ohiya
Canaan ed wai kta ce:
Hed wiconi,
Ed ciyataŋ kta, O Christ. AMEN.

168 Vespers. L. M.

"Wakaŋtaŋka Iye Ciŋhiŋtku iśnana icaġe ciŋ He makata uśi."—1 John iv: 9.

From "Tunes Old and New" by permission of Rev. Dr. Tucker.

2 Ate kiŋ Towaśtedake,
Oŋ Jesus Christ uŋqupi ce;
He ed taŋyaŋ ikduha po,
Wawiciya Itaŋcaŋ ce.

3 Wanikiya Itaŋcaŋ kiŋ,
He tona ȟciŋ waciŋyaŋpi
Hena wicakici uŋ kta·
He oŋ aiçiciya po.

4 He Woniya wicaqu ce,
Qa wowaoŋśida owas,
Wicoowotaŋna nakuŋ,
Qa Towicake kiŋ hena.

5 Niś ohiŋni waciŋyaŋ po;
Iye etaŋ wiconi ce,
Qa heced oŋ sutaye ȟciŋ
Wiconi ed yaipi kta. AMEN.

Miscellaneous.

169 Asaph. S. M.

"Wakaŋtaŋka oknikdewicaye ciŋ owasiŋ Iye itokab caŋkpeśka makakde eŋajiŋ kta ce." — Heb. i: 6.

[*Schumann, Hymn 115, may be used.*]

From "Tunes Old and New" by permission of Rev. Dr. Tucker.

2 Wanikiye ciŋ He,
Yataŋ idowaŋpi,
Oȟaŋpi kiŋ oknaye ȟciŋ,
Uŋkiś uŋśkaŋpi kta.

3 He Toye, Toȟaŋ ko
Awaŋyag uŋpi, qa
Iś śkaŋpi kiŋ, uŋkiś eya
Eced uŋyaŋpi kta.

4 Wanikiya waśte,
Nitaniya Wakaŋ
Okihiuŋyaŋpi kta e
Uŋkukiyapi ye.

5 Wakaŋtaŋka Ate,
Ciŋhiŋtku kiŋ nakuŋ,
Qa Woniya Wakaŋ kiŋ He
Wakaŋtaŋka Niye. Amen.

Miscellaneous.

170 Heavenly Father, We Beseech Thee. 8s. 7s.

"Itaŋcaŋ, tuwe ekta uŋyaŋpi kta he? owihaŋke waniŋd wiconi wicoie duha kiŋ." —St. John vi: 68.

FANNY J. CROSBY. REV. ROBERT LOWRY.

2 Jesus, yus uŋkayapi ye,
Qa wayutakuni śni
He aohomni uŋśkaŋpi,
Oŋ waciŋuŋniyaŋpi.

3 Woniya Wakaŋ uya ye,
He uŋyuskəpi kta e;
Qa caŋku okna uŋyaŋpi,
He Niye kiŋ Ee kta. AMEN.

172 "Guide Me, O Thou Great Jehovah." 8s. 7s.

"Maka akaŋd oyate tokeca qa ikdaka uŋpi kiŋ heca ikdaotaŋ-iŋpi." — Heb. xi: 13.

TRUST.

From "Tunes Old and New" by permission of Rev. Dr. Tucker.

2 Mui wicoui kiŋ etaŋhaŋ
U kiŋ he yuhdoka ye;
Qa maṭiŋ kte ciŋ hehaŋyaŋ,
Christ, iyoyaŋbmayaŋ ye.

3 Ded hewoskaŋd hciŋ wauŋ kiŋ
Manna kiŋ yudmayaŋ ye;
Qa wahacaŋka mitawa
He Niye kiŋ Ee kta.

4 Jordan ohuta kiŋ he ed,
Wikopešnimayaŋ ye;
Qa wicoŋṭe kiŋ ohiya
Canaan ed wai kta ce.

5 O Wakaŋtaŋka Ate kiŋ,
Qa Ciŋhiŋtku kiŋ nakuŋ,
Woniya Wakaŋ hena ko,
Ohiŋni yataŋpi ye. AMEN.

173 "Through All the Changing Scenes of Life." C. M.

"Ohiŋniyaŋ Itaŋcaŋ kiŋ bdawašte ece kta, woyataŋ Tawa kiŋ ohiŋ-niyaŋ mii ed uŋ kta." — Ps. xxxiv: 1.

FIRST TUNE. THAXTED.

From "Tunes Old and New" by permission of Rev. Dr. Tucker.

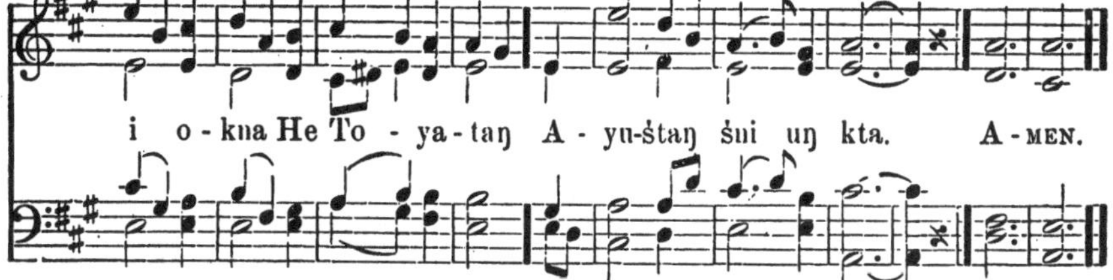

2 Itaŋcaŋ oŋ minaġi kiŋ
Iyuśkiŋ kta; nakuŋ
He oŋśiĥaŋpi kiŋ naĥoŋ,
Qa wiyuśkiŋpi kta.

3 Itaŋcaŋ kiŋ awakita,
Namaĥoŋ qa eced
He wokokipe kiŋ owas
Etaŋ imicu ce.

4 Itaŋcaŋ oŋśike ciŋ he
Howaya caŋ naĥoŋ,
Qa tokakije tona keś
Etaŋhaŋ ekdaku.

5 Itaŋcaŋ kiŋ kokipapi
Hena wicikdukśaŋ
Taoknikde wakaŋ waŋji
Wicayaŋka ece. AMEN.

173 "Through all the Changing Scenes of Life." C. M.

"Ohiŋniyaŋ Itaŋcaŋ kiŋ bdawaŝte ece kta, woyataŋ Tawa kiŋ ohiŋniyaŋ mii ed uŋ kta." — Ps. xxxiv: 1.

SECOND TUNE. ST. AGNES.

From "Tunes Old and New" by permission of Rev. Dr. Tucker.

2 Itaŋcaŋ oŋ minaġi kiŋ
Iyuśkiŋ kta; nakuŋ
He oŋśiĥaŋpi kiŋ naĥoŋ,
Qa wiyuśkiŋpi kta.

3 Itaŋcaŋ kiŋ awakita,
Namaĥoŋ qa eced
He wokokipe kiŋ owas
Etaŋ imacu ce.

4 Itaŋcaŋ oŋśike ciŋ he
Howaya caŋ naĥoŋ,
Qa tokakije tona keś
Etaŋhaŋ ekdaku.

5 Itaŋcaŋ kiŋ kokipapi
Hena wicikdukśaŋ
Taoknikde wakaŋ waŋji
Wicayaŋka ece. AMEN.

Miscellaneous.

174 All Saints. C. M. D.

"Taku śica nakicipa yo, qa taku waśte e ecoŋ wo, wookiye akite, ça okna uŋ wo."—Ps. xxxiv: 14.

From "Tunes Old and New" by permission of Rev. Dr. Tucker,

2 Itaŋcaŋ Tokokipe kiŋ,
Ho po, wakaŋheja,
Oŋspeciciyapi kta e
Namaȟoŋ ȟca u po.
Wicaśa ni kte ȟciŋ nakuŋ
Waśte waŋyakiŋ kta
E, oŋ aŋpetu ota ciŋ,
Tuwa henica he?

3 Niceji taku śice ciŋ
Etaŋ kduha yo, qa
Niiha taku woknaye
Eyeśniyaŋ, nakuŋ.
Qa śice ciŋ ayuśtaŋ yo,
Waśte kiŋ he ecoŋ,
Qa wookiye kiŋ ode
Qa he ekna uŋ wo.

4 Itaŋcaŋ kiŋ iśta kiŋ oŋ
Awicatoŋwe, ça
He noġe oŋ nawicaȟoŋ,
Owotaŋpina kiŋ.
Itaŋcaŋ Taitoknake
Iś ś capi owas
He itkokibwicauŋ oŋ
Henanapi kta ce. AMEN.

175 Bedford. C. M.

"Hoyekiyapi, uŋkaŋ Itaŋcaŋ kiŋ naȟon, qa tokakijepi kiŋ owasiŋ etaŋhaŋ ewicakdaku."—Ps. xxxiv: 17.

[*Horsely, Hymn* 105, *may be used.*]

From "Tunes Old and New" by permission of Rev. Dr. Tucker.

2 Itaŋcaŋ oŋśiȟaŋpi kiŋ
Wicikiyena uŋ;
Iyopeiçiyapi kiŋ
Niwicaya ece.

3 Itaŋcaŋ kiŋ tuwa toȟaŋ
Owotaŋna uŋ kiŋ
He tokakije ota śa
Etaŋhaŋ ekdaku.

4 Itaŋcaŋ kiŋ huhu owas
Awaŋkiciyaka,
He oŋ waŋjinaka eśa
Kaweġapi kte śni.

5 Qa śice ciŋ he śicapi
Wicakte kta, nakuŋ
Waśte kiŋ śicedapi kiŋ
Wicayasupi kta.

6 Itaŋcaŋ kiŋ Taokiye
Naġi opekitoŋ,
Qa tona He waciŋyaŋpi
Wicayasu kte śni. AMEN.

Faith

176 My Faith Looks up to Thee.

"Ahimatonwan po, kinhan yanipi kta." Isa. 45:22

OLIVET. 6.6.4.6.6.6.4. LOWELL MASON, 1833.

2 Nitowaśte kin he
Mayuwaśakin kta,
Nimayin kta;
Miye on niçiçu,
Waśtecidake cin
Owihankeśniyan
Eced hin kta.

3 Woiyokiśica,
Qa okpaza kin ed,
Mici un ye;
Iśtamnihanpe kin,
Micipakinta ye;
Ake wanuni kta
Anapta ye.

4 Tohan wiconte kin
Mahiyohi kinhan,
Wanikiya;
Nitowaśte kin on,
Wikopeśniyan ȟcin,
Wankan niye ekta,
Imacu ye. Amen.

CHANTS

Hinhanna Cekiyapi

From "Tunes Old and New."

Venite, exultemus Domino

Kuwa miye,★ Itancan kin iyuśkinyan unkidowanpi kta:
Wowanikiye unkitawapi Wowaśake kin★ ekta iyaunkiś'api kta;
Iye ite kin wopida yuha unkakipapi kta;★ psalm on iye ekta iyaunkiś'api kta.
ITANCAN kin Wakantanka tanka kin heon:★ ho, taku wakan owasin iwankab Wicaśayatapi tanka un.
Maka ośbe kin hena iye nape okna kduha;★ qa he towaśake kin hena iye tawa.
Miniwanca kin he tawa, qa iye kaga:★ qa iye nape kin maka puze cin he piya.
Kuwa miye,★ ohoundapi qa unpatujapi kta:
ITANCAN, Unkagapi kin itokab,★ canpeśka makakde inaunjinpi kta.
Wakantanka unkitawapi kin he iye heon:★ qa towiḣan kin en oyate kin, qa iye nape en taḣcaskana kin he unkiyepi.
Wowitan wakan kin on ITANCAN kin ohoda po;★ iye itokab, maka kin ai cancan nunwe.
He u kin heon,★ maka kin kdasu u kta heon:
Woowotanna on maka kin yasu kta,★ qa oyate kin towicake kin on.
Ateyapi kin, qa Cinhintku kin,★ qa Woniya Wakan kin, wowitan yuha nunwe;
Otokahe ekta hecetu qon, dehan hecetu,★ qa ohinniyan hecetu kta, maka owihanke wanin. Amen.

HINHANNA CEKIYAPI

3 "ROSE OF SHARON."

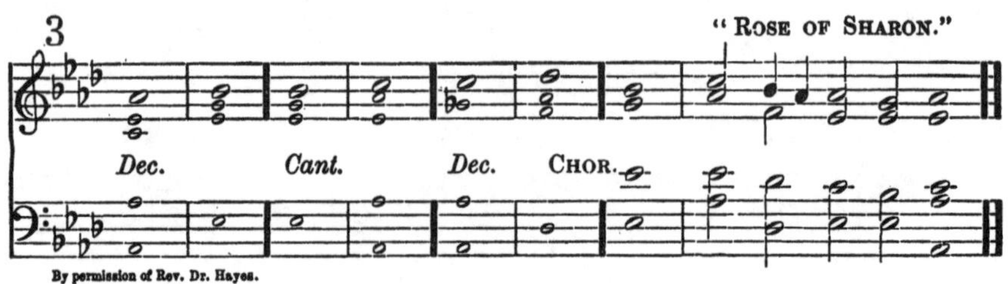

By permission of Rev. Dr. Hayes.

4 J. ROBINSON.

Te Deum laudamus.

Wakantanka, unniyatanpi:★ Itancan kin he niye unkonikdakapi.

Maka kin owancaya ohonidapi,★ Ateyapi kin ohinniyan.

Niye, Oknikde owasin hotankakiya hoyeniciyapi;★ Maħpiya kin, qa ekta Wookihi kin owasin.

Niye, Cerubim qa Seraphim★ ohinniyan hoyeniciyapi,

Wakan, Wakan, Wakan,★ Itancan, Sabaoth Wakantanka;

Maħpiya, maka ko★ Nitowitan Towinihan kin ojuna.

Wahośiyepi wowitan ośpaye kin niyatanpi.★ Waayatapi okodakiciye waśte kin niyatanpi.

Martyr obe wookinihan kin niyatanpi.★ Okodakiciye Wakan kin maka owancaya wicanida;

Ateyapi kin, tawookinihan wopteca śni kin he;★ Nicinkśi ohodapica, wowicake, qa hecena kin;

Nakun Woniya Wakan,★ Wicakicanpte cin.

HINHANNA CEKIYAPI

Wowitan Itancan kin,★ he ni—ye—, Christ.

Ateyapi Cinhintku kin★ ohinniyan he niye.

Wicaśa niwicayayin kte çehan,★ Witanśna un wan etanhan nitonpi kta onśiniçiye.

Wiconte ope kin ohiyaye çehan,★ tona wicadapi kin owasin Mañpiya Wokiconze kin wicayakiduñdoka.

Wakantanka etapa kin ekta idotanka,★ Ateyapi Towitan kin en.

Unyadasupi kta yau kte cin★ he wicaundapi.

Heon etanhan nitaokiyepi niwe teñika on opewicayeton kin★ owicakiyin kta, iceunniciyapi.

Wakanpi nitawa kin ob wicayawa ye,★ wowitan ohinniyan en.

Itancan, nitaoyate niwicaya ye,★ qa woaiñpeye nitawa kin kduwaśte ye.

Awanwicakdaka ye,★ qa ohinni yuwankan ewicayaku ye.

Anpetu otoiyohi★ unniyatankapi;

Qa Nicaje kin ohoundapi ohinni,★ maka owihanke wanin.

Itancan, anpetu kin de woañtani cona★ awanunyaka miye.

Itancan, onśiunda miye,★ onśiunda miye.

Itancan, wacinunniyanpi kin iyecen,★ nitowaonśida kin unkuya miye.

Itancan, wacinciya ce;★ tohinni inihanmaye śni ye.

HINHANNA CEKIYAPI

Benedictus Es, Domine.

Itancan atewicunyanpi Wakantanka tawapi kin, niyawaśtepi ce:★ taku owasin iwankab ohinni niyatanpi qa niyawankantupi.

Nicaje towitan tanka kin heon niyawaśtepi ce:★ taku owasin iwankab ohinni niyatanpi qa niyawankantupi.

Woohoda tipi wakan nitawa en niyawaśtepi ce:★ taku owasin iwankab ohinni niyatanpi qa niyawankantupi.

Omahetuya ekta taku owasin wandaka qa oknikde wakan opeya ounyaya niyawaśtepi ce:★ taku owasin iwankab ohinni niyatanpi qa niyawankantupi.

Nitokiconze kin en wowitan oiyotanke en yaun niyawaśtepi ce:★ taku owasin iwankab ohinni niyatanpi qa niyawankantupi.

Mahpiya okotonya en yaun niyawaśtepi ce:★ taku owasin iwankab ohinni niyatanpi qa niyawankantupi.

Ateyapi kin, qa Cinhintku kin,★ qa Woniya Wakan kin, wowitan yuha nunwe;

Otokahe ekta hecetu qon, dehan hecetu,★ qa ohinniyan hecetu kta, maka owihanke wanin. Amen.

HINHANNA CEKIYAPI

Benedictus. *St. Luke* 1:68.

¶ *Advent omaka en Anpetu wakan kin ataya unpi kta, qa idchanyan onśpa inhanke unpi śni kinhan he hecetu.*

ITANCAN Israel Tawakantanka kin yawaśtepi nunwe;★ taoyate ekta wicahi qa opewicaton kin heon.

Qa taokiye David ti kin en,★ wanikiyapi wan tanka eunkicikdepi:

Iye Waayatapi wakan tawa ipi kin eciyatanhan ie ciqon,★ maka tokaheya icage cin ehantanhan;

Hecen tona toka unyanpi etanhan,★ qa śiceundakapi napepi kin etanhan niunkiyapi kta.

Wowaonśida hunkakewicunyanpi wahowicaye ciqon, he ecen econ kta;★ qa wokiyapi wakan tawa kin he kiksuyin kta;

Abraham ateunyanpi kin he taku wakanyan eciye ciqon he hee kta ce;★ decen ionśiunkidapi kta;

Tona tokaunyanpi nape kin etanhan unkiyuśpapi kinhan;★ wokokipe cona waecaunkiconpi kta;

Iye itokab, wicoowotanna qa wowakan kin en;★ tohanyan unnipi kin hehanyan;

Qa niye, wakanheja, Waayata Iyotan Wankantu tawa kin eniciyapi kta;★ Itancan tacanku kin wiyeya yecagin kta on ite kin itokab nin kta;

Taoyate wowanikiye wosdonye wicayaqu kta,★ woaȟtani wicakicicajujupi heon.

Wakantanka unkitawapi canteunkiyapi kin heon etanhan;★ qa heon wankantanhan anpao kin unhiyohipi ce;

Hecen okpaza qa wiconte ohanzi kin ekna iyotankapi kin hena iyoyamwicayin kta;★ qa unsihapi kin wookiye canku kin okna unkayapi kta heon.

Ateyapi kin, qa Cinhintku kin,★ qa Woniya Wakan kin, wowitan yuha nunwe;

Otokahe ekta hecetu qon, dehan hecetu,★ qa ohinniyan hecetu kta, maka owihanke wanin. Amen.

HINHANNA CEKIYAPI

9

DEAN ALDRICH.

10

DEAN ALDRICH.

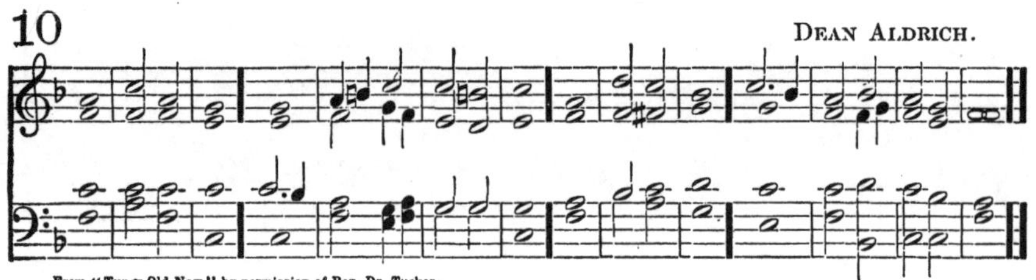

From "Tunes Old New" by permission of Rev. Dr. Tucker.

Jubilate Deo. Psalm 100.

Maka kin ataya,★ ITANCAN kin ekta hotankaya iyakiś'a miye,

Wowiyuśkin on ITANCAN kin okiya po,★ wowiyuśkin odowan yuha iye itokab u po.

ITANCAN kin he Wakantanka e sdonya po;★ he iye unkagapi qa unkiçicagapi śni,

Taoyate kin,★ qa towiḣan kin en taḣcaskana kin hena unkiyepi.

Tatiyopa kin mahen wopida yuha ya po,★ tahocoka kin en woyatan yuha ya po;

Wopida eciya miye,★ iye Caje kin yawaśte po.

ITANCAN waśte kin heon,★ towaonśida-waśte kin owihanke wanica;

Qa towicake kin★ wicoicage owasin iciyaza suta ece.

Ateyapi kin, qa Cinḣintku kin,★ qa Woniya Wakan kin, wowitan yuha nunwe;

Otokahe ekta hecetu qon, dehan hecetu,★ qa ohinniyan hecetu kta, maka owihanke wanin. Amen.

Ḣtaṗetu Cekiṗapi.

11 W. LEE.

12 R. LANGDON.

From "Tunes Old and New" by permission Rev. Dr. Tucker.

Minagi kin Itancan kin yatan:★ qa mitaniya kin he, Wakantanka Wanikiya mitawa kin en wiyuśkin ce.

Taokiye onśiya waun kin,★ ekta ahimatonwe cin heon.

Iho, heon detanhan★ wicoicage kin owasin yawaśtepi kin emakiyapi kta.

Ecin, Tuwa Waśake cin He taku tanka ecamicon;★ qa Caje kin wakan ce.

Qa tona kokipapi kin hena, wicoicage qa sam wicoicage owasin en,★ Towaonśida kin en wicaun ce.

Iye isto kin on wowaśake kdutanin;★ waḣaniçidapi kin hena cante mahen taku wacinyuzapi kin en wicayuobdeca.

Waśakaśakapi kin hena toyankcpi ctanhan kun kdicuwicaya,★ qa onśiya unpi kin hena wankan ewicakde.

Docinpi kin hena taku waśteśte on imnawicaya,★ qa jicapi kin iś cokakana kikdewicaya.

Iye Towaonśida kiksuye cin on,★ Taokiye, Israel he okiya;

Abraham, qa owihanke wanin cincawicayin kte cin,★ onśiwicada kta keye ça hunkakewicunyanpi iwahowicaye ciqon he oknayan.

Ateyapi kin, qa Cinhintku kin,★ qa Woniya Wakan kin, wowitan yuha nunwe;

Otokahe ekta hecetu qon, dehan hecetu,★ qa ohinniyan hecetu kta, maka owihanke wanin. Amen.

ḢTAYETU CEKIYAPI

13

TALLIS.

From "Tunes Old and New" by permission of Rev. Dr. Tucker.

14

J. TURLE.

By permission of A. S. Barnes & Co.

Bonum est confiteri. Psalm 92.

Itancan kin wopida eciyapi kin **he** waśte,★ qa Nicaje psalm idowanpi kin, **Iyo**tan Wankantu.

Hinhanna eca nitowaonśida-waśte kin oyakapi,★ qa hanhepi iyohi nitowicake kin,

Dowankiyapi ikan wikcemna, qa mazayuhotonpi kin on,★ mazadowankiyapi akan dowanpi oqo kin on.

Ecin, IT'ANCAN, nioḣan kin iyuśkinmayaye,★ ninape oḣan kin eciyatanhan wowiyuśkin **on** wadowan kta.

Ateyapi kin, qa Ċinhintku kin,★ qa Woniya Wakan kin, wowitan yuha nunwe;

Otokahe ekta hecetu qon, dehan **hecetu**,★ qa ohinniyan hecetu kta, maka owihanke wanin. Amen.

ĦTAYETU CEKIYAPI

15

J. Barnby.

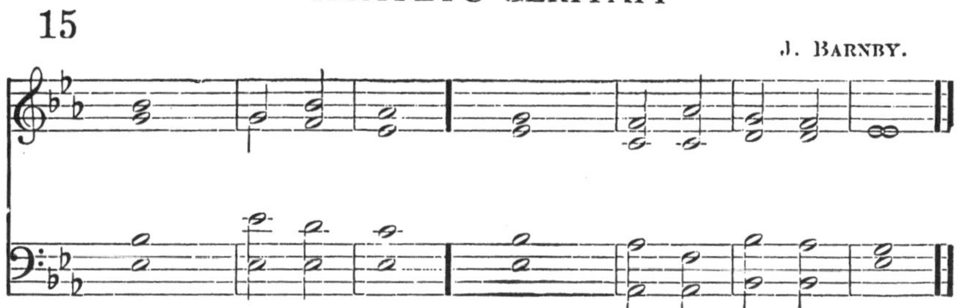

From "Tunes Old and New" by permission of Rev. Dr. Tucker.

16

Tonus Regius.

From "Tunes Old and New" by permission of Rev. Dr. Tucker.

Nunc Dimittis. St. Luke 2:29.

Itancan, Nitaokiye kin wanna wookiye yuha iyayeyaya,★ ehe ciqon oknayan;

Ecin miiśta kin★ wanna Wowanikiye Nitawa kin wanyaka.

Oyate owasin wicitokab★ wiyeya eyaknake cin he;

Iyoyanpa wan oyate kin aiyojanjan wicayin kte çin hee,★ qa Nitaoyate Israel towitan kte cin.

Ateyapi kin, qa Cinhintku kin,★ qa Woniya Wakan kin, wowitan yuha nunwe;

Otokahe ekta hecetu qon, dehan hecetu,★ qa ohinniyan hecetu kta, maka owihanke wanin. Amen.

ĦTAYETU CEKIYAPI

17

W. Hine.

By permission of A. S. Barnes & Co.

18

T. Norris.

By permission of Rev. Dr. Tucker.

Benedic, anima mea. Psalm 103.

Minagi kin, ITANCAN kin yawaŝte wo,★ qa taku mahen maun kin owasin, iye Caje wakan kin.

Minagi kin, ITANĊAN kin yawaŝte wo,★ qa taku wowaŝte econ kin owasin akiktonje ŝni wo;

He woaħtani nitawa kin owasin nicicajuju★ he wowayazan nitawa kin owasin asniniyan,

He nitoni kin hades etanhan niyan,★ he wowaonŝida-waŝte qa wocantkiye on wateŝdagnicaton,

Oknikde niyuhapi kin, ITANCAN kin yawaŝte po,★ wowaŝake en waniŝakapi kin,

Iye oie ecen ecanonpi kin,★ iye oie ho anayagoptanpi kin.

Taobe kin owasin, ITANCAN kin yawaŝte po,★ taokiyeniyanpi toiyokipi ecen ecanonpi kin.

Taku kage cin owasin, tokiconze ounye kin owasin okna, ITANCAN kin yawaŝte po.★ Minagi kin, Itancan kin yawaŝte wo.

Ateyapi kin, qa Cinhintku kin,★ qa Woniya Wakan kin, wowitan yuha nunwe;

Otokahe ekta hecetu qon, dehan hecetu,★ qa ohinniyan hecetu kta, maka owihanke wanin. Amen.

Wotapi Wakan

19 Three-fold Kyrie

ST. PHILIP — WILLIAM H. MONK 1871

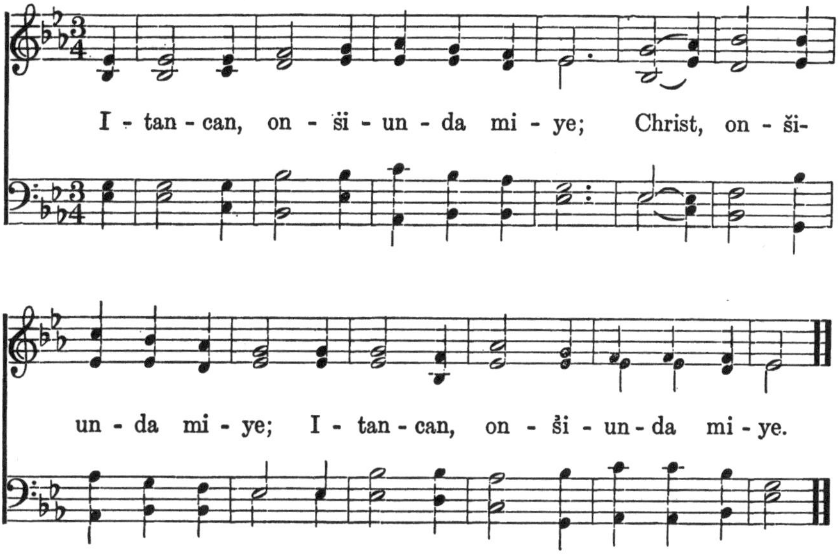

I - tan - can, on - ši - un - da mi - ye; Christ, on - ši-

un - da mi - ye; I - tan - can, on - ši - un - da mi - ye.

Kyrie Eleison
(After the Ten Commandments)

20

From BEETHOVEN.

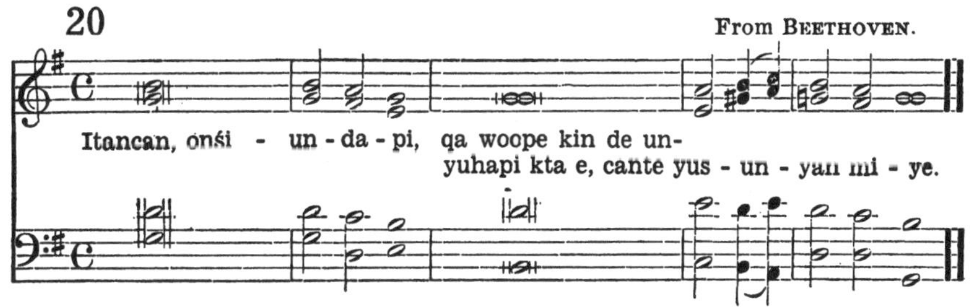

(After the 10th)

Itancan, onśiundapi,★ qa woope kin dena owasin unkicantepi en oyawa kta, iceunniciyapi..

WOTAPI WAKAN

21

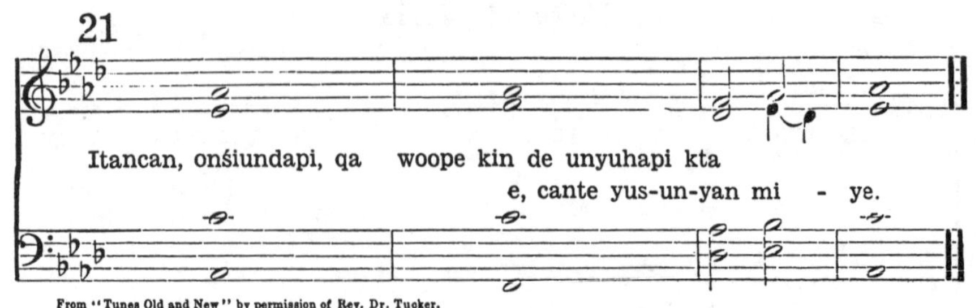

From "Tunes Old and New" by permission of Rev. Dr. Tucker.

(After the 10th)

Itancan, onśiundapi, qa woope kin dena owasin unkicantepi en oyawa kta, ıceunniciyapi.

22 Gloria Tibi.

23 Laus Tibi

Christ Niye ȟca, Christ Niye ȟca, Woyatan, woyatan, woyatan duha nunwe.

24 Offertory ANON.

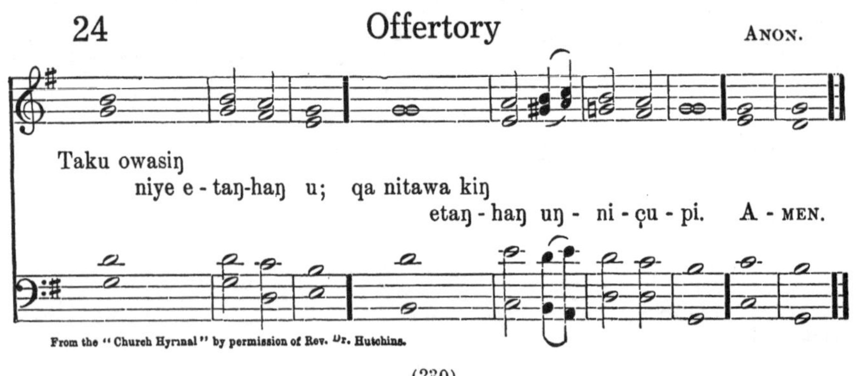

From the "Church Hymnal" by permission of Rev. Dr. Hutchins.

WOTAPI WAKAN
25
HUMPHREYS.
Taku owasiŋ
Niye e - taŋ-haŋ u; qa nitawa kiŋ
etaŋ - haŋ uŋ - ni - çu - pi. A - MEN.
Sanctus
26
MERBECKE
Wa - kan, Wa - kan, Wa - kan, wicota en Itancan Wakan - tan - ka,
mahpiya qa maka Ni - to - wi - tan kin o - ju - na:
Wowitan duha nunwe, I - tan - can Iyo - tan Wan-kan - tu. A-MEN.

WOTAPI WAKAN

Gloria in Excelsis.

27

CANTUS ECCLESIAE.

Wankan Wakantanka wowitan yuha nunwe;★ qa maka akan wookiye, wicaśa ekta wicotawacin waśte.

Unniyatanpi, unniyawaśtepi, ohounnidapi,★ unniyaonihanpi, wopida unniçupi nitowitan tanka kin heon,

Itancan Wakantanka, mahpiyata Itancan,★ Wakantanka, Ate Iyotanwaśaka.

Itancan, Cinca hecena-icage cin, Jesus Christ;★ Itancan Wakantanka, Wakantanka Tacincana tawa, Ateyapi Cinhintku.

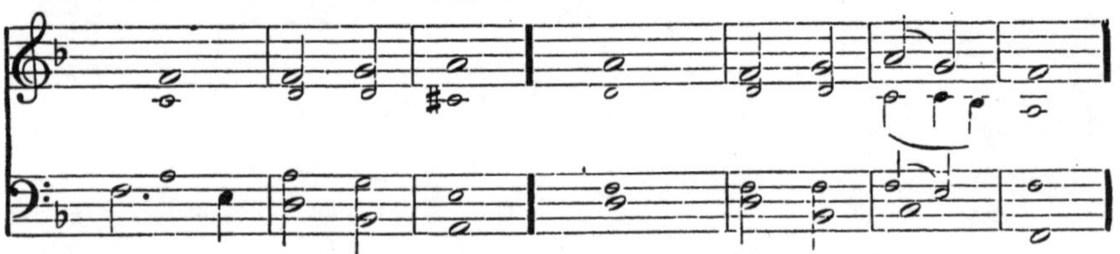

Maka etanhan woahtani yutokan iyeyaye cin,★ onśiunda miye.

Maka etanhan woahtani yutokan iyeyaye cin,★ wocekiye unkitawapi kin eyaku ye.

Wakantanka Ate nape etapa kin en idotanke cin,★ onśiunda miye.

Niśnana niwakan heon,★ niśnana Initancan;

Nisnana, Christ, Woniya Wakan kin kici,★ Wakantanka Ate towitan kin en, iyotan wankan yaun. Amen, Amen.

WOTAPI WAKAN

28

Gloria in Excelsis.

OLD CHANT.

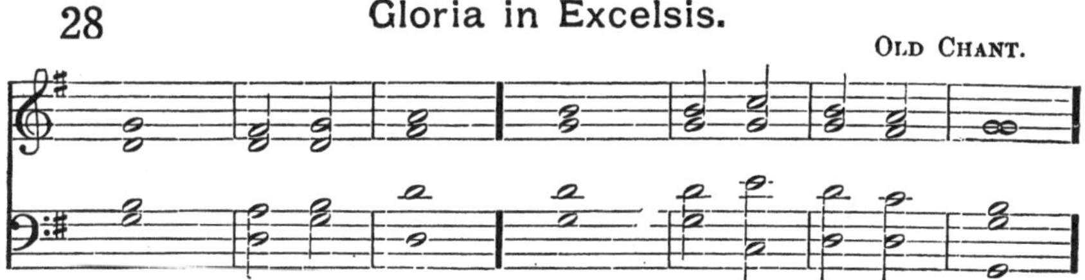

Wankan Wakantanka wowitan yuha nunwe;★ qa maka akan wookiye, wicaśa ekta wicotawacin waśte.

Unniyatanpi, unniyawaśtepi, ohounnidapi,★ unniyaonihanpi, wopida unniçupi nitowitan tanka kin heon,

Itancan Wakantanka, maħpiyata Itancan,★ Wakantanka, Ate Iyotanwaśaka.

Itancan, Cinca hecena-icage cin, Jesus Christ;★ Itancan Wakantanka, Wakantanka Tacincana tawa, Ateyapi Cinhintku.

Maka etanhan woaħtani yutokan iyeyaye cin,★ onśiunda miye.

Maka etanhan woaħtani yutokan iyeyaye cin,★ wocekiye unkitawapi kin cyaku ye.

Wakantanka Ate nape etapa kin en idotanke cin,★ onśiunda miye.

From "Tunes Old and New" by permission of Rev. Dr. Tucker.

Niśnana niwakan heon,★ niśnana Initancan;

Niśnana, Christ, Woniya Wakan kin kici,★ Wakantanka Ate towitan kin e n, iyotan wankan yaun. Amen.

29

BRIDGE.

30

DOWNES

By permission of Rev. Dr. Hutchins.

Psalm 39. Dixi, Custodiam

ITANCAN, omawihanke kin sdonyemakiya ye, qa mitaanpetu kin tohanyan kta hecinhan;★ hecen wamaśake śni ħca sdonwakiyin kta.

Wanyaka ye, mitaanpetu kin nape okdakinyan iyecen yakaga, qa wani kte cin he nitokab takuśni iyececa;★ awicakehan wicaśa otoiyohi, sutaya najin eśa, oniya wanjina iyececa.

Awicakehan wicaśa kin ohanzi wan en icicawinwin omani: awicakehan oniya wan on nihinciyapi;★ woyuha waeknaka ece, tka tuwe hena pahi kta sdonye śni.

Unkan nakaha, Itancan, taku e ape waun he?★ Woape mitawa kin he niye etu.

Wawaħtani kin owasin etanhan imacu ye;★ wicaśa witkotkoka wowiħaħamayanpi kta makage śni ye.

Wawiyopeyapi on wicaśa waħtani kin iyopeyaya, wayakukes'a iyecen owanyagwaśte kin dutakuniśni ece:★ awicakehan wicaśa otoiyohi oniya wanjina hececa.

ITANCAN, wocekiye mitawa kin naħon ye, qa hoyewaye cin ninoge naħonkiya ye;★ waceye cin on inina yanke śni ye;

Niye en wicaśa matokeca heon, unkdaka waun,★ atewicawaya owasin unpi qon he iyecen.

Mitokan etonwan ye, hecen waśagmiçiyin kta,★ detanhan ibdabde śni, qa icinonpa en waun śni itokab.

Ateyapi kin, qa Cinhintku kin,★ qa Woniya Wakan kin, wowitan yuha nunwe;

Otokahe ekta hecetu qon, dehan hecetu,★ qa ohinniyan hecetu kta, maka owihanke wanin. Amen.

WICAĦAPI

Psalm 90. Domine, refugium.

ITANCAN, wowinape unkitawapi kin he niye,★ woicage iciyaza uye cin.

Ħe kin hena icage cin itokab, maka kin qa makoce ko kagapi śni itokab,★ ho, otokahe qa owihanke wanin, Wakantanka kin he niye.

Wicaśa woatakuni śni ekta wicaduhomni,★ qa akeś wicaśa cincapi kin, kdicu miye, eha ece.

Omaka kektopawinge kin, he niiśta kin en ħtanihan wanna henakeca he iyececa,★ qa hanhepi en woawanyake wanjina iyececa.

Kahin iyewicayaya woiśtinma wan iyececapi;★ hinhanna eca wato iyecen ataninpi śni.

Hinhanna eca to, qa wankankiya icaga;★ ħtayetu hehan kaśdapi, qa śnija qa puza.

Ecin nitocanniye kin on unsotapi,★ qa nitocanze cin on wikounpapi;

Waunħtanipi kin nitokab eyaknaka;★ woanaħbe unkitawapi kin niitoknake iyoyanpa kin en.

Ecin anpetu unkitawapi kin owasin nitocanniye kin on tokan iyaya:★ omaka unkitawapi kin wicowoyake wan iyecen unkdusotapi:

Omaka unkitawapi anpetu kin hena omaka wikcemna śakowin, qa wowaśake yuke cinhan omaka wikcemna śakdogan,★ hececa eśa wowaśake tawapi kin wokakije qa takuśni, ecana owihanke, qa najica unkiyayapi kin heon.

Hecen anpetu unkdawapi kta onspeunkiya miye;★ kinhan wicoksape ekta cante yeunkiyapi kta.

Ateyapi kin, qa Cinhintku kin,★ qa Woniya Wakan kin, wowitan yuha nunwe;

Otokahe ekta hecetu qon, dehan hecetu,★ qa ohinniyan hecetu kta, maka owihanke wanin. Amen.

Burial of a Child

31

W. Hine.

32

R. Farrant.

Psalm 23. Dominus regit me.

Waawanyaka mitawa kin, Itancan **kin** hee;★ wimakakijin kte śni.

Peji owiĥankiye en waĥanmakiya;★ wooziiçiye mini kin icakda yus-amayan ece.

Iye minagi kin yuecetu;★ wicoowotanna canku kin okna amayan, iye Caje kin on.

Ho, wiconte ohanzi kaksiza kin okna mawani eśa, taku śica wanjina kowakipin kte śni,★ niye mici yaun kin heon; cansakana qa cansagye nitawa kin, hena micanptapi.

Mitokab waknawotapi wan miyeciknaka, tokamayanpi kin wicitokab;★ wikdi on pa sdamayakiya, wiyatke mitawa **kin** iyatakde.

Awicakehan anpetu tona wani kin owasin wowaśte qa wocantkiyewaśte ko miyakna un kta,★ qa ITANCAN ti kin anpetu ohinniyan en ounwayin kta.

Ateyapi kin, qa Cinhintku kin,★ qa Woniya Wakan kin, wowitan yuha nunwe;

Otokahe ekta hecetu qon, dehan hecetu,★ qa ohinniyan hecetu kta, maka owihanke wanin. Amen.

WAKANHEJA WICAȞAPI

Psalm 121. *Levavi oculos.*

Ȟe kin hena ekta iśta yuwankan ewekdaku;★ tokiyatanhan wowawokiye mitawa kin u he.

Wowawokiye mitawa kin, ITANCAN kin;★ maȟpiya maka ko kage cin he eciyatanhan u ce.

Iye nisiha yutokanpi kte cin iyowinyin kte śni;★ iye niyuha kin iśtinbe śni nunwe.

Wanyaka wo, iye Israel yuhe cin;★ ȟba qa iśtinbe śni ece.

Awanniyake cin he ITANCAN kin hee;★ nietapa ekta wowinape nitawa kin he ITANCAN kin ee.

Anpetu icunhan, anpetu-wi kin kiunniniyin kte śni,★ qa hanhepi-wi kin hanhepi icunhan.

Taku śica owasin etanhan, ITANCAN kin niyuha kta,★ iye ȟca ninagi kin awanyakin kta.

Tankan idade ça tin yaku kin hena ITANCAN kin awanyakin kta,★ detanhan tokatakiya qa owihanke wanin.

Ateyapi kin, qa Cinhintku kin,★ qa Woniya Wakan kin, wowitan yuha nunwe;

Otokahe ekta hecetu qon, dehan hecetu,★ qa ohinniyan hecetu kta, maka owihanke wanin. Amen.

Easter-Anpetu kin.

33 LORD MORNINGTON.

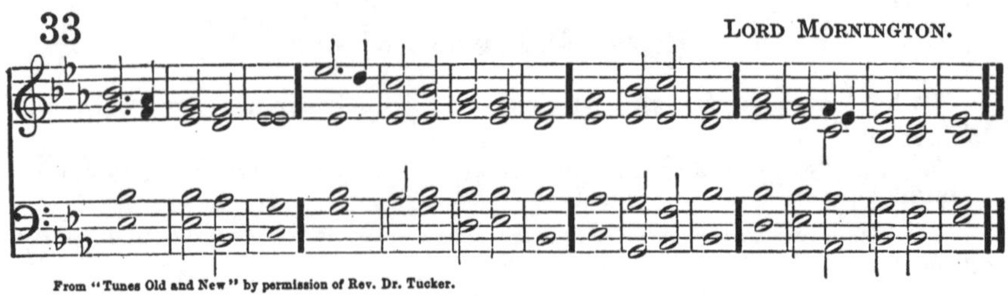

From "Tunes Old and New" by permission of Rev. Dr. Tucker.

34

¶ *Hinhanna Cekiyapi en, Easter Anpetu kinhan, Venite kin eekiya, Woahiyaye kin de eyapi kta.*

Christ, Woacakśin unkitawapi kin unkiyepi on wośnapi:★ heon etanhan woahope kin ahounpapi kta;

Napoȟyapi tannina kin, nakun wokipajin qa oȟanśica napoȟyapi kin he on śni;★ tka woknayeśni qa wowicake aguyapi napoȟyapi kin on.

Christ wiconṭe kin etanhan inajinkiyapi qon, he ake icinonpa ṭin kte śni;★ tokata tohinni wiconṭe kin yuha okihi kte śni.

He ṭe ciqon, wancana woaȟtani on ṭa;★ tka He ni kin, Wakantanka on niun.

He iyecen niś eya woaȟtani en ṭe nikdawapi kta,★ tka Wakantanka en niyaunpi Jesus Christ Itancan unyanpi kin he eciyatanhan.

Christ wiconṭe etanhan kini,★ qa tona iśtinmapi qon etanhan waskuyeca tokaheya icage cin hee.

Wicaśa kin eciyatanhan wiconṭe u kin,★ he iyecen wicaśa eciyatanhan wiconṭe etanhan kinipi kin u ece.

Adam en owasin ṭapi kin,★ he iyecen Christ en owasin niwicayapi kta.

Ateyapi kin, qa Cinhintku kin,★ qa Woniya Wakan kin, wowitan yuha nunwe;

Otokahe ekta hecetu qon, dehan hecetu,★ qa ohinniyan hecetu kta, maka owihanke wanin. Amen.